❧ *Ybor City Chronicles*

Ybor City Chronicles

❦ A MEMOIR

Ferdie Pacheco

❦ University Press of Florida

Gainesville Tallahassee Tampa Boca Raton Pensacola Orlando Miami Jacksonville

99 98 97 96 95 94 6 5 4 3 2 1

Library of Congress Cataloging-in-Publication data

Pacheco, Ferdie.
    Ybor City chronicles: a memoir/Ferdie Pacheco.
    p.   cm.
    ISBN 0-8130-1296-1 (acid-free paper)
    1. Pacheco, Ferdie—Childhood and youth.
    2. Ybor City (Tampa,Fla.)—Biography. 3. Ybor
    City (Tampa, Fla.)—Social life and customs.
    4. Tampa (Fla.)—Biography. 5. Tampa (Fla.)—
    Social life and customs.   I. Title.
    F319.T2P33   1994
    975.9'65—dc20
    [B]   94-822

Frontispiece: A gala evening at El Pasaje Hotel,
1939. Courtesy of *La Gaceta,* Ybor City, Florida.

The University Press of Florida is the scholarly
publishing agency for the State University System
of Florida, comprised of Florida A & M University,
Florida Atlantic University, Florida International
University, Florida State University, University of
Central Florida, University of Florida, University
of North Florida, University of South Florida, and
University of West Florida.

University Press of Florida
15 Northwest 15th Street
Gainesville, FL 32611

I dedicate this book to the immigrants from Spain, Cuba, Sicily, and Italy who melted together to form the utopia that became Ybor City. Specifically, I dedicate it to Tony Pizzo, who was the first to recognize the importance of preserving our history and who has worked unceasingly to record our passage.

❧ Contents ❧

❧ Preface ❧

After a lifetime of reading, painting, and writing history, there is one thing I am sure of: the greater the distance from the event, the more nebulous it becomes. The facts become fuzzy and every witness tells a different story.

In writing this light-hearted reminiscence about growing up in Ybor City, fifty years ago, I became aware that there were many Ybor Cities. Anyone who lived through these years has his or her own Ybor City.

This memoir covers a period from 1935, the depression years, through the war years to 1945, when I finally left Ybor City to seek my education. That span of ten years remains frozen in my mind as the happiest years of my life, and seems more real and immediate than the many decades that followed. With time to reflect, with the ability to record, with the desire to leave the descendants of the Ybor City immigrants with a record of "how it was," I dedicated myself to putting down my memories in the form of stories, each independent of one another, yet strung together with the thread of my personal evolution to manhood.

If the reader can feel the joys, the vibrancy, the laughter of those days in this unusual community by viewing it through my eyes, then I have achieved my purpose. For I wish, more than anything else, to capture the ambience of the times. I want to share my voyage and bring you into the utopia that was my Ybor City.

So with that in mind, let me reassure the reader that this book is not a history of Ybor City from 1935 to 1945. Take it for what it is: my reminiscence about a short ten years of my youth. These stories may not be the strict truth as other witnesses remember it, but they *are* the truth as I remember it. They are *my* truth.

❦ Acknowledgments ❧

This book of stories was the fallout of research done for a massive novel on Ybor City based on the life of the lector Victoriano Manteiga. I interviewed him when he was in his eighties and was so impressed by his fire and his remembrances of past life in Ybor City that I started to do the research for the novel, during which I got the idea for this book.

Since I have talked to half of Ybor City while writing the book, I can only give them a collective nod of the head and my heartfelt thanks.

Professional help was overwhelming; several men contributed generously of their time and encouragement. The first of these is Roland Manteiga, the son of Don Victoriano, who still publishes and edits *La Gaceta,* the country's only trilingual newspaper. He not only was a source of information but opened his photography files for our use.

Of particular significance was the work of my editor, Sandy Richardson, who not only supervised the writing but encouraged me to add more to the growing stories of Ybor City. Mr. Richardson has been the editor of four works which received Pulitzer Prizes, and for two decades was known as the golden boy of publishing in New York. A resident of New York, Sandy has become a fan of Ybor City, and he welcomes any chance to return. His was a major contribution.

Gary Mormino, professor of history at the University of South Florida, was a great help, and his huge file on Dr. Avellanal was responsible for the accuracy of the chapter on this charming rogue.

Joe Guidry of the *Tampa Tribune* editorial staff has been a great source of encouragement and his non–Ybor City viewpoint kept the text open and interesting to non-Ybor City readers. Joe also made the *Tribune* photo files available, particularly for the Charlie Wall chapter.

Anyone attempting to write about Ybor City must first consult with Tony Pizzo. A very successful businessman and political activist, Tony patiently collected photos and stories about Ybor City over the years, for he saw what the others in Ybor City did not see. He understood the historical importance of the community, reveled in its past, and believed in its future.

All of us who know and love Ybor City lore owe a huge debt of gratitude to Tony Pizzo. He wrote the epilogue of this book with style, grace, and practicality too—ever the master salesman, he closes with a pitch to come visit Ybor City and see for yourself the places written about in the book. At eighty years of age, Tony stands as the spirit of the resurgence of Ybor City; he is its soul and pilot light.

Finally, of course, my deeply felt thanks go to my partner in life, my wife, Luisita. She continues to amaze me with her capacity to learn and grow. She has conquered the word processor and remains the keenest critic of my work and its best supporter. I always felt I was blessed to marry a beautiful girl who was a master of flamenco dance. Imagine my surprise when she turned out to be a master of the word processor as well. Will my good fortune never end?

Chapter 1

Sweet Sam

A slanting cold December rain pounded Sam's face as he urged his two mules to a final effort. He had come a long way in his wagon, carrying a grand piano and his ailing wife Leona. Sam knew he had to go as far from New Orleans as the mules would take him. From the look of the swaying mules, Sam knew he had gone as far as he could go.

Sam saw a sign swinging wildly in the howling wind, lit by a flickering electric light bulb. He read the words WHOLESALE DRUG COMPANY, but couldn't make out the foreign name.

Gently he laid Leona on the driver's seat, pulling a large poncho over her so that she would keep dry. He pulled a wet felt hat over his eyes, pulled up his collar to ward off the cold rain rolling down his back. His hands felt numb and were raw from many days of holding the reins. The downpour soaked through his thin cotton gloves. He dropped a large weight, tied to the reins. He wanted to keep the mules from wandering off, although they were exhausted and stood in the driving rain with their heads drooping almost to the ground.

Sam could see through the window that the man inside was greatly agitated. He knew it was not the moment to knock on the back door, but he was at the end of his rope. He rapped softly on the door. Nothing happened. He rapped harder.

The door swung open, and Sam looked at the angry face of one of the biggest white men he had ever seen.

"What is it? What do you want? It's Christmas Eve, we're closed."

**And They Came to a Shelter
on Christmas Eve.** *1993.*
Ferdie Pacheco.

"Yassuh," Sam averted his eyes but held his ground. The fact that it was Christmas Eve surprised him. Had they been on the road that long?

"I must ask for your help. We come a long way, suh. My mules done played out. My wife, Leona, is very sick, and we at the end of the road."

The big man looked beyond Sam at the two scraggly mules, leaning in their hitches against each other, and the small poncho-covered bundle on the driver's seat. Behind them a large tarp-covered object loomed in the dark.

"Kin you help my woman? She's mighty weak. Almost done in."

"You bring her in. I'll set up the cot next to the heater. I'll put a pot on and make hot chamomile tea with lemon and honey."

"Suh, I don't have no money."

"If you think about it, I didn't ask for none."

"I can work."

"Doing what? Tap dancing?"

"Nossuh, I can't tap dance, but I can work hard for you." Sam looked at the boxes and bags of drugs with the white invoices stuck to the front with straight pins.

"Can you drive a Model T?"

"Yassuh."

"Can you read?"

"Yassuh."

"If I give you a map of Ybor City, could you find Trelles Clinic, the Centro Asturiano, the Centro Español, the St. Joseph's Hospital, and Lodato's Drugstore?"

"Yassuh, if you help my wife to feel better."

"What wife?"

"She on the seat, covered up. If she get any wetter, she'll die of the fever."

"What are you carrying? Looks awful big."

"A piano," Sam said, looking at the floor.

"A piano?" The big man squinted his eyes, waiting for the flickering light to illuminate the piano. "Are you a piano player?"

"Nossuh," Sam said, and offered no further explanation.

The big man appeared to soften. He brought Sam in to warm himself by the kerosene heater. He offered him a drink of rye whiskey, but

Sam turned it down. He was cautious around whites and he knew better than to drink with one, even if it was Christmas Eve.

"What's your name?"

"Sam. My wife's name is Leona."

"Good to know you, Sam."

The big man took Sam's hand and shook it in a strong grip. "I'm J.B. Pacheco, and I own this warehouse. I sell medicine."

"Yassuh."

"Bring your wife inside."

Carefully they laid Leona on a cot. J.B. motioned for Sam to unbutton the back of her blouse.

The big man put a water glass to Leona's back as she lay on the cot. He put his ear to the thin glass and she breathed deeply. She could not breathe without coughing. Patiently he thumped her back with his fingers. He had big powerful fingers and it sounded as if he were hitting a drum.

"Where does it hurt?"

Leona looked frightened.

"She don't talk," Sam said quietly.

"Mute?"

"Yassuh."

J.B. looked at her pale fingernails, pulled her eyelids down, noting their pink color. He then looked in her mouth. He stood up and shook his head.

"This woman has pneumonia. She should be in a hospital."

"We ain't got no money."

J.B. looked out of the front window at the two exhausted mules standing in the driving rain. He was adding up the pluses and minuses.

"Hell, it's Christmas Eve, Sam. I wouldn't be a Christian if I didn't give you both safe harbor on a terrible night like this."

"Thank you, suh. I'll be obliged to you and pay you when I can."

"You know what J.B. stands for?"

"Nossuh."

"J is for Joseph, Jesus Christ's father, and B for Baltazar, one of the three wise men."

"The only wise man who was black," Sam said, looking J.B. in the eye at last.

And they shook hands on a contract they both honored for as long as they lived.

※ The shiny blue Ford delivery truck pulled into the driveway at twelve o'clock, and a ten-year-old boy was waiting with a dust rag in his hand.

Sam carefully rolled up the window and locked the door. He pulled on his big gold chain and took out a large pocket watch, clicking the lid open with his thumb. A beautiful melody filled the air, and he showed the watch to me.

"Right on time," I said.

"Master Ferdie, prepare to go to work." Sam let me take the watch key and wind the watch, a ritual we had performed hundreds of times. As Sam went to the back porch, I began to polish the gleaming blue delivery truck

"Good day, Mrs. Pacheco," Sam said, washing his hands with a garden hose. "How are you today?"

"Fine, Sam, just fine, and I've got your favorite lunch today—picadillo, black beans, rice, and plantains."

Sam sat at an old linoleum-covered table, on a straight-back chair. His place held a blue tin plate, a set of cheap silver from Kress's, and a large-mouthed jar of ice tea. He carefully placed the large napkin in his celluloid collar, covering his tie. He hiked up his sleeve garters so that the white cuffs on his striped shirt were out of the way. Sam was a fastidious dresser and could not abide spots on his vest or shirt.

I remembered the many nights when guests would ask J.B. about Sam's strange ways. After all, he certainly wasn't just a run-of-the-mill helper. J.B. treated Sam as a family mystery and a source of hilarity.

"Don't you think it strange that my delivery man is better-dressed than the druggist he calls on in a truck shinier than the bank president's Buick? Well, here's one for you. Sam owns a grand piano."

"Can he play it?"

"That's not the point. Either he can't, or won't, play it. And that's not all. He has a wife, Leona, who can't or won't talk."

"You mean he won't sell the piano? Hell, he could live for five years on what he could get for his piano."

"I know, but don't ever mention it to him or he'll clam up for a week."

The thought of a black man owning an expensive piano and not playing it, nor attempting to sell it, made everyone laugh in Ybor City. I would flinch when I heard some man say, "The dumb nigger, owns a piano and can't play it."

When I heard Sam called a dumb nigger I would wince. I knew better, but in a Spanish home, small boys never spoke at the supper table unless we were spoken to first.

⚜ Ybor City was a Spanish enclave stuck in the middle of the South Florida town of Tampa. About half of its inhabitants were Spaniards, with the rest equally divided between Cubans and Italians. They furnished the work force for the expanding cigar industry.

By the late 1930s Ybor City was a self-contained community, boasting a cradle-to-grave socialized medical system and its own banks and social clubs. An immigrant arriving from Spain could spend the rest of his life in Ybor City without having to learn the English language, nor change his life in any way, because Ybor City *was* Spain.

But most Spanish immigrants who came to a new country were eager to be assimilated into the current social order. So many a Spaniard landed in Tampa, free of racial prejudices, only to discover a new racism. The Anglo establishment who had inherited the legacy of the Civil War and Reconstruction placed blacks at the bottom of the social scale. They were considered only one step above slavery, and as workers, barely human.

Spaniards, however, had a moderate view of blacks. They were hired to work in the cigar factories, although they never had lunch with their Spanish co-workers. They rode to work in the back of Ybor City's trolley cars.

As I grew, I questioned my mother about why Sam had his own utensils and ate on the back porch, even in the rain.

"It's the way things are in this country, son. I can't explain why."

So when J.B. came home with the great news that I would be

allowed to accompany Sam for the whole summer on his daily delivery of drugs, I was filled with questions. Why did my father trust Sam with his most cherished possession, but they didn't eat together?

"This is wrong, son, but it's just that way in America. When you grow older perhaps you can change it."

"I will," I said, my jaw jutting out. This always made my father laugh. He patted my head affectionately.

"First, you will be a doctor. Then you can be a crusader," he would say, tucking me in at night.

I sat on the porch at the top stair of our large house on Columbus Drive, looking down the empty thoroughfare and watching for the arrival of the blue truck. My mother dressed me in a seersucker shirt which she had hand-made for the occasion. She had even made the buttons, an item that caused me embarrassment. Why couldn't she just buy me a shirt at Fernandez and Garcia, so I could look like the other boys? *Well,* I thought, *at least I won one argument,* and I stood up so I could feel the grown-up sensation of long pants. I even put new white shoestrings in my Kinney's sneakers. I checked my work utensils over and over again: a pencil, a jackknife, a large handkerchief with a dime tied into a corner knot, and my comb. I leaped to the curb as I spotted the blue Ford turn the corner and pull in front of my house.

As far back as I could remember, Sam always shook my hand solemnly and left a piece of candy in it. This ritual led me to call him Sweet Sam.

I hopped into the truck, smelling the new leather and the clean aroma of pharmaceuticals. Sam handed me a clipboard of invoices.

"Right on time, Sam," I said, the first of many times. I always tried to say the right thing to Sam.

"Procrastination is the thief of time," Sam said, shifting smoothly into first gear.

"What did you say?" I asked, dumbfounded.

Not taking his eyes off the road, and continuing to shift gears, Sam pointed to the glove box. I opened it to find a thick dictionary and a pad of papers, principally the backs of used invoices.

"Now, Master Ferdie. Today is your first day at work. I told your daddy I'd take you to all the clinics, hospitals, and drugstores in town

The Word Is Procrastinate, Look It Up. *1993. Ferdie Pacheco.*

and would teach you the drug delivery trade. But what you are really going to learn is to use the English language properly."

I was astonished by this amazing change in Sweet Sam. I had only heard him speak with a yassuh and nossuh. Now he sounded like the man on the radio.

"Take the pad and write down the word *procrastinate*." Sam patiently spelled it out for me. "Now, look it up under P. You do know how to use a dictionary?"

"Yes, Sam, I think so," I said, unsure of what I was being instructed to do. I took the book and finally found the word *procrastinate*.

"To put off doing something until a future time," I read slowly.

"Good. Write it down." Sam stuck his left arm out the window as he turned into 12th Avenue. "Now tomorrow when you get in this truck I want you to spell it, and to use it in a sentence."

"Did my father ask you to do this?"

"Your father doesn't know I speak like this, and we are going to keep it that way, otherwise he might gravitate into an untenable position."

"Gravitate?" I was leafing through the dictionary, trying to find how to spell the word.

Sam smiled as I buried my head in the book. "Those two words are enough. That takes care of my part of your education for the first day. From here on out, we'll take care of Mister J.B.'s deliveries."

The day passed in a blur of activity, visiting the emergency room at Tampa General, where I saw a man with his skull split open and a boy with a broken arm. I met the pharmacists at Lodato's and Trelles Clinic, and they all said how much I looked like my father, which gave me a great deal of pleasure. Sam made me carry the lighter boxes and he allowed me the job of having the customers sign for the goods. In this way Sam made me feel important and responsible.

When lunch came, Sam drove to our house on Columbus Drive and went through his ritual of wiping off the Ford, locking it, and washing his hands with the garden hose. I saw my plate of food and glass of milk on the dining table, waited until my mother was in the kitchen, then hurriedly took my lunch to the back porch and put it next to Sam's.

By the middle of that summer I felt the joys of maturing under the tutelage of an unusual professor. In addition to dictionary work, Sam brought small books of poems and short stories which he made me read out loud as we made our rounds.

One day, when I had saved up twenty-five cents, our delivery route took us to Palmetto Beach, and I decided to introduce Sweet Sam to the succulent joys of a cuban sandwich. Sam was flattered by the offer. We drove to the Columbia Restaurant, where my aunt Lola was the day cashier. Bashfully I asked her to put a cuban sandwich in a bag along with a cold S.B. beer. The total of twenty-five cents caused me to skip having a Coke, and I hoped Sam would not offer to buy it. It was the first time I had bought a grown-up his lunch. The idea that I spent the princely sum of twenty-five cents on Sam's lunch was making me feel giddy.

Knowing that we should not be seen eating together, Sam drove to Palmetto Beach and backed the Ford to the water's edge. Opening the back door, so that a cool breeze blew through the truck, we sat on the back bumper. I opened the bag and pulled out the long sandwich, cut diagonally in two.

Sam walked to the water's edge and removed his rimless spectacles carefully, placing them in his vest pocket. He washed his face and hands in the warm water. I did the same.

Finally, Sam took a bite of the hard-crusted sandwich, filled with ham, roast pork, cheese, dill pickle, and mustard. I watched him intently. Would he like it? Had he ever eaten one before?

A smile spread on Sam's face, and a quick nod of his head indicated his approval.

"Succulent, Master Ferdie, delectable." Sam took a second bite. "You can write those words down later."

We sat with our backs to the side of the truck, chewing contentedly, until I realized that I had not offered Sam his drink. I reached into the brown bag and brought out the fat green bottle and handed it to Sam, realizing at the same moment that he didn't have an opener. He accepted the bottle and promptly set it against the bumper, popping the top with one quick motion of his hand.

The hard bread crust made the sandwich difficult to eat without some liquid to wash it down. Sam took a long swig of the cold beer. Small droplets remained on his moustache, and with the rag he was using as a napkin he wiped his mouth.

"Perfection," Sam sighed, taking another long pull from the bottle. He closed his eyes for a long moment, savoring the refreshing brew. I felt a glow of satisfaction from providing pleasure for a person I cared for. Suddenly Sam's eyes popped open. He looked over the top of his glasses.

"Where's your drink, Master Ferdie?"

"Ah, I didn't get one."

"Now, I appreciate the beer, but we could have had two R.C. Colas with the ten cents the beer cost."

"My father says a cuban sandwich ain't a cuban sandwich unless you have a beer with it."

"Isn't," Sam corrected me, and thought about it for a moment. "Have you ever tasted beer?"

"No, sir. In my house I can only have watered wine with meals."

"Hm, I think it's time you tried it. You think we could share a secret? I mean Mister J.B. wouldn't mind, I'm sure, but your mother might be upset. So, it's our secret."

"Yes, sir!" I reached for the cold bottle, my dry mouth sorely in need of something cold.

As I started to take a drink, I was aware of a terrible dilemma. I had been told by my family never to drink from another person's bottle without first wiping off the top of the bottle, but I was aware that Sam might interpret this movement in a racial way. What if he was insulted that I would not drink from a black man's bottle without first wiping it off? I looked at Sam, who was chewing his sandwich, a hint of amusement in his eyes.

Well, if I die, I die, I thought, imagining hordes of death-dealing microbes parading into my mouth.

Gingerly I tilted the bottle, trying to pour the beer into my mouth without letting the lip of the bottle touch my lips. Sam watched in silent amusement. I gulped down the beer and handed the bottle back to Sam.

Deliberately Sam took the bottle and wiped it with the palm of his hand, then popped a finger in the bottle.

"Master Ferdie, didn't your daddy ever teach you about the Germ Theory?" He took a long pull of the golden brew. "Never drink from another man's bottle unless you wipe it off first."

In that way Sweet Sam taught me a lesson about the ways of the adult world, the ways of the South, and about friendship.

As the summer heat reached its peak in early August, Sam began to speed up the deliveries so that he would be finished by four o'clock. From this felicitous turn of events an unexpected bonus resulted.

In the late thirties the kidnapping of white children by blacks was a fear that had survived after the Reconstruction era. The fact that no such cases had ever been reported didn't seem to diminish this fear. So when Sam turned the Ford into Morgan Street, I thought it odd, since this street led into the central Negro district, and I knew that we had finished with the deliveries.

***Didn't Your Daddy Ever
Teach You about the Germ
Theory?*** *1993. Ferdie
Pacheco.*

There was a row of small, identical clapboard houses which took up the entire block. Most were shabby and in need of paint; others were in the final stages of disrepair. Sam stopped in front of the only house that was so neatly kept that it seemed like a model home.

It appeared to me like a single pearl in a row of grey oysters.

"Now, Master Ferdie, you will reap the harvest of your diligent labors." Sam smiled at me. My own smile was hiding a sea of troubled thoughts.

The white picket fence stood out like a Band-Aid on a black finger. No other house had a fence. The front yard was neatly trimmed and a small flower bed added a touch of color. The porch had two green cane rocking chairs. The house was bright white with dark green trim.

My heart beat fast as Sam fumbled for the key to the front door. I thought it odd that all the other front doors were open, as were the windows. But in the August heat any expectation of a breeze needed maximum ventilation. A closed front door shut out the hope of a breeze coming through the front door and blowing through the straight hallway and out the open back door.

Next door a disheveled man sat in a broken chair with a beer bottle in his hand. His face was troubled, and a three-day stubble heightened the effect.

"Sam, what you got thar? A white boy?"

Sam did not look at the man but continued in his precise way to open the front door. I tried not to notice the man and quickly stepped into the house and the welcome safe harbor of Sam's parlor.

The walls were made of grooved pine, painted white with enamel. The floor was a highly waxed varnished oak. The most amazing thing about the room was its lack of furniture.

With the afternoon sun beaming off its polished ebony top, a majestic grand piano sat, like a great sleeping watchdog, at the entrance to the rest of the house.

Sam told me to look at the photographs on the wall, and on the piano top. He would return in a moment.

The pictures on the wall seemed old and faded, like my grandfather's books about Spain. I saw a grim-faced man, who looked a bit like Sam, in a Union uniform. The Civil War was still talked about. Any schoolboy knew the difference between a Yankee and a Rebel. This Yankee held a large Dahlgren revolver in his crossed arms. On his chest he proudly displayed a medal that I had never seen before.

On the piano were photographs of more recent vintage. They were clearer and better prints.

These photographs were mostly of musicians, holding their instruments in the act of playing. One large photograph was a beautiful group of ladies on the stairs of a mansion. Most were white, although the back row was all black. I didn't recognize Sam in any of the photographs. I thought they were photos of family and friends.

"Master Ferdie, come with me to collect your bonus," Sam said, leading me through the small hallway to the kitchen.

The kitchen was spotless, and on the white enamel-topped table I spotted a big pie. Two large wedges had been cut from it and placed in front of the two chairs. Beside the plates were two barrel glasses of ice-cold milk.

"Lemon meringue pie, à la Leona, *la specialité de la maison*," Sam pulled out a chair and motioned for me to be seated.

The back screen door opened and a trim, lovely, sweet-faced lady came in holding a quart bottle of milk, the beads of condensation coalescing and running in rivulets to spot the linoleum floor.

"Master Ferdie, we owe this delightful refresher to Mrs. Leona," Sam said. By his tone of voice I understood that I should muster an effort to thank her.

"Pleased to meet you, ma'am." I stood up and walked toward her with my hand extended, as I had been taught by J.B. "And thank you for the pie. It's my favorite kind."

Putting down the milk bottle, Leona wiped her hands on her apron and took my hand in hers. She smiled a beautiful smile, her eyes crinkling in an attractive way. I could see that she was happy to meet me, yet she never spoke a word.

"Now we have only one rule about this bonus. If I hear from your mamma that you haven't eaten your supper without wiping up your supper plate, then the bonus is finished forever."

"No problem, Sam. We don't eat at my house until Papa comes home. And he doesn't come home until eight o'clock."

Sam put a generous piece of the fresh pie in his mouth, and wiped his lips with the clean napkin.

I had trouble sleeping that night, my head reeling with the images of what I'd seen, my stomach aching from the big supper I had eaten.

Yet I felt a sense of accomplishment. I'd been taken into an adult's confidence. Not just any adult, not an uncle or one of J.B.'s friends, but the most important one in my immediate life, Sweet Sam.

Sam had taken a big chance by taking me to his home. This act was a gesture of real friendship that was not lost on me. I had never believed friendship could exist between a boy and an adult, much less between a white boy and a black man.

I was bursting to tell somebody of my afternoon of discovery. I would have told Manolin, my best friend at the corner garage, but he would just tell his parents, and that would put an end to my bonus afternoons. Certainly J.B. or my mother could never be told. Gossip could go hard on Sweet Sam. The thought that Sam had cleared it with my father never entered my mind.

Determined to guard our secret with my life, I rolled over in my bed, putting my leg on the window sill to try to get as much of a breeze as I could. I fell asleep, my mind a blur of images. The row of dingy houses, Sam's white palace, the frightening man next door, the fresh aroma of the front room, the smell of cedar furniture polish, and the magnificent, monstrous grand piano. At last, to see the grand piano after years of hearing about it. It was even grander than I had imagined. The pictures that were ghosts of Sam's past were clearly in my mind. But which one was Sam? Was there a picture of Leona? Questions, until sleep came and the last thing I thought about was Leona. How beautiful she was. How soft her hands were. She had a lovely smile. While she never spoke, I felt she had transmitted to me her wordless feelings, like the dolphins I played with at the beach. Finally I realized that only my father had ever met Leona. Yet Sam had trusted *me* to meet Leona.

Summer was coming to an end. I was already regretting starting school, giving up the daily rounds with Sweet Sam and his late-afternoon bonuses.

My father was happy that I had worked most of the summer, instead of playing with my friends. I had chosen to ride around in a hot truck making deliveries; more surprising, I had relished the time I spent with Sam. Already my father had detected a marked change in my vocabulary, which he attributed to my accelerated reading. With Sam I had witnessed a surgical operation at Trelles Clinic. I'd seen an autopsy at Tampa Municipal Hospital and met most of the important doctors in the town. It was one of the brightest ideas Sam had ever had. After this summer there would be no doubt that I would choose a career in medicine.

On a stormy late August afternoon, I stumbled on the threshold of a great mystery, and would live to remember the afternoon for the rest of my days.

❧ Dark clouds were blowing in from the Gulf, and the waves on Tampa Bay were battering Bayshore Boulevard, sending up columns of grey spume over the Ford truck. The little truck swayed in the strong wind and Sam was having a difficult time keeping it from hitting the curb. Other cars were lined up on the other side of the boulevard, stalled out and helpless as the water in the road became deeper and crept over their running boards. It was well past four o'clock when Sam pulled up in front of his house. Carefully he put on his black oilskin rain gear and took his rimless glasses off, folding them as he placed them in his pocket. I did the same, loving every minute of walking in the rain with rain gear protecting me. I had never owned rain gear before. Rain was either an occasion for a frolic in the backyard with my old clothes on, or discomfort when I walked home from school in it.

The wind battered Sam's house, the screen door was banging rhythmically, and the two porch chairs were rocking as if two ghosts sat in them. Sam's face showed a moment of worry. But he turned the chairs around and leaned them on the front wall. He stopped the door and held it motionless with his foot while he fumbled in his pocket for his keys.

I was shocked to hear a loud, angry voice coming over the fence, yelling above the wind.

"Sam, you dumb nigger. I tole you to quit bringing that white kid into the neighborhood. You gonna get us kilt by the Klan."

Sam continued to fumble in his pockets for the key, not giving any attention to the boisterous man next door.

"The Klan will come one night and burn a cross on your lawn." The man took a long pull from a whiskey bottle. "Now, I don't care if they burn your house down, but I don't want mine to go with it!"

Sam turned the key, but the sodden door remained stuck for a moment and he had to put his shoulder against it to open it.

The man was becoming more and more agitated. Sam ignored him. He was now trying to crawl over Sam's picket fence.

"Dumb nigger! Own a piano and cain't play it. Has a wife that cain't talk. And now he gonna bring a white boy here who's gonna bring the Klan to fry his ass."

For the first time since I had been coming here, I was afraid. I had never experienced such hostility. And I had never seen grown men fight.

The man was tangled up in the picket fence, and in his exasperation he drew out a straight razor and opened it. It looked long and cold and evil.

"What I gotta do, Sam, cut you, to keep that boy outta here? Maybe I gotta cut the boy!"

For the first time Sam reacted. First he gently pushed me inside, then he turned to the man and spoke in a low voice, clear, but laden with menace.

"You're drunk, Snow, so I'll let this pass this once. But from this day on, if you so much as look my way or Leona's way, or this boy's way, there isn't any place far enough away to run, no hole deep enough to hide in, where I won't find you and kill you."

The air seemed to come out of the drunken neighbor. He released his grasp on the picket fence and fell backward into a pool of muddy water. Sam entered the front room and latched the screen door, then closed the wooden door behind him.

"I'm sorry if he scared you, Master Ferdie. Snow is not really a bad man. But drink turns him into a monster."

Sam went to the kitchen to look for Leona. Obviously she was not at home.

I leaned against the gleaming grand piano. I felt weak, as though I might faint. Then slowly my fear changed to anger. Who was this worthless man who called Sam a "dumb nigger"? And Sam constantly withstood jokes about his piano and his mute Leona. Why did he keep taking it? Why didn't he sell the piano and be done with it?

When Sam entered the room he found me with my fist clenched, tears in my eyes, my jaw thrust forward. Sam had seen the look many times in my father's eyes.

"Why do you let them call you a dumb nigger? You're not! You're not! Why do you let them make fun of your piano? What does it mean to you? Why don't you just sell it?"

The lace curtains blew in the wind and rain that came in the half-open window. The floor darkened as the rain pooled under it. Sam looked undecided. Obviously Leona had left to go shopping before the storm blew up, and she was stuck at the store until the rain stopped. We were alone. We were isolated from the outside world.

Sam moved to the piano, adjusting the sleeve garters so that his cuffs were halfway up his arm. He was deliberate in the way he lifted the lid from the keys. His face was a mask. Without the rimless glasses he looked different. He ran his hands over his wet, straight hair.

The first notes hit me like a thunderbolt. They were slow, harmonious, deep notes, and they were dirgelike.

"I went down to St. James Infirmary . . . to see my baby there . . ."

Sam's eyes were closed. His high cheekbones and straight nose gave me the impression of a High Plains Indian chanting a funeral tune. His voice was strong and sure and very pleasing to the ear. For the first time I heard a dialect in Sweet Sam's voice. I had never been out of Tampa in my life so I didn't know it was New Orleans Creole patois.

Let her go, let her go, God bless her!
Wherever she may be,
She may roam the whole world over,
She'll never find a
Sweet Sam like me . . .

The tempo now picked up and Sam swung into another tune, joy leaping from the keyboard and replacing the sadness of the opening chorus. I watched his hands fly over the keys, feet beating time, eyes closed, and his smile as wide as the Mississippi River.

Sam came to a stomping, swinging finale, and when he stopped he put his hand on my shoulder.

Let Her Go, Let Her Go, God Bless Her! *1993. Ferdie Pacheco.*

"That, Master Ferdie, was jazz. That's what I did long ago, but I can't do it no more. And let that be our secret."

"Please. Please, play some more. What is jazz? Why don't you play it? It sounds great! I never heard no one play like that . . ." I was excited, happy, and curious all at one time. I couldn't stop begging for more.

Sam looked out the window to check the storm. The wind was dying down, the rain letting up.

"All right, but only one more. If I'm going to tell you about jazz, we have to begin with Scott Joplin," Sam started a tinkling happy tune, "who invented ragtime."

Sam was playing his happy tune when he stopped and looked at the hallway. Leona stood there with a hurt and furious look on her face. Sam instantly closed the piano and walked me to the front door, as though to get me out of her sight.

❧ The truck pulled up in front of our house on Columbus Drive. No words had passed between us, but we both knew that the summer was over. There would be no more deliveries, no more vocabulary tests, no more cuban sandwiches, no more late-afternoon bonuses, and no more piano concerts.

Without being asked, I turned to Sam and said, "Don't worry, Sam. I won't tell a soul about jazz and the piano."

Impulsively, Sam hugged me as he had at the end of every day since I was a toddler.

"I know you won't," he said, and rode off down the red brick street, ending my introduction into the adult world.

❧ When the war came, J.B. went into the retail drugstore business, and Sweet Sam was lost in the shuffle.

By 1948 I was in college. During the Christmas break I was visiting a friend who worked in a hospital emergency room. An old, rough-looking black man was being tended to, and as he talked I became aware that he was Snow, Sam's argumentative neighbor. I asked him about Sam.

"Sam, he be in bad shape. Leona died a few years back. Cancer, they say. Spent all his money on her illness. Sold the house. Now Sam's sick.

His heart is bad. Cain't work. Gets a piece of change from the gub'ment."

"Where does he live?"

"Oh, on Morgan Street, in Miss Ella's Boardinghouse. Has a room there to hisself. But he don't see nobody though."

Impulsively I got into my car and drove straight to the Morgan Street boardinghouse. I found that Sam had gone to the cardiac clinic and would not be home until late afternoon. Miss Ella proved to be a warm, expansive, church-going lady who had a soft spot in her heart for Sam. She told me that Sam had often spoken highly of J.B., and that he was following my educational career and was proud of my achievements. Of course, she said, looking me sternly in the eye, Sam had fallen on hard times, but would accept help from no one.

Without much persuasion Miss Ella allowed me to go into Sam's room. It was Christmas Eve, and I told her I was here to buy Sam anything he needed.

The room was a smaller version of the front room that was so vividly etched in my memory. Sam had painted the walls antiseptic white. The old wooden floor was painted dark brown. It gleamed.

There was no furniture in the room except the grand piano, which occupied most of the space. In the corner was a washbasin and a medicine cabinet above it with a clean white towel neatly hung from a small rack by its side. Under the basin was a folded army cot, and in the other corner a small cardboard closet containing Sam's black coat, striped tie, and shirt hanging on wire hangers.

"Sam likes to keep it simple," I smiled, looking at the sparse room.

"Sure do," Miss Ella said, shaking her head. "He done all the painting hisself. I just buy the paint."

"What does he need most?"

"Need? That man don't *need* nothin'. He could use his watch back. He hocks it at Detroit Red's at the end of every month when he runs out of cash. Tell Red I sent you. It ain't much."

"Is that all?"

"Well, I spect he could stand some company," Miss Ella fixed me with a hard, church-lady stare, in the event I was contemplating just applying a white folk's money poultice to my aching conscience.

"I'll be back before Sam gets home from the hospital."

"That be round six."

"I'll be here before then."

I went home with the news that I had found Sweet Sam, and asked my mother to make a lemon meringue pie, using only fresh lemons and making real meringue, as only she could. While it was being made I drove fast to Detroit Red's, where I picked up the big gold watch. I wound it with the tiny key, and opened it to hear the beautiful tune which I now identified as the "Marseillaise."

By late afternoon I was back at Miss Ella's. I took a white towel and spread it on the black ebony piano bench. I placed the fresh pie on the towel with the two plates, and two of my mother's best silver forks. Beside the plates I put a large quart bottle of milk, the beads of condensation on the sides, the cream at the neck.

In the fancy case I had bought from Detroit Red I placed the gold watch. Miss Ella, getting in the spirit, opened the cot and made the bed with fresh linen she had just taken down from the clothes line. As an additional touch, she picked some zinnias from the yard and made a bouquet which she put in a chipped chamber pot in the corner of the bare room.

Christmas Eve, 1948, was notable because Bing Crosby had introduced Irving Berlin's "White Christmas," and so everywhere you went, whether to O'Falk's Department Store or Maas Brothers, or the Yellow House Bar, or the Columbia Restaurant, you heard this song.

Miss Ella's front porch was no different. A ragged assemblage of boarders were drinking heavily, laughing at old stories, and ignoring Bing Crosby's "White Christmas," which played over and over again on Miss Ella's phonograph. From time to time they would look across the street at a black 1941 Chevrolet, where I sat slouched down in the seat waiting for Sweet Sam to return from the hospital. As the evening wore on and the sun went down, a thin string of Christmas lights flickered on, and the derisive laughter of the front-porch celebrants grew in volume. The idea that a white boy was waiting for Sam on Christmas Eve in this neighborhood seemed to fill them with merriment.

I was growing uneasy as a few men directed remarks in my direction. Although they were contemptuous they weren't menacing, but I felt uncomfortable anyway. Maybe I was intruding. Maybe I wasn't welcome, but my excitement at seeing Sweet Sam again overcame my doubts. I resolved to stay put and see it through.

Finally, as the street lights were being turned on I saw him. He came walking down the street, much slower now, bent, but still somehow giving the impression of being erect. It was Sweet Sam all right, as distinctive as ever in his white celluloid collar and cuffs, his striped shirt, and his perfectly buttoned vest. No way to hide him behind old age and grey hair. You might as well try to hide the Statue of Liberty under a coat of red paint.

The men on the porch stifled their laughter and respected Miss Ella's instructions to keep my secret. They chided Sam as they always had.

"Go on up there, Sam, and play us some real back-home Christmas music, we be tired of the White Christmas shit."

"Yeah, Sam, give us Black Christmas . . ."

Sam nodded, accustomed to their jibes, still refusing to answer, or explain. They waited expectantly as they guessed what Sam would do when he saw the watch and the pie and the milk.

"White Christmas" was coming to yet one more finale, when the first chords of a funereal dirge were heard. The men stopped laughing to listen, and I jumped from my car to hear the music.

Soon the men recognized the sad chords, and one man, with a deep voice, sang along.

"I went down to St. James infirmary . . . to see my baby there . . ."

Then the tune stepped on into ragtime tempo, which slipped into stride piano with amazing ease. My heart jumped as I raced into the house.

"I *tole* you that nigger could play the piano if he wanted to . . ." a voice cackled behind me on the porch.

I found Sam at the piano, a smile on his wrinkled face. The moustache was white now, and the straight hair was thin, but to my eyes he still looked like Sweet Sam, the man who had taught me so much about medicine, the English language, music, and about life in America. Suddenly I was ten years old again.

"Boy, didn't your father ever teach you about the Germ Theory?"

We fell into each other's arms, squeezing hard, afraid to let go lest we break down and cry.

Finally, we ate the pie until it was all gone, and drank the cold milk and talked about what had happened since we last spent a wonderful summer together, trying not to mention how we both had changed, and how different things were.

Sam looked at the gold watch lovingly, and opened it to hear the beautiful, tinkling "Marseillaise." He looked at the time, as if thinking that he didn't have much time left.

It was then that I could not withstand my curiosity about Sam any longer. Who was he? Why did he and Leona come to Tampa? Why didn't Leona speak? Why didn't he play the piano? Why didn't he sell the piano, particularly now when he was sick and needed the money? Why?

Sam nodded when I burst forth with my rush of questions.

"I see that you have gravitated to the central question and polarized me into a position where I'm obligated to answer." Sam's eyes had the old mocking gleam in them, and he started by telling me about his father, Jethro, who although a slave on a Louisiana plantation was also the son of the master. When the Civil War came, the white son of the master took a commission in the Louisiana Tigers and took Jethro, his half-brother, to Virginia. He was killed in the Seven Days Battle. Jethro could only save his watch and his Dahlgren revolver. He went on to serve in the Yankee army, received the Medal of Honor, and came back to New Orleans, where he opened schools to teach freed black men to read and write. His partner was an educated Englishman, and when Sam came along, he was taught English by the same professor and was then put in a music school to learn to play the piano.

Sam played a small segment of an etude, then stopped as he felt his strength going. In short, direct sentences, stopping to rest or play to illustrate his story, he told me of his young manhood in Storyville, of his wanton years as the star piano man at the bordello Le Chien Rouge, and of the tragic story of Leona. As a young teenager Leona was kidnapped out of the cotton fields of Mississippi and brought to Le Chien Rouge, where a chain of events occurred which rendered her mute, and resulted in Sam escaping from New Orleans in a mule-drawn carriage. Leona had killed a white man, the savage pimp of Le Chien Rouge, and Sam was afraid that they would be identified if he ever played the piano. If they were caught Leona would be brought back to Louisiana and

Now When I Die, Bury Me in Edwin's Clapp Shoes. 1993.
Ferdie Pacheco.

hung for killing a white man, and Sam along with her for helping her to escape.

He finished with the last lines of the "St. James Infirmary Blues":

Now, when I die,
Bury me in Edwin's Clapp shoes,
A box back suit, and a Stetson hat.
Put a twenty-dollar gold piece on my watch chain,
So the boys will know I died standing pat.

I tucked Sam in his bed, my head whirling from the story and the music. We made plans for Christmas Day. J.B. had insisted that Sam be invited to sit with the family and eat the Christmas meal. There they would discuss Sam's future.

Some stories are meant to end when they end, and Sam, having told me his story, ended it that night. When I went to pick him up on Christmas Day I found a tearful Miss Ella. She held my hand and told me that Sam had gone to join Leona, and that she had found him that morning as I had left him: his hands holding the gold watch, with the faint suggestion of a smile on his lips.

Remembrances of J.B.

I had a strong father to guide me. He gave me room to grow and develop my own personality. He was a pillar of strength, intimidating, daunting, and protective of me. His was the greatest influence on me, and he wholly supported my freedom to choose my own way of life.

J.B. hated to fly. No one ever convinced him that people were meant to fly. I on the other hand believed that my future would be tied up in aviation. In the mid-thirties my heroes were aviators. Lindbergh had flown the Atlantic. Jimmy Doolittle was renowned as a closed-course champion flying a Gee Bee at the Cleveland air races, and every boy could name the aces who had flown in the First World War.

Every morning I put on my flying helmet and goggles. I took my pathetic tricycle, encumbered by a side mount, and sped down the sidewalk imagining I was Captain Eddie Rickenbacker on the tail of a red Fokker tri-plane.

So I was overjoyed to hear J.B. tell my mother, Consuelo, that Captain Fernandez was coming by for lunch. He told me that Captain Fernandez had flown in the Lafayette Escadrille. He was now a stunt pilot who earned his living doing dangerous aeronautic tricks for the movies. When things were slow, he gave people rides at county fairs. J.B. seemed to consider the captain a fool, a clown, and not to be taken seriously. After all, he drove a beat-up Pontiac with bad brakes. He came to a stop by downshifting and aiming at something cheap. When he came to dinner, his irresponsibility was the subject of conversation and there were lots of laughs at his expense. Playing with my model Spad under the table, I was highly excited.

Captain Fernandez was a rumpled, ragged, lanky man. His clothes were covered with oil blotches, his cavalry breeches tucked into leather puttees. His face was weather-beaten. I could swear I saw the faint outline of goggles marked on his face. The bottom half of his face was darker than the top half. His hair was tousled and uncombed. In short, he was my idea of what a pilot should be.

Captain Fernandez was the first man I ever saw roll a cigarette. My father offered him an Old Gold, but he waved it away, as though accepting a machine-made cigarette was the first step toward decadence. "Real men roll their own," he appeared to be demonstrating, squinty-eyed. J.B. laughed and called for *café solos* ("coffee alone," or black coffee). When the makings were in the thin, neatly channeled paper, Captain Fernandez expertly folded over the white paper and licked it with his thick tongue. He knew I was watching him, mouth open, amazed by his display of manly expertise. He decided to top off his performance with a show-stopper. He took a big kitchen match from the gas stove, and struck the match on his grizzly chin. My father laughed heartily at the astounded look on my face.

"Who's this? Eddie Rickenbacker?" Captain Fernandez plucked me out of my hiding place under the table. He picked me up and sat me on the oilcloth-covered kitchen table.

"This is my son Ferdie. He's going to be a doctor," said J.B., pointedly cutting off any reply that would suggest another option.

"Looks like he's going to be a pilot."

I was aghast. The thought that anyone would contradict my father was incredible.

J.B. was a huge man in my eyes. He was a six-footer in a town of small European men. His shoulders were broad. He had an air of authority about him that seemed to bode violence. Men gave way to him, and deferred to his wishes. No one contradicted him. At least not so far as I had heard.

"Have you ever seen a real airplane before? Have you ever thought of flying in a real airplane?"

The captain was talking to me directly. He wasn't asking J.B. about me. He was asking *me*. I looked at my father for permission to speak. He was puffing contentedly on his Old Gold cigarette, sipping the fresh, steaming expresso my mother had just served. He nodded slightly and I blurted out, "No, but I would like to."

"Well, J.B., looks like we got us a birdman."

"Not on your life, bub." J.B. returned me to the cockpit of my pedal airplane. "That's the closest he'll ever come to an airplane."

My hopes, which had risen like a full-power-packet rocket, came crashing to earth. J.B.'s word was final. I'd never heard anyone dispute it. Not my mother, nor even my grandmother.

Captain Fernandez blew a lazy white smoke ring in the air and watched as it rose to collide with the flypaper banner hanging from the electric light.

"J.B., you want this boy to be a sissy? To grow up afraid of his shadow? Or do you want him to be a tough guy, like you, not afraid of anything."

"Flying isn't 'anything'. Birds fly. People don't."

"Nonsense, J.B., I survived the Great War, Hollywood, and county fairs. All in my trusty Jenny. Let me take the boy up once. Just once around the field. No stunts. No tricks."

"Please, Poppa, please!" I was at his knee, amazed by my audacity. "Just once."

For all his tough demeanor, my father was a pushover for his family, and I had had palpable evidence that I was his favorite child. Once he came home and found me crying in pain, lying on the kitchen floor. I had stepped on my grandmother's prized family heirloom, a primitive, twisted black iron fork. It had been in her family for centuries. As soon as he found the errant fork he took it to the back porch and hurled it as far as his mighty arm could fling it. It was never found again. An offender that had attacked his son had been dealt with. Although it brought a year of silence from my indignant grandmother, it assured me that I was unquestionably his most valuable possession. Now, Captain Fernandez was pushing his luck, but my tearful pleading and the idea that I had to start becoming a man wore down J.B.'s better judgment.

"OK, but just once around." J.B. stood up and put on his straw boater. "And let's do it now before I change my mind."

We followed Captain Fernandez in his battered Pontiac, my father's resolve weakening every time he heard the grinding gears and saw the intrepid captain hit a curb, or barely miss a tree, or the car in front of him.

Tampa's airfield was called Drew Field, and it was a large cow pasture edged by the bay. At one end stood a large, dilapidated hangar, a limp wind sock on its roof. In front of the hangar were a few yellow Piper Cubs. Off to the side was a gigantic bi-wing aircraft, all struts and wires. It was painted a faded olive drab and had Allied roundels on the wings. It looked like a condemned building.

Captain Fernandez drove toward the tired war bird, his arm hanging out of the Pontiac, waving us on enthusiastically.

My heart was pounding. I feared that J.B. would change his mind. His face reflected his inner doubt. Surely this elaborate bedstead couldn't fly.

The Pontiac came to an abrupt halt against a concrete culvert, its radiator emitting a white cloud of steam, and the captain spoke to a young mechanic.

"Jake, remove the chock blocks, prime 'er for me. I'm going up for a spin with this young pilot here. We're going to see what the university minarets look like from up above." He winked at J.B., who had brought his majestic black Buick to a halt next to the wrecked Pontiac. "Once around the city," J.B. grunted, as though the words tore at his heart.

Captain Fernandez put me in the front cockpit. It had a wicker chair and a tattered cushion. The safety belts looked like old cowboy belts. They smelled of oil, of gasoline, of castor oil. It was heaven!

He climbed in behind me and cocked his head to one side so he could see Jake, who had given the propeller a few turns.

"Switch on!" Jake called.

"Switch on!" the captain responded.

"Contact."

"Contact."

The enormous engine, which was a foot away from my cockpit, coughed a few times and then, to my amazement, roared to life. I had never heard anything as loud. I put my hands over my ears. It was as though two jackhammers were pounding in my helmet. I felt a fine spray hit my face and speckle my goggles. The taste was familiar—castor oil.

The plane waddled out to the middle of the field, and Captain Fernandez pointed it at the bay. The take-off was bumpy because the grass field had never been smoothed out.

I felt the magic moment of flight, the lift-off. My heart sang with joy. The powerful motor roared and we gained altitude over the bay. Flocks of seagulls scattered in the path of the lumbering plane. A pelican dived for the safety of the azure bay.

Suddenly the motor stopped. We banked smoothly and approached the grassy strip again. From Captain Fernandez issued a muffled laugh. The figure of my father waited, arms crossed, lips compressed, a look of relief in his eyes.

We rolled to a stop, and the captain reached down into the fuselage and produced a large can with a spout. Gracefully he jumped from the plane and walked past J.B., who grabbed his arm.

"Hey, I told you once around. You barely got off the ground."

"Yes, I forgot to check the gas. We're out of gas."

Those were the last words I ever heard Captain Fernandez speak.

I watched in fascination as J.B. crashed a resounding right cross to the face of the surprised pilot. Life did not leave his body, but consciousness certainly did.

My father snatched me out of the cockpit of the airplane, my thin body sliding out of the crossed safety belt like a pea being shucked from a pod.

My experience in aviation had ended abruptly. My last sight of Captain Fernandez was through the rear window of J.B.'s Buick: a man lying on his back, arms and legs outspread, totally unconscious, with a surprised look on his face.

I never saw or heard of Captain Fernandez again.

Life with J.B. was like that. Sometimes his good nature gave way to sudden solutions. I was never used to it but I was proud of it. It didn't happen many times, because he was well-known and well-liked. For reasons I did not discover until I was a middle-aged man, my father was greatly respected.

Consciousness Left Captain Fernandez's Body. *1993. Ferdie Pacheco.*

He was kind and considerate to my mother, but his ways were those of the old country. For example, he never put on his own shoes, or tied the laces. His ritual was to wake up with my mother standing by the bed with a cup of expresso and a glass of ice water. When he finished drinking his coffee, she would put his socks on, then his shoes, and tie them. In time, he would allow me to do it for him. It was the highlight of my day to be able to begin his day happily.

He always took siestas after lunch. He would wait for my mother to finish cleaning the kitchen, then she would come and sit on one side of the sofa. He would put his massive bald head on her lap and drop off to sleep. He usually slept for an hour. She fanned him and remained still. He would wake, wait for his expresso, kiss her, and return to work.

Supper meant full-course meals. We all dressed for supper, which meant we bathed and dressed in clean clothes. Sometimes, when he was overcome by a familial sense of duty, he would ask my brother and me if we would like to go to the movies.

"I want to see the Garbo picture," my genius brother would say. He was sensitive and loved MGM romances.

"Phooey! Let's see Gary Cooper in a western," I would argue.

My father would wait until our argument grew heated. Then he would rise and give a Solomon-like verdict.

"If you guys can't agree, I guess we just won't go."

And before we could compromise, he was gone. Latin men of Ybor City did not stay home in the evenings. Their social clubs were the Centro Asturiano, the Centro Español, and the Círculo Cubano. They all had game rooms where chess and dominoes were played, where a hearts game was always in progress, and where the conversations were often heated, never dull. In all my childhood years I don't remember ever attending a movie with my father.

I learned the profession of pharmacy from my father, and I learned much more than just how to mix and make a prescription. Working next to him, I also learned about life. I saw him give medicine to people who could never pay him, yet he found ways to preserve their dignity. They never asked for charity. They were too proud. But they did accept credit. It was the same thing in a different package. My father never spoke of it.

"Don't do something and then brag about it. If you do, then you haven't done a damned thing."

Brother Joseph (left), Mother Consuelo, and me, 1936. Dell'Elmo Studio.

❧ At the end of four years of hard work at Spring Hill College, just weeks away from a degree, months away from medical school, I got expelled for a prank which can only be described as dumb.

My heart raced as I headed home. J.B. will kill me, I thought. He'll take a baseball bat and work me over. Strange thoughts from a young man who had never felt his father's hand in anger. Why was I having them? I had felt only a sense of shame and embarrassment when I faced my main teacher, Father P.H. Yancey, S.J. He was a terror—harsh, demanding, driven, and intolerant of student errors.

Yet Father Yancey had cried when he confronted his prize pupil who had squandered his chance to become a doctor.

"It's my fault," he said. "I was too hard on you."

The surprise of Yancey's forgiving attitude was nothing compared to facing J.B.

Now I waited in the parlor for J.B. to come home from the drugstore. He entered, walked to me as he always did, took me in his strong arms and squeezed me. With one motion he expressed his forgiveness. No words were needed.

"What do you want to do now?" he said. His voice was even and sympathetic.

Suddenly I was that tiny boy in the kitchen, enthralled by the sight of a heroic father grappling with my assailant, the family heirloom fork, and throwing it beyond any hope of recovery.

J.B. was protecting his boy. Suppressing any manly urge to cry, I answered in a clear voice that I would go on to pharmacy school and then proceed into medicine. He agreed. He drank his expresso and headed for the Centro Asturiano, and the never-ending game of hearts with Al Lopez, Tomate, Tudela Cuervo, Diaz, Alonso and his gang.

He never mentioned my trouble again.

❧ My father never spoke of his childhood, nor did I ever hear his brothers, John and Ralph, speak of their past. It took me years of research to discover what I do know.

Their father, like J.B., was a pharmacist, and his father before him. He was in the Spanish army and apparently ended up on the wrong side of the Spanish-American War. When that war ended in Cuban

*Brother Joseph (left) and I
when we were in the navy,
1932. Maas Brothers Photo-
graphic Studio.*

My father, J.B., in his twenties, 1915.

independence, he elected to stay in Cuba. He had come from Valencia, with a wife and three boys. When his wife died, Dr. Pacheco, as pharmacists were called, married a concert pianist with the unique name of Pennsylvania.

With a paucity of purse that continually dogged the Pachecos and with three bright boys to educate, he took the traditional Spanish way out: he made a deal with the Catholic Church. In exchange for a university education the boys would enter the priesthood. A careful study of the Pacheco boys would have revealed a two-thirds chance of failure.

Serious Ralph was a possibility. The handsome, skirt-chasing John, and the puckish, irresponsible J.B. were sure bets to abandon the project.

The way out was provided by the Vatican. Ralph progressed far enough in his training for the priesthood to be sent to Rome. The pope took it upon himself to save the Catholic world by issuing an encyclical banning motion pictures as a mortal sin. One good look at Charlie Chaplin would condemn the sinner to eternal and everlasting damnation. Ralph retained enough of the Pacheco contentiousness to want to see for himself. In one of the dumbest, or smartest, moves in his life, Ralph, dressed as a priest, attended a nickelodeon on the Via Veneto. It was a historic moment for the Pachecos. Ralph was kicked out of the Church, and John and J.B. were instantly relieved of their obligations.

Dr. Pacheco opened his apothecary in Ybor City around 1905. Only J.B. was attracted to pharmacy, and he apprenticed under the tough old bird. If the father had any redeeming qualities, none were recorded in family stories. The only time J.B. ever mentioned him to me was when he was telling me how easy I had it as a child, as far as corporal punishment was concerned. His father carried a heavy walking stick, and if J.B. ever slipped and called him "Poppa" instead of the more formal "Dr. Pacheco," he would whack J.B. on the back with his stick. I guess it's no wonder none of the three boys ever spoke about him.

My step-grandmother Pennsylvania was a delightful, educated, cultured piano teacher who loved a good story. She was a fantastic musician and an atrocious cook. She would serve her guest a burnt quail, smile, and tell a funny story while playing Chopin. She had a daughter, Delia, but I never clearly understood where she fit in.

Uncle Ralph was a quiet, shy man who lost his legs in a streetcar mishap and was reduced in size and fortune to making his living as a stationary bookkeeper. He would come to J.B.'s La Economica Drugstore when I was a kid, and he always gave me a dime tip. When I was a twenty-five-year-old registered pharmacist, he would come to do the books and he still gave me a dime. I never knew why.

Uncle John was more fun. He was famous in Ybor City. He had a matinee-idol air about him. No photograph could capture his handsomeness; it had to do with attitude. He was tall and took pride in his physique. In my eyes John was as close to royalty as you could get.

Grandfather Pacheco as a Spanish Army officer, 1895. J.A. Suarez y Cía Fotografos. Courtesy of John Pareja, M.D.

A notorious womanizer in his youth, he had stood up so many girls at the altar that there was a saying in Ybor City which still exists today: "She stayed waiting like Pacheco's bride."

When he did marry, Ybor City was shocked, for he married a cute American girl who was shy and very quiet. Bonny was her name, and she was a favorite person of mine. They had two beautiful daughters and a Huck Finn son.

John was an alderman and had an active part in building Cuscaden Park. He presided at the openings of parks and streets in Palmetto Beach. As long as he stayed in office, the riches and prestige never stopped. My greatest Christmas came in the midst of the Great Depression. John showed up at the house the day before Christmas and gave us fifty dollars. It was enough to outfit a football, baseball, and basketball team.

Politics was neither easy nor safe in Tampa. Election Day in Tampa was like D-Day in Normandy with proportionately the same casualty rate. It was open war. Uncle John's nerves finally gave out and he had a nervous breakdown, which was spoken about in whispers at my house. I felt bad about it, especially since I would not able to see my oldest cousin, the gorgeous Dorita.

John, with the knowledge of an incurable Don Juan, did not trust anyone near his two beauty queens. That kind of suffocating parental love always results in the precipitous escape of the shackled girls. Dorita married a local boy, and Nena fled to Miami and married a hairdresser who was every bit the womanizer Uncle John was. Is this psychodrama familiar to you?

Dorita's husband contracted tuberculosis and had to be sent to Denver for a year. She had borne him a son named, what else, John. The

Dr. Pacheco in front of his apothecary shop with sons, John, Ralph, and J.B., 1917.

Step-grandmother Pennsylvania Pacheco, a grand personality and an extraordinary pianist, 1913. Burgert Bros. Studio.

poor baby was soon tagged "Doody," which in those days was not a scatological reference. The only other such nickname was given a fraternity brother of mine. His was Cagalata (He who Defecates Tin Cans) because his family owned goats.

Does it surprise you to know that both Doody and Cagalata turned out to be psychiatrists?

Toward the end of his life Uncle John tried to bond with me. Of all his nephews I suppose he saw more of himself in me. I was also a skirt-chaser, I was "going places," and I was a worker.

Going anywhere with Uncle John was an adventure. He would meet me at the Centro Asturiano cantina, invite me to a movie at the Tampa Theater. Whether I had seen the movie or not, I would accept. Who could turn down royalty?

*Handsome John Pacheco,
1920. The ladies adored him.
Courtesy of John Pareja, M.D.*

We would be seated on the aisle and the program would start. John was always on the outside seat. First, he was claustrophobic and couldn't stand people sitting on both sides of him. Also, some people say his nervous problems started when he inadvertently ran over a Mafia don's mother. In spite of assurances from the gangster that he knew Uncle John was not at fault, John remained wary, hence that aisle seat.

After ten minutes of newsreel and coming attractions, the main feature would begin. The Tampa Theater was an MGM theater, so the feature would start, as it does today, with the roaring lion. As soon as John saw the lion, he would get up and walk briskly up the aisle.

"Come on, I've already seen this movie!"

Before you could say "Gable's back, and Garson's got him," we were back at the Centro watching J.B. play dominoes.

Uncle John lived to a ripe old age, accompanied wherever he went by the angelic Dorita, who managed to raise a family and still cater to Uncle John's needs. They taught me a lesson. Just because a girl is incredibly beautiful does not mean she is not a good person. I pass this on to young people who are scared of beautiful girls. And I hate to sound cynical, but they're also easier to divorce.

 The Korean War came, I joined the air force, married, got my discharge, and was admitted to the University of Miami Medical School.

I couldn't wait to tell J.B. and drove straight to La Economica Drugstore. I found him with his head on the prescription counter, fast asleep. It was only ten o'clock in the morning. I was shocked; my father was a ball of energy. He never dragged around, never kept still, never sat down.

"He catnaps all the time," explained the other pharmacist, Gus Moreno. "It's the diabetes. He doesn't always take his insulin. He doesn't always stick to his diet."

He woke up to give me his warming smile. J.B. the superman was now a worn, tired man. His clothes hung from his shoulders. The belt that once barely encircled his girth now needed new holes to make it hold up his pants, which hung in folds.

What happened? When I had left for the air force he was indestructible. He would live forever. Now, as I held him in an embrace, he seemed old, frail, and pitiful.

Front row, left to right: Henry Tudela, Joe Diaz, Tomate. Back row, left to right: a worn-out J.B., Larry and Libby Hernandez, 1951. Robertson-Fresh Commercial Photographers.

That Christmas we celebrated my start in medical school. His happiness at seeing me in school knew no bounds. I was on top of the world knowing of his happiness.

New Year's Eve proved unlucky. I was awakened by the news that J.B. had been taken to the Centro Asturiano Hospital suffering from a heart attack. *Why there?* I wondered. His hospital was Trelles Clinic. Sensing the worst, I jumped in my clothes and headed for the hospital. It was a freezing cold night. I was told at the emergency room that they had no record of a J.B. Pacheco.

"You don't need a record for J.B.!" I shouted. "Everybody knows him."

An intern—a middle-aged man, a Cuban refugee—heard me. He took me by the arm and brought me to a gurney parked in a freezing hallway.

"Is this the man?"

He was covered by several blankets. His face was a deathly white, made more so by a large dose of morphine.

"How long has he been here?"

The intern shrugged. "Two, maybe three hours. Quien sabe?"

I brushed past him, took the phone, and arranged for immediate transfer. Trelles, now old and fat himself, was waiting. An EKG machine cranked out the picture. It was hopeless. They had waited too long.

So I sat with him. His once beefy paw, the fist that knocked out Captain Fernandez, was now a shriveled claw in my hand. I prayed that he would wake up and see that he was being cared for, that he was not alone.

My prayers were answered. For a brief moment his eyes opened. He saw me. He recognized me. He smiled his beautiful smile, and he closed his eyes forever.

I've lived a long time, I now understand things better. I see J.B. with greater clarity. He was an unusual father. He gave me life. He gave me direction and instruction. Every time I told him what I wanted to do for him when he got old, and I got rich, he would smile.

"Just do for your children what I tried to do for you. That's the way you can repay me."

And even now, when honors or praise come to me I think of J.B. and hope he is watching. I was fortunate to have a strong, loving father.

Chapter 3

Tampa's Toonerville Trolleys

On a bitter cold Sunday afternoon my brother Joseph and I stood wrapped in sweaters, a large muffler covering our faces to keep the cold wind from our lungs. My grandmother's hand held my muffler firmly in place, and I could not wait for her to loosen her grip so that I could breathe fresh air. My grandfather Gustavo Jimenez (my mother's father and the Spanish consul) held my bare hand and looked down Michigan Avenue for the familiar sight that would end our frigid wait.

I heard the streetcar before I saw it. The clang, clang, clang of the little yellow Michigan Avenue trolley, its green and red lights blinking as it hit the bumps in the track, carried through the cold air. It came fast, looking as though it would never stop. My grandfather, a calm, placid man, did not even wave. His ruddy old face, turned toward the trolley, was contented. And why not? Sunday was an important day at the Consul's house. First there was a sumptuous meal, prepared by my grandmother, Carmen. Then, repairing to his upstairs study with his two grandchildren, the Consul spent a joyful hour listening to NBC Symphony with Arturo Toscanini conducting. Then, dressed in our Sunday clothes, we walked to the corner of Michigan Avenue and 12th Street across from Arñiella's Latin American Garage, and awaited the regal transport of one of the Tampa Electric Company's streetcars to take us to the Tampa Theater to see a first-run movie.

After the movie we stood by Walgreen's at Franklin near the railroad track, my face again covered by a scarf, this time to protect me from "El Sereno," the dreaded night air which was a menace to young children.

El Sereno was a holdover from medieval Europe, where the miasmic night air was fraught with pathogens. Streetcar after streetcar would arrive, each with distinguishing lights, and I would lean back on my grandfather's sturdy legs, his hands comfortably holding me, pressing me to his rough suit. I would listen sleepily as he recapped the movie for my grandmother's sake, for only he had understood the English version, and only he could retell it in a vivid way. My grandmother, who stubbornly refused to learn English, would wait for a pause in the narrative, and invariably she would say in an exasperated voice, "I know all that," when we were aware that she had not understood a word.

Now the familiar green and red lights came into view. At this hour, the trolleys coming down Franklin Street would usually be lined up, end to end, and your car would not be visible until it just pulled up to the corner.

The glass doors opened with a bang. A little wooden step descended and, grabbing an iron railing, you would pull yourself into a familiar and comfortable car. The first thing you noticed was the smell. A faintly electrical smell, yet it was a clean clear smell. So unlike the exhaust fume smell of a bus: there were no fumes in a Tampa Electric jewel. Pure, clear Tampa air and, always, the faint evidence of electricity. My grandfather would hand the conductor a quarter. Clicking the change counter strapped to his waist, the conductor would count out five nickels. Handing them to my grandfather, he would beam a friendly smile and nod. Most conductors knew my grandfather because of one of his peculiar habits. He invariably tried to tip the conductors a nickel. While it may not seem generous today, in the middle of a depression a nickel was a mighty tip.

My grandfather was a princely man. A diplomat, educated in Europe, a concert flutist who owned a beer brewery in Mexico, he was brought up to look after the masses. Doggedly he offered his nickel tip, but most of the time he was graciously refused. Yet every conductor on the Michigan line talked about him years after his death in 1938. I often met conductors who asked about him. It wasn't often a man offered a nickel tip for a nickel ride. That's a hundred percent tip. It would be considered large in any era.

We found our seats. My grandmother sat with my brother, seating

Left to right: Grandmother
Carmen, Brother Joseph,
Cousin Junior, me, and
Grandfather Gustavo, 1933.

herself next to the window and thereby thwarting El Sereno from one last chance of hurting little darling. My grandfather would let me sit next to the window, my favorite seat, to watch our progress down Franklin Street, as its dives and juke joints passed by. Then as we passed through the residential section we watched the houses drift by, only a few recognizable to me in the dark, with small lights dimly shining from front windows, and porches illuminated so that a late-arriving husband could find the front door. We passed Robert E. Lee Grammar School, where we went to school, and George Washington Junior High, where we were later to attend. Then we went by my step-grandmother's house, the fun-loving piano teacher Pennsylvania Pacheco, known to us as Vannia, who lived on Michigan Avenue. Only three blocks to go. Finally, my grandfather would reach up to pull the cord. The streetcar would squeal to a halt, the glass door would clang open, and the wooden step would appear. We could step down, we were home. All too soon, I had to leave my wonderful trolley. I heard the yellow trolley, alive with its crackling electrical smells, creaking, groaning, and swaying as it went on to another destination.

It's funny what sticks in my mind when I try to remember the Tampa streetcars of the 1930s and 1940s.

I remember the seats, made of wood and beautifully lacquered. They had wicker seats and wicker backs for comfort. There were brass handles on the end, so it was easy to turn them. When a car reached the end of the line, the seats were flipped over to face the opposite direction, so the passengers would be facing forward on the return trip. The cool thing to do, when we reached the wise-guy high school era, was flipping the seat in front of your seat to put your saddle oxford shoes on, looking both sharp and careless.

The front seats were reserved for whites, and the rear seats were for blacks. During the mid-war years, feeling a sense of injustice because black soldiers were fighting in the war but had to sit in the back, I clearly recall trying to make a statement when a beribboned black GI got into the streetcar and had to sit in the back. He did it quietly, without objection, understanding and accepting "his place." I felt very angry, and as a gesture of defiance, I got up and sat in the back of the car with him. The response was unexpected. The blacks got up and moved back one row away from me. The conductor, observing my intrusion into the back seats in the reflection of his front window, just shook his head at the pathetic simplicity of my ill-conceived and poorly received gesture. It was a lesson that carried over into the civil rights struggle of the sixties and seventies, when I opened an office in the primarily black Overtown section of Miami.

My streetcar gesture, my defiance of social order began in the little yellow streetcar, continued in the corner of the boxing ring with Muhammad Ali, and ended with the burning of my Overtown office in 1980. A full circle. A futile gesture and an unexpected result.

I recall the four parallel iron railings that ran the length of the outside of the car, covering the car windows. I could never figure out whether they were there to keep the passengers from falling out or to keep freeloaders from jumping in. But all it meant to me was an effortless means of propulsion, since it furnished a dandy grip when I rode a bicycle alongside the streetcar. With good luck, one could make it from Ybor City to downtown Tampa without having to pedal once.

Streetcars also furnished me with experience in guerrilla warfare. The Dawkins boys and I became experts in ambush tactics.

When my grandfather died in 1938, my father bought a grand two-story house on Lamar Street. We had arrived in Tampa Heights, quite a departure from Ybor City. There I became part of the infamous Dawkins Oak Street Gang, made up of Byron, the older and more devilish brother, Marvin, the younger and more docile one, and myself. Our purpose was to disrupt the boring status quo of our neighborhood. One method was the systematic ambushing of the Tampa Electric streetcars.

We accomplished this by waiting in the bushes for the streetcars to approach a bypass double section of the track, where one streetcar would wait for another streetcar to pass in the opposite direction. Byron stole enough grease from his dad to grease the track, which would cause the trolley wheels to spin, making the car a stationary target.

Our ammunition was primitive. We would take a small brown paper bag, fill it with loose grey Tampa sand, mix in Tampa sandspurs, tie the top, and fling it with all our might at the four parallel black iron railings of the streetcar. The bags would break, the sand would spill all over the

Trolley in front of the post office, 1941. Courtesy of Stephen McGee and Clem Heilan.

passengers, and we would run through the neighborhood back alleys to our secret hiding place. On really boring days, we would spray the passengers with a neighbor's garden hose, then bomb them with our sandy Molotov cocktails. Mosby's Civil War guerrillas never operated more efficiently than we did. The conductor always fumed and stomped around in apoplectic anger. All of this was very amusing and provided us with a great afternoon of fun. This was many years before daytime television, you see.

The sadness of growing old away from your hometown is that people are forever coming up to you and saying, "I guess you're too much a big shot to remember me?" This is tricky. I have been on national TV for many years and everyone has watched me get old, so they know what I look like, but I do not have that advantage, so I am always being shocked.

Once when I was devouring one of Bibi's delicious cuban sandwiches at the Tropicana Shop in Ybor City, an old man with a cane came up, and stood looking at me. I felt one of those "I'll bet you don't know who I am" questions coming, and smiled a weak smile. I decided to take the offensive.

"Give me a hint," I said.

"There's a streetcar waiting for us at the turnaround," he said, his face weathered in a million wrinkles.

"Byron Dawkins!" I exclaimed with obvious pleasure.

"Didn't recognize me, did you?" he said good-naturedly. "I knew who you were," he added.

"Byron, when was the last time I saw you?"

"The night of our high school graduation at Jefferson."

"That was in June 1944, Byron, forty-five years ago."

"Doesn't seem that long," Byron said. I guess it wasn't.

I have never heard anyone speak about the extra-long streetcars. The big trolley was the one you took to go to the delights of Sulphur Springs, an ice-cold aquatic spring. Why the streetcar was extra long, I'll never know. It was fun to run up and down its extra length. It rocked and rolled much more than the short trolleys, so you could ride in the back conductor's station and imagine you were in the navy, riding on the bridge of a destroyer or an admiral's barge. I got my sea legs on the Sulphur Springs streetcar. I also got seasick.

Sulphur Springs was both a pleasure and a pain. It was where the boisterous guys from Ybor City went when they wanted a good fight. Not a clean fight. Just a good fight. I must confess that I did not enjoy the prospect of losing my front teeth in a punch-out at Sulphur Springs. I remember riding to the springs with Charlie Otero, who was just back from the Pacific, his chest full of ribbons, his sailor hat squared almost on the bridge of his nose. Charlie couldn't wait to get in a good fist-fight. I sometimes think about how life turns out for some of us. Charlie had just come from a real fight, the all-out hell of the Pacific war, but he couldn't wait to fight some more. He ended up the police chief of the city of Tampa. Is there a message in there somewhere?

There was no corner of our community that wasn't accessible to the little yellow streetcars of my youth. They were our perfect and complete circulatory system. We went to school on them, went to work, to dances, to movies, to the downtown shopping areas, to Sulphur Springs to swim and to Ballast Point to enjoy the factory picnics.

The greatest bargain in town was the long ride down Bayshore Boulevard for a nickel. As the streetcar picked up speed, the refreshing wind off the bay would whip through the open windows of the car, creating the excitement of anticipation, for you could taste the salt in the air and by the time Ballast Point hove into view you were ready to jump into the bay.

The ride home was equally delicious. The crowd had eaten and drunk their fill, and were relaxed, happy, and carefree. Momentarily the economic worries of the depression were on hold. Singing would break out, and spirits soared. The clacking of the wheels and humming of the wires seemed to accompany the mirthful voices. The ride was long, all the more rewarding when one considered the price, one shiny nickel.

In all my years of enjoyment aboard a trolley, I wish I could tell you one story of romance. Of the many functions the trolleys served, a love transport it was not. They were too open, too well-lit to do young lovers any good. If you got to put your arm around your date, or held hands, you were doing good.

I do remember a tale of frustrated, unrequited love, and the trolley played an integral part.

When I started Jefferson High School, I was two years younger than anyone in my class. I had known most of my classmates since grade school, so I did not feel the difference.

The difference came with high school and puberty. The little girls I used to punch on the arm, and pull the hair of, suddenly developed into highly desirable young ladies. Out came the sweaters, pleated skirts, bobby socks, and saddle oxfords. Instead of playing volleyball at lunchtime, they now jitterbugged to Benny Goodman, Artie Shaw, and Glenn Miller.

The war was in full swing, and suddenly there were officers in green tunics and pink pants, driving Ford convertibles, and sailors in tight-fitting snappy blues, and marines in blindingly brilliant dress uniforms. A sixteen-year-old boy is to an eighteen-year-old beauty as a can of Spam is to caviar.

I had worked up a king-size crush on a beauty named Joyce, who had grown up with me in the next desk to mine for five years. She was Miss Everything, being as bright as she was good-looking. In the last two years, as her hormones kicked into effect, she had advanced several quantum leaps ahead of me.

She was of humble origins and had to work. She was the cashier at a movie theater, the Franklin, a second-run house across from the palatial Tampa Theater. While I spent all day with her, I never really talked to her. Sometimes I was lucky enough to walk her home, but since the hormonal assault she had a variety of guys waiting in convertibles to give her a ride home.

Finally, in our senior year I hatched a plan that was beautiful in its simplicity. Joyce had to get home, bathe and dress, and catch the Jefferson Avenue streetcar to work. This occurred daily, so that if I hustled home on my bike, I could dress and be standing on the corner waiting for the streetcar which was carrying Joyce to work. Here, feigning amazement at finding her in this car, I would talk to her. Person to person. Boy to girl. This would cost me a nickel a day, which I could save from my lunch money by the simple expedient of not buying a

Coke. A nickel for the streetcar was all it would take, and I was resigned to walking back. Joyce was worth it.

It is my sad confession that in all of my entire senior year I never once got on the Jefferson streetcar when Joyce was on board. My master plan flopped due to inadequate intelligence on my part. Had I but asked, I would have found that there was a guy that drove her home from school, waited and drove her to work, and returned and drove her home from work.

It was one of the few times I can report that the Tampa Electric Company failed me. It would not be the last time that my heart would cancel out my brain. That phenomenon exists at any age.

The rest of my family regarded streetcars with ambivalence. Twice they had been the instruments of great harm.

Once my father's brother, a bookish accountant named Ralph, got on a streetcar on Seventh Avenue in front of the Ritz Theater. Streetcars were still open affairs then. A buxom woman got on after Ralph was seated. An Iberian gentleman to his fingertips, he got up and offered the lady his seat. The car started with a lurch. Ralph felt himself in danger of falling overboard. His only hope was to reach out to take hold of the buxom lady, but they had not been introduced, so quite obviously he could not save himself. He fell in the path of a Model T, which bumped him under the streetcar. The immediate unpleasant effect of his misguided act of courtesy was that Uncle Ralph lost both legs.

The Tampa Electric Company gave him a pair of beautiful mahogany legs, with large straps that cut into his shoulder. The Ford Company provided him a new car every two years, with all the instruments for driving—gas, brakes, etc.—on the steering column.

This they did until he died. He lived into his eighties, and if there is a moral in there somewhere, you tell me.

My uncle Fidencio, a *cacique* (political boss) in Monterrey, Mexico, married my mother's sister. He had survived Villa, Zapata, Carranza, and the gringos only to succumb to a streetcar. When he was ninety-three he was told that his chauffeur, a lifelong employee of eighty-five, was dying at home and couldn't come to drive him. A suspicious man by nature, and imperious to a fault, he decided to see for himself. Without telling anyone he took a streetcar for the first time in his life.

A young Uncle Ralph Pacheco, 1905. Buchanan Studio. Courtesy of John Pareja, M.D.

At the street where the chauffeur lived, he got off. Now Don Fidencio was a man used to having people open doors for him, and stop and bow to him. He lived his life as if he were still in the nineteenth century.

Don Fidencio got off the streetcar and stepped into the twentieth century. A Carta Blanca delivery truck ran him over and left him on the street flat as a postage stamp, his imperious airs crushed out of him by the realities of present-day life.

Every kid had fantasies. I wanted to fly in an airplane. I wanted to play in an important game. Most of all I wanted to pilot a streetcar. I wanted to control the little yellow streetcar as it hurled through the night, past houses where grown people were asleep, or making love, or listening to the late-night news on the radio. Of course, I knew I had as much chance to do that as I had to ride in a big red fire engine.

But good things come to him who waits. One night, when I was fourteen, I was finishing up working late at the Columbia Restaurant, and a conductor friend of mine came rushing in for his demitasse. No one was around to serve him, so I quickly poured the cup of black coffee.

He saw I was walking out, so he asked me if I wanted to ride to the end of the line. The Palmetto Beach streetcar did not have far to go, and it was empty, and he felt like talking.

The night was hot and humid, and I felt like unwinding, so I agreed to go with him. The air blew in the open front window and felt wonderfully soothing. We began to talk and he confessed to me that his ambition was to be a fighter pilot. Although the war in Europe was winding down, there was still plenty of war left in the Pacific.

I confessed my childhood fantasy of piloting a trolley. We had gone by most of the civilized part of Palmetto Beach and a dark road lay ahead illuminated by weak light bulbs, obscured by swarms of mosquitoes. He offered to make my fantasy come true.

Eagerly I accepted and took the source of all power, which was shaped like a coffee grinder, in my right hand. With minimal instruction I launched my space craft into orbit.

The electric lights inside the streetcar reflected off the front glass, obscuring my vision. The copilot saw the trouble and pulled the black curtains down around me creating a cozy cockpit. I increased to max speed. We were zooming down the old tracks, rattling, rolling, groaning, and humming. Cats and dogs took their chances, for braking would not save them. We were on the outer edge of the envelope. We were at re-entry speed, in danger of burning up, when we came to the end of the line. He let me turn the car around, which was a routine where one went down the aisle, hands out to either side, flipping over the seat backs so that they faced in the opposite direction. The cash box, power switch, and brake handle were taken to the other end of the car. The power pole on the outside was pulled down and rehooked. And then I returned command of the streetcar to its rightful conductor.

Few fantasies ever turn out as good as you imagined they would be, but this one proved the exception. I have now experienced many wonderful moments, but few of them stuck in my mind like this simple pleasure.

Perhaps before I leave this earth, streetcars will run again down 7th Avenue, and I can board on Franklin Street, on Walgreen's corner by the Tampa Theater, and ride to the Columbia Restaurant and have a nice hot cuban sandwich and a cold S.B. beer. God, I hope so.

⟨⟩ Chapter 4 ⟨⟩

The Greening of Cousin Paul

Why are children so mean? Surely they are not taught to be by their parents. Before TV, in the era of rigid movie censorship, and in peaceful times, where did our devilish ideas come from?

My brother and I were so well behaved that we appeared docile. My parents bragged about our exemplary behavior for hours on end. In the house we were very good. Outside it was a different matter.

My mother had six siblings. All were successful. They made my grandparents proud. Yet in all large families, there was always a black sheep. In the Jimenez family, my uncle Paulino marched to a different drummer. When the family moved to Tampico, my grandfather was aghast to find that Paulino had left school for a full month and was hanging out on the waterfront with some dock rats. This cost him two days of hanging by his thumbs in the cellar. Spaniards are harsh in disciplining a wayward child. My stern grandfather was secure in the knowledge that his errant son was learning an important lesson. However, Paulino was actually enjoying himself being pampered by Indian maids who adored him. They would cut him down, feed him delicacies and wait on him hand and foot, then quickly hang him back up when my grandfather approached.

Uncle Paulino was handsome and lovable. He was a devastating storyteller and a great wit. He had touches of François Villon and Errol Flynn in his personality. It's not difficult to conclude that he never changed. He was chronically unemployed as an adult, and my grandfather became resigned to the impossibility of ever civilizing his playboy

58

son. After moving to Florida, he built him an automotive garage next to his consulate. Thus the large house at 1019 Columbus Drive housed the family and the Spanish Consulate; the garage adjoining the house provided employment for Paulino.

Paulino married a lady who had the misfortune of being tubercular. She gave him a boy, naming him Paul in a spate of unimaginativeness. Soon afterward they moved to New York, and a few years later my aunt died. My uncle Paulino faced a crisis: what to do with little Paul during the long three-month summers. Characteristically, he sweet-talked my grandmother into bringing the boy to Tampa. He would not be in the way. He also had ready-made playmates in my brother and me; he and I were the same age.

When the poor little kid appeared for the first time in our big house, he seemed in shock, and was dreadfully frightened.

To begin with, he knew only a New York Puerto Rican ghetto. Uncle Paulino was a great storyteller, but he was abysmal in teaching his son the ways of life. His eating habits were odd. He didn't seem to know the difference between a knife and a fork or a spoon. My grandmother tried to correct him, but she would freeze up because of his innocent uncouthness. She was also accustomed to being called "Abuelita," the loving diminutive of *abuela* (grandmother). Where my brother and I had soft, loving voices, Paul had a foghorn of a voice. When he blurted out loudly "Abuela," my tiny grandmother would recoil as if she had been slapped in the face. My grandfather, whose fatherly spirit had been broken by Uncle Paulino's resistance to his instruction, would take a spoonful of sodium bicarbonate and trudge wearily upstairs to his bed.

I felt sorry for Paul, who had a well-scrubbed, angelic face, and who obviously was frightened of everything. I decided to cure him. He seemed like a good sort. He was worth a summer of instruction. He became my summer project. After all, I owed at least this much to my Uncle Paulino, who was a particular favorite of mine since he had always let me play in the cars in his garage. The dirtier I got, the more he laughed. I guess the thought of causing my mother, his sister, to go to the trouble of cleaning me up was satisfying to him.

Paul's phobia was a fear of heights. My gang prided themselves in jumping off high places. After all, these were the same kids who devised

Paul arrives on the Silver Meteor. 1938. Courtesy of Gus Jimenez.

a test of courage where we took off our shoes and stood on white-hot iron manhole covers to see who could take the pain the longest. I never won. I never equated senseless pain with bravery. On the other hand, I was good at jumping off high structures.

The education of cousin Paul seemed simple to me. First we would jump off the third stair of our five-step stoop. By the next day I had him comfortably jumping off the porch. The next step was jumping off the porch railing. It seemed much higher, but by holding my hand and jumping together he felt safe.

The next day we went to the empty yard beside Paulino's empty garage. There was a fence about six feet tall, our next objective. It took coaxing but I solved the problem by raking some leaves and cut grass to form a cushion. Cousin Paul closed his eyes, held my hand, and jumped. He came up grinning. He believed he had graduated. "Not quite," I said.

The last goal was to jump about nine feet. It was a roof that looked very high. Cousin Paul blanched. That night he went to bed early, laid low by acute anxiety. I sneaked off to the yard where we were to jump and dug as deep a hole as I could. Carefully I covered it with a network of twigs and a pile of leaves.

We practiced all day. The jump would take place at dusk. We had all day to work up to it. We went back to the front steps and started our progression of jumps. Lunch was dismal. My grandfather thought Paul looked feverish and gave him a dollop of castor oil in orange juice. He took a nap and woke up to find me by his bedside. We worked in the yard. He jumped from the fence, landing comfortably in the bed of leaves, all the time glancing at the high jump from the roof. I pointed out the huge pile of leaves I had put at the spot he would land. It was getting dark when I decided it was time for our jump. Cousin Paul, seized by a sudden fear and feeling the effects of the castor oil, relieved himself in front of me. I was horrified because in addition to the sight of a human being moving his bowels, I also saw three feet of a wriggling worm emerging. I was amazed and repulsed. I had never heard of worms, much less seen one. Now, more than ever, I determined to save this poor ghetto kid and make him over in a new mold. Mine, for example.

I took him up to the roof full of resolve. This lesson would be good for him. First, he would learn to jump from heights; second, the fall would kill what remaining worms he had in his stomach; and third, he would learn never to trust strangers.

Cousin Paul held my hand tightly. It was wet and clammy. The sun was rapidly disappearing behind the large oak tree, and a faint breeze relieved the heat of the summer day.

I lined him up with the pile of leaves. Holding his hand, commanding him to close his eyes, we jumped together. He let out a terrifying scream and disappeared under the surface of the yard and into the hole. He had done it! He had broken every record for the high jump.

"Congratulations, Paul. See? Now you're the best. A champion. You see, you don't have to be scared of heights, do you?"

I took the piteous whimper I heard emanating from the bottom of the pit to mean he agreed.

What? Me worry? Cousin Paul in 1938. Courtesy of Gus Jimenez, Jr.

The next problem we needed to solve was Paul's fear of cats. The appearance of a cat would send him running for the shelter of the garage. No amount of coaxing from the family could reduce his terror. I took it as my solemn familial duty to remedy his fear. After all, had I not cured his fear of heights?

In Ybor City we had a surplus of stray cats. This was before Dr. Avellanal began his experiments in cryogenics. For a while, only the smartest of cats avoided Dr. Avellanal's freezing treatment.

My gang's unofficial secret clubhouse was a tool shed the size of a small room. There, amidst gardening tools, we would hold nocturnal gang meetings. To add a touch of intrigue, our only light was a candle stuck in an old large-size Evening in Paris cologne bottle.

Paul desperately wanted to be admitted into the gang. In fact, the gang consisted of my brother and me. Paul envisioned barrio gangs like he saw in Spanish Harlem.

My brother and I spent a full day catching cats. Paul had been taken by my uncle Gus to the beach, so we had a day to work out a therapy for Paul's cat phobia. Catching cats was not hard work. In those depression days, cats were always looking for a handout. We put bowls of milk by the toolshed. As the cats came to feast, we caught them and threw them in the hot tool shed.

By the time Paul returned from the beach, sunburned and in a panic (he also feared water), we had collected an army of fourteen angry, hungry, thirsty cats in the tool shed. They were in evil humor.

"Good news, Paul," I said, slapping his sunburned back. "The gang has decided to ask you to meet tonight in the tool shed." This news was so exciting that Paul forgot to cry about his sunburn.

After supper, when it was dark, we went out to play. Paul was in a state of high excitement. We went directly to the tool shed.

The cats were quiet. Darkness had placated them. I prepared Paul for the darkness, telling him it was a ritual to light the candle only after all the members were present.

Paul went into the dark shed in happy anticipation. There was a moment of silence as the cats adjusted to the new prisoner. Then all hell broke loose. Paul screamed inhuman yells and beat on the locked door. Finally my soft heart could not stand it any longer, and I opened it. A human rocket shot by me, a few cats hanging onto his T-shirt by their claws. A comet tail of cats followed him to the alley.

Eventually, the shocked new member of the gang ran home to complain, only to be met by a stern look from his Abuela. She was used to trouble from a boy named Paul.

Many years later I met a large black man at a jazz concert who told me he had been Paul's boss. He had laughed many times at Paul's stories reliving the many things I did to cure him of his phobias. Since I had not heard from Paul for forty years, I was amazed to discover that he remembered his traumatic summers with fondness. He credits me for curing his major phobias.

"Except one," the man smiled broadly.

"Oh. Which one?"

"Cats."

"I can see why," I said, picturing little Paul fighting for his life in a closet with fourteen hungry, evil cats.

"He hated cats so much it cost him his live-in lady. She had a cat, and Paul did so many things to it that it died of harassment. On the day of the funeral, the lady told Paul to jump off a tall building."

Of course, I reasoned (with a modicum of pride), Paul was ready for that. High jumping was no longer his problem.

🐟 Water in any form, except the drinking kind, gave little Paul fits. Baths were not his favorite things. Swimming was unthinkable.

In the interest of life-saving, I undertook my most serious challenge. It took most of the summers he spent with us to get him to accept water as a friend. Wading was the first step, and this led to his first quasi-belief that he would not lose his life if water ever touched him.

Years ago some well-intentioned dolt introduced water hyacinths to the waterways of Florida. At the time of Paul's education, hyacinths clogged the Hillsborough River. We often played at the waterworks at the foot of 7th Avenue, next to the library. We would tell my mother we were off to the library, and spend the time playing Huck Finn on the river.

One day it occurred to me to tell Paul that hyacinths were so thick and so strong that we could walk on them. He regarded me with a suspicious stare. After all, he had fresh memories of the great heights and the cat cure. Not to mention his scars.

I had preceded him to the riverside by a few hours and had put several big boxes under the hyacinths. I walked out to show him it was safe, then returned. Remembering the treachery of the high jump and the deep hole, he suggested that he should walk in my footsteps, like a man walking through a mine field. Of course, this was my intention, since he would walk the first few feet in absolute safety.

Carefully he put one foot in front of the other until he was sure the hyacinths would indeed hold him. I blissfully waved him on, shouting words of encouragement.

I remember well how he was looking back, smiling a confident smile as he came to the end of the boxes. Then he took one more step. The look on his face as he sank into the river, under the hyacinths, was pitiful. I actually felt sorry for him.

Paul graduated at the end of the summer when I taught him to swim. Well, perhaps not quite swim, but certainly to flail about in the water until help came.

We had been playing Huck Finn, and I had yet to get him to understand

The Lamar Street Cavalry: Junior and Paul above, me below, 1938. Courtesy of Gus Jimenez.

that before my brother and I let him play Huck he had to ride the raft we had built on the river. Shortly before he was to return to Spanish Harlem, he summoned up a burst of pride, and volunteered to ride the currents of the Hillsborough River on our raft.

Knowing our raft was not very sturdy and aware that Paul's flailing could not be mistaken for swimming, I decided to take an inner tube and fasten it to him, in case the raft disintegrated.

Ideas for teaching the lessons of life were never in short supply. It was while instructing Paul how to propel his inner tube to the bank in the event of raft disintegration that I got the *pensamiento máximo* (the maximum idea) which would cap the summer.

I launched Paul on the raft at a bridge and raced to the next, where I had found and stored a big chunk of cement. Paul floated serenely on the current, safely tucked into his big inner tube. He was playing Huck Finn for all he was worth when he came to the next bridge and saw, to his horror, that I was poised with a chunk of cement over the railing.

My marksmanship was accurate. The block fell on the unoccupied forward section of the raft with a sickening thud. The raft disintegrated, expelling Paul and his tube into the swiftly moving currents of the black river.

Many years have passed, but I still count this as one of my greatest cures. Paul made landfall just before he reached the downtown area. He reached home by suppertime serene in the knowledge that he knew how to survive a maritime disaster. He had beaten the Ol' Debbil Ribber, and he now knew never to take anyone's word for anything.

Years went by, and our summers with Paul ended. I became a teenager. One day when I came home from working at La Economica, there was a sixteen-year-old boy waiting for me on the porch. He was painfully thin, white as a sheet, and he had a leonine head of hair. His young face was handsome, marred only by a moustache drawn on his upper lip in eyebrow pencil. He had on a white shirt with a black bow tie tucked into his top pocket. He wore zoot suit pants, high in the waist, long in the fly, ballooned out in the knee, and narrow at the cuff. They were the first I had ever seen. His black and white wingtips were on the porch railing.

I survived the summer, 1938.
Courtesy of Gus Jimenez, Jr.

It was Paul. He now had an anglicized last name. He affected the airs of a mature man.

Feeling a little self-conscious riding up on my Schwinn bicycle, I gave him a warm handshake. He whipped out a Chesterfield cigarette and offered me one. The thought of smoking around my house made my blood run cold.

"Been tending bar at the Waldorf in the Big Apple. Pop wanted to spend a month in Tampa, so here I am. Got a job tending bar at the Floridan." He blew a cloud of blue smoke in the air, away from me.

"Hence the moustache," I smiled, pointing at the ridiculous line on his upper lip.

"Yeah. I gotta look old."

"Sure had me fooled." I sat by him on the glider. "Thought you would have joined the merchant marine by now."

His eyes widened in horror. "One torpedoing per lifetime is enough," he said, resurrecting images of the inner tube drifting down the river toward the Gulf Stream.

We talked about his romantic adventures. He seemed not to bear any animosity for the cures I had inflicted on him.

"What's happening tonight?" He had the night off and was looking for action.

"Nothing much. I'm going horseback riding at sunset," I said, beginning to set a trap, just to keep in practice.

"Hey, I ride. I ride all the time. I ride in Central Park."

Click. The trap closed.

"Well, I dunno. These are real horses. Not walk-down-the-path horses. They're gallop-over-the-fields horses."

"So what? The horse ain't been born I couldn't ride, pahdner." He did a fine imitation of Gary Cooper.

The stables were out in the boonies behind Sulphur Springs. The horses were pretty wild, and the price was therefore cheap. The black stableboy eyed Paul suspiciously. His experienced eyes fixed on the zoot pants and the thin-soled, pointy shoes.

"Looks like a city boy to me."

"Yeah. He's from New York, but he can ride."

"We'll see," the boy said, spitting on the ground.

Paul picked a large grapefruit from a tree next to the barn that had a big sign which read DO NOT PICK FRUIT.

"Looks like he could handle Ol' Debbil Fury." The boy looked at me for approval.

"I'd say so," I smiled. "He's ridden in Central Park."

"Yes sir, Debbil Fury do just right."

In a few minutes he returned with my horse, a bay I was used to riding. Speedy but controllable. I was up in the saddle in a moment, looking down on Paul, whose face was filled with impatience. He wanted to show me he could ride.

The boy brought out a dark, snorting, prancing horse. His eyes looked crazed, and he seemed angry to be disturbed at this late hour. The stableboy handled his bridle roughly, pulling his head sharply.

"Now you got to git Ol' Debbil's attention or he run you clear to Tallahassee." So saying, he balled up his fist and struck the horse as hard as he could on the side of his head. The horse seemed to buckle, and stayed quiet as Paul mounted. He looked oddly out of place in a western saddle. His zoot pants rolled up, showing black silk hose, and his pointy shoes stuck in the stirrups created a picture that made the stableboy laugh.

"Git on witcha then, Ol' Debbil!" He struck the horse again, this time on his rump. The horse took off at a moderate canter. Paul jiggled up and down like a shaker of martinis.

We had gone two miles when Paul's head began bobbing as though he could not control it. His thin-soled shoes slipped out of the stirrups from time to time. He held onto the big grapefruit with one hand, the other trying to rein in the horse.

About a mile ahead I knew there was a cutoff trail which would lead back to the barn. I also knew it took a super horseman to keep Ol' Debbil Fury from heading for the barn. I determined that our best course was to race, in the hope that Debbil Fury would gallop right by the turnoff.

Putting spurs to my bay, I yelled, "Let's race!"

Paul's body flew back in the saddle as Ol' Debbil Fury accelerated. The horse passed me with Paul horizontal to the earth, bent backward, still holding onto the grapefruit.

**That Boy Got to Like Grape-
fruit a Whole Lot.** *1993.*
Ferdie Pacheco.

The high-speed turn at the cutoff was a thing of beauty. Ol' Debbil Fury turned on a dime. Paul's body flew out of the saddle and seemed to hang suspended in midair for a moment, then was pulled back by the G-force of the turn. His only contact with the horse was the hand that held the mane in a death grip. His other hand hung on to the grapefruit.

Now Ol' Debbil Fury caught sight of the open barn door, and he headed for it at tremendous speed. He must have had an extra gear and a booster jet in his tail. Paul's mouth was open as if in a permanent scream, but I could hear nothing. Perhaps he was flying faster than the speed of sound.

The stableboy opened both doors and seemed to be yelling something frantically. At about the time Ol' Debbil Fury was re-entering the barn, I heard the yell clearly:

"Duck! Duck! Duck!"

Paul hit the upper part of the door and flew backward in a sitting position, landing in a generous mound of dung. His hand still holding the grapefruit.

"Hm-hmmm. That boy got to like grapefruit a *whole lot,*" the stable boy said with a straight face. I looked at Paul's face, which had a purplish tinge and Little Orphan Annie eyes.

Add horses to heights, water, and cats.

❧ I have never seen him since, although every decade or so I get word of him. He's had another name change. Another job. Another wife. So it was incredible that I was standing at a urinal in Bay Front Park talking to a big black man about my cousin Paul, who, claimed the man, talks about me all the time, and talks about how much I taught him.

I wonder why?

Chapter 5

Tales of the Columbia

The Youngest Waiter

It is the burning desire of every young man to get a paying job to help his family during difficult cash-short days. It also makes a boy feel like a man. It gives him both prestige and pocket change, but most important of all, it gets him out of the house and away from the dreaded chores his mother has devised for him, all of which are unpleasant and unpaid.

The most glamorous establishment in Ybor City was the Columbia Restaurant. To be a waiter in the Columbia provided the best money in Ybor City. For a fourteen-year-old it was a quantum leap into manhood, fame, and wealth. That is, until the first day at work.

❦ A heavy early-morning June sun beat down on Byron Dawkins and me as we bent to the task of greasing the streetcar tracks and packing our sandbags to ambush the eight o'clock trolley. Our preparations were rudely interrupted by the call of my mother from the front porch. From the sound of her voice, I knew it was urgent, which in my house meant anything relating to my father's immediate needs.

Wiping my greasy hands on Byron's overalls, I scampered home as fast as my fourteen-year-old legs could carry me. It took a moment to adjust my eyes to the darkness of the front room and I slowly perceived the worried faces of my *abuelita,* Aunt Lola, and Mother hovering over

The Columbia Restaurant at night, 1945. William W. Carnes Photography. Courtesy of Adela Gonzmart.

the ever-crying, ever-despondent small figure of my older brother Joseph, the genius-in-residence of the family.

The moment of truth had come for Joseph, but once again he had failed miserably. My father was a gruff, no-nonsense man's man. He had devised a new way to get Joseph out the house and into the world of Ybor City and manhood. His other attempts had met with shattering failure, protected as Joseph was by his genius and by three clucking females.

World War II had brought a manpower shortage to Ybor City. At the Columbia Restaurant, "The Gem of Spanish Restaurants," the need for waiters was acute. Lawrence Hernandez, the personable owner and a friend of my father, had suggested that their eldest sons, Lorencito and Joseph, both sixteen, be drafted to wait on tables in the bustling café, the coffee shop at the front of the restaurant.

My father eagerly accepted and telephoned home to break the good news to my mother, who would in her kind and gentle way tell my brother. My brother responded with his usual nonviolent resistance: he tried to hang himself with my only necktie. Unfortunately, it was a new knit tie and it stretched so far that they cut down Joseph with his feet still planted firmly on the floor of the closet. Point to Joseph.

The time-honored way to get around a confrontation with my father was to have me volunteer to do whatever had been chosen for Joseph. This I accepted happily because it got me out of the house, which meant avoiding the housekeeping chores and "doing the yard." Doing the yard was to be avoided at all costs. Once I volunteered to join Joseph to have his tonsils removed at El Bien Público solely to avoid doing the yard.

Imagine the joy and pride I felt at eight o'clock the next morning when I stood in the hot sun at the corner of Oak Avenue and Lamar Street, awaiting the streetcar which would take me to my first grown-up job. I straightened my new black bow tie for the tenth time. My white shirt was stiff with starch, freshly pressed by my mother. My black pants had a razor-sharp crease and my black shoes glistened from the shine I had spent the night applying. *No doubt about it,* I thought, *anyone can see I am on a man's mission. I am a waiter at the great Columbia Restaurant.* Oh, the pride of that moment.

Columbia Café. 1945. Courtesy of Adela Gonzmart.

The Columbia Café, on the corner of 22nd and 7th Avenue, was the meeting place of all Ybor City. In those days it never closed and so attracted the early-morning hunters, fishermen, produce dealers, dairymen, and farmers and then throughout the day the businessmen and workers of Ybor City. At night the players, lovers, crooks, and sports people came in and stayed until the wee hours.

I was greeted by Lorencito (Little Lawrence), the tough sixteen-year-old son of Big Lawrence. There is a saying that the apple doesn't fall far from the tree. Well, I can testify that the proverb is all wrong. The apple, in this case Lorencito, did not even fall in the next county from the tree.

Lorencito was a tightly muscled collection of mean thoughts. While his father was the patron saint of the handout, Lorencito was an evil-spirited bully, adept at punching people silly. Such was his malevolence that Big Lawrence was able to get him an appointment at the Naval Academy at Annapolis—the feeling being that if he was such a terror on land, he would be even worse on water. Time proved Big Lawrence correct.

I was unafraid of Lorencito, because we had grown up together. He

The Georgia Military Academy tries to tame Lorencito Hernandez, 1942. Paramount Studios, Orlando. Courtesy of Casey Hernandez.

viewed me more or less as his personal property. His own fourteen-year-old brother, Casimiro, was an easy target to hit, and Lorencito liked a challenge. So I started off my first day of adult employment with a large hickey on the triceps of my skinny, dish-carrying arm. Lorencito had a grip like Charles Atlas, which was not surprising since he had been squeezing a Charles Atlas coiled spring grip since the age of puberty. A handshake from Lorencito was not an experience you would soon forget and you would rather jump into the frigid waters of Sulphur Springs fully clothed than shake his hand.

❧ The coffee shop was humming with the mid-morning coffee-drinking crowd. They each had their own personalized order and everyone assumed that you knew his preference. The Columbia Café specialized in the best coffee in town. It was expresso but was made in large vats. The turnover was so rapid that the coffee was always fresh. Next to the vats of *café cubano* was a larger vat of boiled milk with a pinch of salt.

Coffee was served *solo* (alone), which meant black, *cortadito* (cut a little bit), which meant a small demitasse of much coffee with a dash of milk, very dark, and *café con leche,* coffee with boiling milk. The variants depended on the personal whim and pathology of the drinker. Strong men, like my father and Frank Alonso, liked their coffee very dark (*obscuro*); politicians, lawyers, and burglars liked it half and half (*mitad y mitad*), and men with the weight of the world on their shoulders, with weak or failing digestive systems, liked it mostly milk with just a drop of coffee (*clarito*). The builder Domingo Rañon once went a whole week drinking pure hot milk before he got wise to my experiment.

Size of cup was never stated but indicated by finger signals, undecipherable to anyone but the waiters of the Columbia Café. It was said the signals dated back to the days of King Alfonso the Absurd. I had to learn them before I was issued my badge of office, an apron. I had been eating in the café since I was little and my aunt Lola was the much-feared, asp-tongued cashier, so I did not wander into Lawrence's wonderland unprepared. I was ready.

Just before the lunch crowded in, I was given the "go" sign by Pete the bartender. He looked at my skinny body in disgust, as if to say,

"Look what we have come to." It was as if a high school football player had been dropped into the starting lineup of the Miami Dolphins at the Super Bowl. Pete did not inspire confidence. Fear of failure, yes. Confidence, no.

In order to get my attention the customers would rap on the marble table tops with coins, purse their lips, and make a kissing sound. I hated that, but there was a waiter named Kiki who seemed to like it a lot. Customers also clapped their hands, snapped their fingers, or made a hissing sounded to call the waiter. Others yelled "Oye, tu!" (Hey, you), which was acceptable, or "Oye, chiquito!" (Hey, kid), which was not. I hated that. I felt it was demeaning.

Things began at a reasonable, normal pace. I had large hands, so I learned to juggle as many as six cups in one hand. This was an indispensable qualification for a good Columbia Café waiter. First, you had to guess what everyone wanted. Second, you must not forget the water. Third, you hoped everyone paid you. Pete the bartender was death on waiters who got stiffed.

It was about eleven-thirty in the morning when the first of several unusual incidents occurred. These made such a great impression on me that when I think back, it seems the Columbia Restaurant influenced the course of my life even more than when I studied philosophy with the Jesuits.

Harry the Porter, an older black man, had brought a ladder behind the bar and climbed to the top in order to clean the crystal of the big clock over the cash register. Below him, to one side, Aunt Lola was working the register. On the other side, Pete was slicing ham at the sandwich counter, preparing for the lunch rush.

Santo Trafficante the younger came in, greeted Pete in Italian, and asked for a sliver of ham in order to taste its goodness. Pete reluctantly offered up a slice on the end of his long knife and asked for a nickel, which caused many raised eyebrows since Santo was a big spender, a popular figure, and the crown prince of the Trafficante family. At this point one of his crowd came in who was known for his boorish behavior. He was Jimmy, the principal nemesis of Harry the Porter.

Harry the Porter suffered from a rare psychological-neurological disorder which rendered him unable to tolerate certain sounds. A prolonged kissing sound drove him into a convulsive state. At such times he would throw whatever he had in his hand in the direction of the offending sound.

Jimmy liked to taunt Harry by pointing to him and pursing his lips, as if to suggest he was about to make the sound. This would drive Harry into an agitated condition, and he would raise whatever he was holding in his hand and babble, "You want it, you want it, you want it, you want it? You can have it . . . you want it?"

At which point Jimmy would emit a loud kissing sound with his lips. Then Harry would throw the object at Jimmy and stagger from the room.

I did not know about Harry's condition. I was at the front table serving Dr. Rex Myers, a one-armed dentist (this was before root canal), and his guests their pre-lunch coffee.

Jimmy entered the café, following Santo the Younger in his lap-dog way, and spotted Harry, high atop his ladder. He pointed at Harry and pursed his lips.

"You want it? You want it?"

Harry held out his soapy bucket of suds and Jimmy smiled, seeing the chance for an all-time Hall of Fame gotcha.

I had time to look up and see Harry as he came crashing down on the freshly cut ham, the ladder skittering on the register, and my astonished aunt Lola. Pete, one hand trying to fend off the falling Harry meteorite, the other protecting the freshly cut ham, cursed as the bucket of soapy water landed on the floor next to me, causing me to jettison my load of cups and spring back to avoid being bathed in soapy suds.

"You got it," said Harry weakly as he staggered to the safe haven of the kitchen, where neither Pete nor Jimmy could get to him. Dr. Myers paid his bill and added a quarter tip in appreciation of the show.

Lunch proved to be well beyond anything a fourteen-year old mind could comprehend. A full lunch, meaning soup, salad, entrée, bread and butter, iced tea, dessert, and coffee, was seventy-five cents. If you wanted, the same was available for fifty cents but you got no soup or dessert. But you always could have another expresso free.

The tables sat from four to six people but in the informality of the café, you could sit anywhere there was a chair. The result was an

Harry's Fall from Grace.

1993. Ferdie Pacheco.

incredible confusion wherein the waiter never quite knew where in the course of the meal the customer was, or whether he had eaten a fifty-cent or a seventy-five-cent lunch.

It was nearly two o'clock now and my arms were weakening. Columbia Café waiters disdained trays and prided themselves on carrying in all plates by hand. Under normal conditions I would have coped well. But I had acquired a complication I didn't need.

Lorencito was waiting for me in the kitchen hallway. I would enter, my skinny arm burdened with heavy plates, and he would grab my neck in his Charles Atlas grip and squeeze. In pro football it is called a burn; later, in medical school, it was termed a pinched nerve. In the life of a fourteen-year-old waiter, it was sheer hell. I would stagger to the dishwasher's counter, barely able to lift my plates to the height of the counter.

"How's it going, kid?" he would say, trying to inflict his hickey-producing straight right to the triceps.

In my mind a debate was raging. Homicide or employment? I looked at the smiling face of Lorencito and knew I'd never kill him. I couldn't figure out how.

❧ The second event that shaped my life took place just as lunch was winding down. This happened in two stages.

If Santo the Younger was liked by everyone at the café, his father, Santo the Elder, was adored and revered. He was feared as well, but nothing in his demeanor indicated that he could kill a fly. He was grandfatherly in those days, beautifully tailored and impeccably groomed. He frequently came to the café and sat at a table by the side door. Prudence dictated that we never ask why.

All day long streetcar conductors would rush in for their *café solo* fix. They would leave their streetcars unattended, dash in, pour the steaming coffee in the saucer, blow on it, and gulp it down. Since an inspector always lurked around the busy 22nd Street intersection, it took skill, daring, fast feet, and an asbestos stomach to pull this off. Their main danger to us was that in their manic haste to get back to the waiting streetcar, they would run over anything in their path.

Any student of physics can predict a disaster if you set three forces in

Trolley Conductors
Slurp Coffee. *1993. Ferdie*
Pacheco.

motion, directed at a single intersecting point. A conductor, running for the door, bumped into me when I was carrying six cups of expresso, all of which catapulted onto the cashmere coat of Santo the Elder as he entered the café.

Santo the Elder brushed off all offers of help, nodded kindly toward me, and mumbled something in Italian that I took to mean "Don't worry, kid, it wasn't your fault." On the other hand, I made a mental note to tell my mother to look both ways before she crossed the street.

The afternoon mercifully came to an end, and with it an end of my hysteria. Now it was time for the characters to appear.

The first of these was Crazy Benny, a ferretlike man dressed in a bilious green suit who carried a rubber briefcase. He sat down, furtively checking the room for signs of FBI agents, death ray machines, or microbe contaminating apparatus. Satisfied that these were not present and overcoming his reluctance to talk to strangers, he ordered his usual *café solo*. He did not speak, he just made a sign.

At the expresso urn, Cuatro Pelos (Four Hairs), a waiter who was bald as a cue ball, was waiting for me.

"Ask Benny about the impossible."

I looked at Benny. He had taken a long piece of yellow paper out of his rubber briefcase and was hunched over writing furiously.

"What's he writing?"

"Ask him," Cuatro Pelos smiled reassuringly.

I put the coffee before Crazy Benny and asked, "What are you writing?"

"A letter."

"To whom?"

"Myself."

"What are you saying to yourself?"

Benny gave me a withering stare of contempt. "If I knew *that* I wouldn't have to mail it. I'll know in two days."

That seemed logical to my exhausted mind, so I probed further.

"What about the impossible?"

Crazy Benny stopped stirring his coffee, which was now mostly in his saucer. He seemed to be gaining strength.

"If the impossible were possible, then it would be no longer impossible, since to be impossible it could not possibly be possible, for to be impossible is to be not possible and so, impossible, because if the impossible were possible . . ."

I recognized where I came in, so I went out toward the front of the café, where Pepe Lu Babo (Pepe the Idiot) had brought in the afternoon *Tampa Times.*

Pepe was an idiot savant, one of those unfortunates who has the mind of an idiot, yet is alarmingly brilliant in a specific field. The fields of mathematics and music have occasionally spawned such savants. Politics has many idiot savants; in fact, it's the rule rather than the exception. Pepe Lu Babo was an idiot savant of newspaper circulation.

He kept accounts by scribbling circular patterns of figures in a spiral-bound notebook. Neither the Egyptians nor the Aztecs ever came close to his obscure method of calculation, yet he was never wrong. Someone would say, "Pepe, give me a *Times* and charge it. Here is a half-dollar for the *Tribune* for the last month and a quarter for *La Gaceta*." Pepe would scribble furiously and then babble in his excited, high-pitched voice. "No," he would insist, "This is what you owe." He was always right.

❧ After a particularly painful triceps hickey I came to a decision about Lorencito the Ruthless. I waited until he entered the room-sized freezer to sneak a smoke. Then I confronted him.

I tried to make myself sound like Gary Cooper doing Wild Bill Hickok. I said, "Larry, I've had enough of you. If you so much as lay a hand on me again, I will order a caldron of bean soup and be waiting for you when you come through that door. Then I'm going to dump it over your head."

My exit was rapid since I reasoned my threat was not in the form of a question, and it required no answer. A few worried minutes passed, and then I got called to see Big Lawrence in his liquor store office.

He was an elegant man. A man of great generosity, humor, affability, and political instinct. His smile was electrifying. I idolized this man who had given me the chance to leave adolescence and jump into adulthood, and I had let him down. I felt miserable.

"Is what Lorencito told me true? Did you say if he hit you again you were going to crown him?" His smile was huge, his eyes crinkling. "With a caldron of garbanzo soup?"

"Yes sir," I said, my eyes focused on the Spanish tile floor.

"That's great! That's terrific!" Big Lawrence was reaching in his pocket. "Tell you what. If he hits you again and you don't hit him with the soup, you're fired. If you do it, I'll give you a raise."

Because I was not expecting to be paid a salary, Big Lawrence's words were more good news than a fourteen-year-old mind could absorb.

"Here's a twenty. Go up front to your aunt Lola and ask her to break it."

I glided to the front, feet barely touching the floor, got my change, and hurried back to find Big Lawrence in a deep conversation with Dr. Rosenthal. He looked at me as if seeing me for the first time.

"What is it, Pachequito?"

"Your change, sir," I said, holding out a handful of dollars.

"I don't know what you are talking about." Lawrence looked at Dr. Rosenthal. "Vic, did you give him a twenty?"

"Not me."

Dr. Rosenthal plucked his eyebrow with yellowed fingers. "You better put that in your pocket, kid. This joint is fraught with marauders."

It was almost time to quit when I spotted Santo the Elder coming in for his late afternoon soup. Determined to make up for my lunchtime disaster, I rushed to wait on him.

The black-marble-topped tables were devoid of cloths, so I took two linen napkins and spread them so I could place the silver and china and crystal on what appeared to be a tablecloth. I rushed to bring him fresh hot Cuban bread and two pats of butter. I used a glass from the *fonda* (restaurant) side, a goblet instead of a plain ordinary drinking glass.

"Buongiórno," I said, groveling, just this side of obsequious.

The old man smiled his kindly smile. He nodded as if he understood my gesture and patted my shoulder.

"Va bene," he said, sitting down with his majestic calm, tucking the linen napkin under his chin.

La Fonda. 1917. Courtesy of Adela Gonzmart.

I sped away like a basketball player on a fast break. I got my order of vermicelli soup and sped back, hoping to impress the old man with my speed and expertise.

Again, he nodded, stopped buttering the bread, and waited for me to serve the soup.

In order for you to understand what follows, I must instruct you about serving soup. If there is more than one order, you are given a caldron and ladle. If, however, only one order is given, then there is no ladle and the small tureen, which has a small handle, is used to pour the soup directly into the bowl.

As I had observed it, it was an easy, graceful, and artistic maneuver. With a flourish, one pours it into the bowl. It seemed to me that the superior Spanish waiters, like Evaristo and El Rey, did it in one amazingly graceful, sweeping, arclike motion. I aspired to show Santo the Elder that he was in the hands of a master waiter.

In one fell swoop I poured the steaming vermicelli soup. It visited the plate, stayed briefly, and continued its course into the lap of a startled Santo. By no stretch of the imagination can a full order of steaming vermicelli soup in the lap be considered a pleasant sensation.

Santo the Elder sat stunned for a moment. Then, grabbing a handful of my white shirt, he pulled me down to his face.

"What's the matter, kid? You got something against me?"

I hid in the kitchen until six o'clock finally came. I realized that I had done it! I had survived, if barely, in a man's world. I took off my black bow tie and walked back into the battlefield of the Columbia Café.

At the corner of the bar next to the coffee urns stood a tall older man, holding a cane, waiting patiently to be waited on but having no luck.

"May I help you, sir?"

"Why, yes," the voice had a soft southern drawl, pleasing to the ear. "I wonder if I can get two quarts of garbanzo soup to go."

Though tired and anxious to get home and leave behind all thoughts about Lorencito, Pete, and Santo the Elder, I felt sorry for the old southerner who was being ignored. I got him the soup, and as an afterthought added two pieces of hot Cuban bread and some tabs of butter.

When I had handed him the soup and he had noticed the added bread and butter, he paid the exact amount.

"Weren't you just getting off?"

"Yes, sir."

"You missed your streetcar."

"There'll be another one in ten minutes."

"Son, I'm going to give you something to remember me by. Do you know who I am?"

"No sir." Robert E. Lee was dead, so it couldn't be him.

"Eli Witt," he waited for it to register in my exhausted mind.

Eli Witt! Not the man that invented the cotton gin? No, that was Eli Whitney. This was Eli Witt, who owned Hav-A-Tampa Cigars, the largest cigar factory in the world.

He handed me a five-dollar bill.

"What you just did shows me you're going far in this world. What do you want to be?"

"A doctor."

"You'll make a damned good one," he said, and shuffled off.

&⋅ The ride back down 7th Avenue was memorable to me. It has its own place in my long list of happy events and I can feel the rocking of the old Tampa Heights streetcar, its electrical smells mingled with the olfactory delights of La Septima. The aroma of fine cigars combined with the heavenly smell of a bakery making bread and coffee being ground. The sights and sounds of La Septima as the street lights were going on, the cool air of the night taking the place of the heat of the late afternoon sun. The streets filled with people, getting on with their happy lives.

And there I was. Finally, I was a part of them. A part of Ybor City. Part of the adult world. I was a waiter at the Columbia Restaurant. I sat on the wicker seat, wanting to tell every passenger on board, "Hey, I did a man's work today. I'm a waiter at the Columbia Café." But surely they must have noticed me already. It's not easy to hide the fact. A waiter stands out.

Since then I have been many things, most of which I have taken great pride in. I have been a pharmacist, a doctor of medicine, a sportscaster, television executive, playwright, screenplay writer, novelist, and painter. And yet, it's hard to explain, the rush of pride and happiness that comes with a job well done was never again as acute, as sharp, or as exhilarating as on that June night when a little yellow streetcar carried an exhausted fourteen-year-old home to a house where he would never again be considered a kid, and where he was given a new respect.

My mother and *abuelita* were there when I came home, their faces expectant, awaiting one of my long, rambling stories.

"Well, how was it? What happened?"

"Oh, nothing. Just another day at the café," I said, and headed for the peace of my room.

Pacheco's Rules Learned from the First Summer at the Columbia

1. Expect the unexpected; it always happens.
2. Face up to a bully; he'll usually back down.
3. Indulge the less smart; they may prove much the smarter.
4. Be proud of your work; no honest job is dishonorable.
5. Accept gifts graciously, especially money.
6. Take any kind of work that gets you out of the hot sun.
7. Never trust a man with a rubber briefcase. Never.

La Septima, 1920s: olfactory delights abound. Burgert Bros. Studio. Courtesy of **La Gaceta.**

The Gem of Spanish Restaurants

The corner of 22nd Street and 7th was at the outer edges of the known world when Casimiro Hernandez, a portly Spaniard from Cuba, decided to open a small coffee shop there in 1905.

The intersection already boasted a bar on each corner. In the middle of the intersection was a watering trough where Col. Teddy Roosevelt had watered his horse while training his Rough Riders to climb hills. Casimiro was very impressed with Colonel Roosevelt, the entire idea of America, and the popular song of the day, "Columbia, the Gem of the Ocean," the title of which he appropriated. His café and *fonda* became "The Columbia, Gem of Spanish Restaurants."

His customers were hunters, fishermen, farmers, dairymen, and cigar workers. Only Casimiro could foresee that the small town V.M. Ybor was building among the scrub palmettos and rattlesnakes was expanding in his direction. The approved extension of the streetcar line would bring life to his small café.

By the time Casimiro was an old man, his vision had come true. Tampa Electric's yellow streetcars trundled to the Columbia from four directions. The Columbia was at an intersection of maximum traffic. The small café grew, and with the addition of a first-class dining room, La Fonda, achieved prominence alongside Las Novedades and other successful eating establishments.

By the time the *fonda* was going full blast, cigar workers could eat three meals a day for five dollars a month while waiting for their families to come over from Spain. It's not hard to understand why when Casimiro died in 1928 he left his sons a whopping $28,000 in debts, and a reputation for softheartedness.

Old Casimiro fathered four strapping boys. He was wise enough to permit the laws of nature to choose his successor. By the time I arrived to work in the café as a boy of fourteen during the war years, the survival of the fittest had determined the inheritors of the beautiful restaurant.

The two eldest boys, Gustavo and Evelio, had not shown enough interest to take over the enterprise. Gustavo still worked there as the chief bartender, and he was as big, gruff, and lovable as his father, whom he uncannily resembled. Evelio was an indifferent restauranteur who had a gift for using his spare time to drink coffee in the café. He was given a store which ground and packaged Colombian coffee.

The son who manifested the greatest interest in the business was the hard-working, serious-minded Casimiro II. When money got short he took in a partner, Manuel Garcia. Casimiro's personable brother Lawrence worked in the insurance business and also got elected justice of the peace. It was not an empty title and gave Lawrence a political base. He was good at it, and he used the position to help the restaurant.

In the late thirties an unexpected turn of events occurred which changed the status quo considerably. Lawrence lost his justice of the peace position in a close election. The times were hard and selling insurance was not easy, so Lawrence decided he wanted to buy back his interest in the Columbia Restaurant. Casimiro was happy at this welcome turn, but Manuel Garcia was not, and bad blood threatened to spill over. Casimiro set a high price, knowing that Garcia could not make the price, but Lawrence, who had heavy financial backing, could.

Garcia left, taking his considerable expertise down the street to Las Novedades. While he was alive he ran the restaurant. It was the equal of the Columbia in quality and popularity. After he died, the restaurant ceased to function and was closed.

From this battle for control there emerged a strong tandem of brothers who formed an unbeatable team and made the Columbia synonymous with fine dining. Together they created the Columbia style. The oddity is that there never were two brothers more disparate.

Casimiro II, the elder of the two, was a quiet, painfully shy man, given to talking in monosyllables and grunts. His area of expertise was the nuts and bolts of running a restaurant. His exceptional talent was in buying the food. His suppliers were sure that Casimiro would be there for the deliveries, smelling, tasting, feeling the goods, questioning the prices, counting the boxes. He worked the kitchen staff hard, and there was scant wastage. The Columbia's profits were directly proportional to the hours Casimiro spent in the kitchen. Nothing was wasted, nothing was stolen. There was never a more efficient kitchen in Ybor City.

His other strength was in labor relations. He was tough, spoke little,

Even the ever-vigilant Casimiro slept sometime. 1940. Courtesy of Casey Hernandez.

but was as fair a man as any who ever dealt with workers. Jobs at the Columbia were avidly sought, for a steady job meant a handsome salary, far beyond that which cigar makers made at the Tampa factories.

If Casimiro II was the invisible force of the Columbia, Lawrence, the youngest of the boys, was the most visible. By the time I worked there, he was Ybor City's rock 'n' roll star. He sparkled. He glittered. He was glamorous.

Lawrence was a small man, impeccably tailored, with a taste for the good life. Once, when my teacher asked me what the term *joie de vivre* meant, I wrote "Lawrence Hernandez" on my paper. He shone in any company, dominated a room, enlivened any discussion, drove away boredom, gave even the poorest man hope.

He had beautiful silvery hair, curly and combed straight back. His smile was dazzling; his eyes crinkled, and every muscle in his face was involved in the act of smiling. It was like the first ray of early morning sunshine. His hands were expressive, and he used them with the skill of an actor.

Physically he was attractive, but if by God's whim he had been born

Big Lawrence: affable, personable and extravagantly generous, 1942. Courtesy of Casey Hernandez.

ugly or deformed, he would still have been an impressive man. His dynamic personality and his inner fire made customers feel that things would work out, because Lawrence was in your corner. What a gift he had. When he concentrated on his end of business, which was the cultivation of new customers, the preservation of old ones, and the business of publicity, he had no equal.

Lawrence came to work at mid-morning. He sat in the empty *fonda*, and waiters fought to serve him. He had a glass of *café con leche* and an end piece of cuban bread and butter. He needed the strong Cuban coffee to kick-start his motor. He accepted company, but did not seek it. He always left a big tip. It impressed me. When the average tip was a dime, Lawrence left a crisp new one-dollar bill.

Ybor City had one abiding passion. True to their Hispanic roots, everyone in Ybor City was politically involved. It was natural that Lawrence with his gregarious personality and his following would gravitate to this field. He kept no office, but the small liquor store behind the café served as his headquarters, where he would sit until late at night receiving petitioners, settling squabbles, and taking care of business problems.

The depression was fading when the brothers decided to hire Iva de Menici to design a fourth room. They had already successfully added a third room in the form of a large hall in a Spanish castle. They called it the Quixote Room and it served as a nightclub. Here Casimiro planned to showcase his talented only daughter, Adelita, who had graduated from Juilliard in New York City.

The fourth room was called El Patio and indeed resembled the courtyard of a house in Sevilla. Its center boasted a fountain with statues of a boy and a dolphin. When disgruntled patrons complained that the dribbling fountain made them visit the rest rooms too frequently, Lawrence smiled his million-dollar smile and informed them that in the rest rooms they would see a new machine which emitted hot air to dry their hands. Lawrence was always putting a new spin on a complaint, turning frowns into smiles.

A mini-boom was taking place in Ybor City during the war era. The shipyards in Palmetto had begun hiring and the demand for workers was so great that they drew them from as far away as the hills of Tennessee and Kentucky.

Lawrence began a policy to attract more dollars into the Columbia. He decided that he would cash customers' checks at the liquor store, provided they bought a pint of liquor and drank it in the café, with free ice and set-ups. Off-duty cops were hired to maintain peace. This policy led to one of my more uncomfortable moments, a moment that almost cost me my health.

A huge mountaineer dressed in filthy overalls, his hair and beard matted with sweat and dirt, sat down at my station. With deliberate movements, he placed a big brown bag on the table alongside his pint of bourbon.

Dutifully, I brought his bowl of ice cubes and a tall glass. He waved the ice aside, opened the pint with one effortless move, poured its contents into the tall glass, and drank it down in a gulp. He disdained the water chaser.

"Git me a clean bowl and a glass of hot milk."

I stood mesmerized by his size and the fetid smell of his clothes.

"You got saltines?"

I nodded yes.

"Bring me a bunch."

As I was at the counter pouring the hot milk into a barrel glass, I caught sight of Pete, the tough, rotund bartender who ran the coffee shop as though he owned it. His lips were compressed; his eyes looked at me in a hard squint. My sense of survival placed both men on a scale. Better to serve the mountain man than discover why Pete was giving me the death ray I dreaded.

I placed the empty soup bowl in front of Man Mountain Dean and put a big soup spoon next to the plate. I had put a number of saltines on a plate with a pat of butter. During these days butter was in short supply.

"Tabasco sauce and mo' butter."

When I returned with the hot sauce and one more pat of butter, the mountain man had already poured out a dozen oysters he had bought at Pardo's Market. It took him longer to season them, with the hot sauce and the contents of an entire pepper shaker, than it did to consume the entire dozen.

"Coffee . . . American," he burped, making "American" sound somehow like an anti-Latin slur. I went back to the urns to pour his coffee.

"What are you charging him?" Pete said in his tight-lipped way.

"Dime for the milk, dime for the crackers and butter, dime for the coffee?" I said weakly.

Pete handed me a menu.

"How much for oyster stew?"

"One dollar fifty for six."

Peter Scaglione: the
bartender and policeman of
the Columbia Café, 1943. Dan
J. Fager for William W. Carnes
Photography. Courtesy of
Adela Gonzmart.

"He had twelve," Pete said, pointedly giving me a pad. I felt as if I was signing my own death warrant.

"Oyster stew, three dollars. Coffee, a dime."

Pete closed his eyes, indicating approval, and motioned me on.

I dropped the green tab at the corner of the table, farthest from him, but a lifetime of catching flies on the porch of his moonshine still had sharpened his eye and his reach. In a flash he got the tab and reacted by grabbing my white shirt and pulling my face down to table level. My clip-on bow tie slid across the white octagonal tiles of the floor.

"What's that?" he roared, his eyes bulging, spittle on his beard.

"That's three ten for your oyster stew." Thankfully I heard Pete's voice behind me. Out of the corner of my eye, from my vantage point on the table top, I saw the massive, squat figure of Pete, his bald pate glistening with sweat, a slight smile on his granite-hard face, his white knuckles gripping a baseball bat. The mountain man considered the price he would pay, and decided to pay the tab.

The only other time I needed Pete was when a local Italian pistolero came in with a bag of freshly baked *pasteles de guayaba* which he had bought at Gus's Bakery across the street. Pete calmly ordered me to charge him a dime for each pastry he consumed, along with a dime for coffee. Again, when my hour of doom arrived, Pete was behind me, the rock-hard face showing a small smile of anticipation. I wondered if Pete ever got to smash anyone with that bat in his forty years as a Columbia Restaurant bartender and peace-keeper. I always felt that when they buried Pete they would place that bat next to him.

Another man who made the Columbia a life's work was the master chef, Pijuan. Every great restaurant owes its reputation to a great chef. If Velásquez was synonymous with art in Spain, Manolete with bull-fighting, Andrés Segovia with the guitar, Antonio with flamenco dance, and Cervantes with literature, then Pijuan was synonymous with culinary mastery. The Columbia Restaurant measured up to any establishment in the South with the sole exception of New Orleans eateries, which were on another planet as far as excellence was concerned.

Pijuan had cooked for Alfonso, king of Spain. When the revolution came, he was urged to come to Ybor City. Francisco Pijuan Alsina was a master chef by any measure, and his artistry marked the Columbia as

**A Mathematical Disagree-
ment.** *1993. Ferdie Pacheco.*

the premiere kitchen in the state. As soon as he had settled into his position of eminence at the Columbia, Pijuan slipped his wife and children into the country. Immigration officials took a dim view of such shenanigans, and soon they were ordered deported back to Spain. This became the major crisis of the Columbia's history, for Pijuan announced that if his family left, he too would leave.

This called for draconian measures, and a bit of Washington D.C. political tap dancing, of which Lawrence had become a master. Calling in a few chits, he was able to obtain passage of Private Law 225 in Congress, "For the Relief of Mrs. Pacios Pijuan," which allowed her to remain in the United States and her husband to continue to set the high standard of excellence for the Columbia Restaurant.

The small, round Pijuan was a tyrant who munched on heads of lettuce like most men eat apples. A waiter who ordered incorrectly was disgraced. One who was not ready when his order was placed on the counter was severely scolded. Pijuan wanted to see the plate when the customer was finished. Had he eaten it all? Had he left any on the plate? More than once he prepared a special dish, then went to the kitchen door to watch the customer. If he ordered catsup or other condiments, Pijuan would roar out, "Take the plate back to the kitchen and tell the customer to go to a diner and order meat loaf."

It was the good fortune of the Columbia to have lifelong employees who would work at their jobs until they died. When Pijuan died, his will specified that a Columbia menu be buried with him.

My old-maid aunt Lola, the head cashier, could not be persuaded to go home until the cash receipts balanced to the last cent. She was also intolerant of waiters' mistakes in addition and, like Pete, acted as though she owned a share of the restaurant.

The headwaiter, Pepin, was an old political crony of Lawrence's. When he tired of his political appointment as meat inspector, he was hired as headwaiter. Possessed of rugged good looks, conservative elegance, and a politician's memory for names and faces, he was a natural for the job. If he had a flaw it was that his years as a meat inspector had instilled in him a horror of microbes. He was the only man who washed lettuce and tomatoes with soap and water before he made his own salad. On the other side of the coin, he piled his plate with all the specialties from the lunch menu and wolfed them down in huge gluttonous gulps. One day we caught a small mouse in a trap and, lacking anything better to do with it, bribed the second cook to put it under Pepin's beans and rice. But that's another story.

To be a waiter at the Columbia at this time was roughly the equivalent of being a New York Yankee. It was the top of the profession, and that is how these waiters viewed their work, as a profession. It was only to be expected that the best of this breed of proud men was a man known simply as El Rey, the King. In part it was because of his imperious manner, in part because he looked exactly like Alfonso XIII, king of Spain.

At a bleak moment in the history of the restaurant, when the Great Depression paralyzed the nation, Casimiro went to the hardware store and came back with some plywood planks and a bucket of nails. The entire take of the previous day had been $12.50.

"One more twelve-dollar day and I'm boarding up the place," Casimiro said, plucking furiously at his eyebrows, as was his habit when things weren't going well. Quietly El Rey walked to the bank and drew out his entire savings of $503. He came back and put the money in front of Casimiro without a word.

So moved was Casimiro by this splendid gesture of loyalty that he vowed never to close the Columbia. He did not accept the money, but he never forgot the gesture, and El Rey became an untouchable employee along with Pijuan, Pete, and Lola.

His name was Gregorio Martinez, although I doubt that anyone knew him as anything but Rey or King. As usual, Tampa storytellers had a story to go with his name. It is much too simple to assume his name was Rey because he looked exactly like El Rey.

He landed in Tampa in the late 1920s and took a job in a speakeasy. The feds raided the place one night and Rey escaped by jumping out of a rear window. In a panic he ran into the Columbia Café, still in his waiter's uniform, and started walking up and down as if he was working there. He looked so good that Casimiro hired him on the spot. Still worried that federal agents might be looking for him, he grew a moustache that made him look exactly like King Alfonso XIII.

Like all Columbia waiters, Rey acted like he understood English.

Patio

Special, Ready to Serve

Spanish Yellow Rice with Chicken .90	Chicken Caserola 1.00
Chicken Catalana 1.00	Half Chicken Country Style 1.25
Chicken Livers with Bacon 1.00	
Broiled or Fried Chicken 1.00	Chicken Liver Omelet 1.00
Spanish Omelet .75	Eggs, Malagueña .75
Spaghetti with Roman Cheese .75	Spaghetti with Meat Balls .90
Eggs "al Plato" .60	Stuffed Eggs .75
Chicken Livers "Broché" 1.50	Mushrooms on Toast .75
Scrambled Eggs with Beef Brains .60	

Columbia's Specials

Chicken Giblets Sauté 1.00	Chicken "a la Ville Rua" 1.50
Chicken Croquette .75	Filet of Trout "Columbiana" .90
Ham, "Roman Style" .60	Steak "Capuchina" 1.25
Chicken Salsa Verde 1.50	Crawfish, Columbia Style 1.25
Chicken and Yellow Rice to order (25 minutes) 1.25	
Chicken Merengo 1.25	Chicken Parisiene 1.25

Desserts

Cream Cheese with Figs .30	Cold Egg Cup Custard .20
Guava Paste and Jelly .25	Roquefort Cheese .25
Arlequin of Custard .10	
Guava Preserves .25	Cocoanut Sherbet .20

Sandwiches

Cuban Combination .25	Roast Pork .25	Club .75
Chicken .50	Ham or Cheese .25	
Coffee .10	Sweet Milk .10	
Buttermilk .10	Iced Tea .10	

Patio

Sea Foods

Crawfish Croquette 1.00	Stuffed Pompano, Special 1.50
Broiled Key West Crawfish, Butter Sauce 1.00	
Broiled or Fried Spanish Mackerel .75	Filet of Trout, Tartar Sauce .75
Filet of Trout with Russian Sauce .90	Crawfish "Siboney" 1.25
Broiled or Fried Sea Trout .60	Shrimp, Creole Style .90
Crawfish, Catalana Sauce 1.00	Broiled or Fried Pompano 1.00
Pompano Papillot 1.25	Trout "Columbia Chef" Special 1.00
Shrimp with Yellow Rice .75	Stuffed Crawfish 1.25
Red Snapper Steak .75	Half dozen Fried Oysters .60
Stone Crabs, Butter Sauce	Crawfish "a la Cognac" 1.25
Lobster "a la Newberg" 1.25	Rice Madrilegna 1.00
Fish al Señor Pijuan	

Steaks and Chops

Tenderloin Steak, French Fried Potatoes .90	Filet Steak "Milanesa" .90
Filet Sauté 1.00	Filet Steak "Columbia" 1.00
Steak "a la Patio" 1.00	Filet Steak "Mushrooms" 1.00
Diamond Steak 1.00	Filet of Beef, Mignon Sauce 1.25
Lamb Chops "a la Ville Rua" 1.25	Steak, Cacerola Sauce 1.00
Lamb Chops, Shoestring Potatoes 1.00	
Pork Chops, French Fried Potatoes .75	Veal Cutlets, breaded .90
Calf's Liver with Onions .50	Beef Stew with Potatoes .50
Filet Steak, "Catalana" .90	Rice "Milanesa" 1.00
Assorted Cold Cuts 1.00	

Vegetables

Hash Browned Potatoes .35	Machine Fried Potatoes .25
Potatoes "Au Gratin" .50	Julienne Potatoes .25
Petit Pois in Butter .35	
Asparagus in Butter .50	String Beans in Butter .30
Boiled Potatoes .25	Lyonnaise Potatoes .35

COLUMBIA MENU RESTAURANT

Patio

COLUMBIA'S ATTRACTIVE AND EXOTIC SETTING RENDERS IT UNIQUE IN AMERICA

Front cover and inside pages of the Patio menu from the Columbia Restaurant, 1938. Courtesy of Adela Gonzmart.

Most words he could make out but inflections, tones, and strange adjectives threw him. Once he was waiting on an air force colonel and a general who were having a last-night feast at the Columbia. They ordered the same food as they had every night: garbanzo soup and steak Pijuan.

Leaning over to light their Perfecto Garcia cigars, Rey felt a glow of pride in the food and his work. Here were two heroes from the fight in the skies above Europe. He was proud that they had specifically requested him, and he felt the warm glow that an impending big tip gives any first-rate waiter.

"The steak was *excellent*," began the general, taking a huge puff of the long cigar, "*but* the soup was superb!"

"I don't know what hoppen, we make-a de sane soup ebery night!"

The use of the word "but" and the change of tone in the middle of the sentence caused Rey's deciphering apparatus to self-destruct. His brain registered this as a complaint. He could see his large tip diminishing in large increments, thus his heart-felt, anguished plea: "I don't know what hoppen, we make-a de sane soup ebery night."

It was not only employees who gave the Columbia their lasting loyalty. Every evening before the supper crowd would come in, a small old man would sit with the waiters as they folded napkins, telling them stories, and ordering his supper.

He was Balbino Alvarez Lopez, formerly a highly respected *capataz* (foreman) at the Perfecto Garcia factory, who had started eating at the Columbia when it was only a café. A lifelong bachelor, Balbino hadn't missed many meals in thirty years.

True to the elder Casimiro's orders, Balbino paid a set price of twenty-five cents, no matter what he ate. Of course, Balbino was a proud and dignified man, so he took pains to order from the left-over-from-lunch specials. However, El Rey, El Curro, and others of the old guard would often slip him a steak or lobster from the night menu. He was kind and people spoke to him with reverence, for he had been a big man in the cigar industry, and had been one of the first important men to recognize the excellence of Don Casimiro's little café.

Balbino started eating at the Columbia in 1918. By the time he died he had only missed thirteen meals, ten in 1945 when he was in the hospital and three in 1952 when all the Spanish restaurants were closed due to a flash strike. Balbino, his faithful attendance at the Columbia notwithstanding, was a loyal union man.

On V-J Day Balbino showed up at his usual hour for supper. To his amazement, he found that the Columbia, in a spate of patriotic fervor, had closed in celebration and in honor of that momentous day. Casimiro, as was his way, was locked inside counting crates of lettuce and doing his never-ending accounting. When he noticed Balbino peering wistfully through the door, Casimiro did the only thing a conscientious owner could do for his most faithful customer: he let Balbino in and fixed him bacon and eggs.

The most spectacular of the Columbia regulars was Pan con Chinches (Bread and Bedbugs) who lived on the largesse of Casimiro. Pan con Chinches was a walking sound machine. He had advanced heart disease, with valvular damage, emphysema, and advanced congestive heart failure—a walking dustbin of a man who slept in doorways long before it was fashionable. He wore a derby hat at a cocky angle over his rheumy eyes. He had no teeth and when he sat in the café, people at adjoining tables moved away because of the sucking, gargling sounds he made as he tried to keep from drooling. If you stood five feet from the table you could hear his heart murmur, which sounded like a steam engine laboring in his chest. He was bent over, but held himself semierect with the help of a broomstick handle.

Casimiro had a standing order regarding Pan con Chinches. He could come in any time except during rush hours. He would be served a big cup of expresso coffee, black. No boiled milk. Whether this was due to Casimiro's fine sense of economy or a secret therapeutic measure, I never found out. He was to be given the leftover tips of the cuban bread used to make sandwiches. There was no shortage of those, so in a sense Pan con Chinches served as Casimiro's disposal unit.

The Columbia Restaurant was owned, run, and patronized by descendants of the Spanish race, and they all had a considerable share of inherited eccentricities and flaws. One of the main flaws was unfounded, stubborn, dogged pride. One day Pan con Chinches arrived with his hat at a jauntier angle than usual, its brim nearly resting on the bridge of his nose. He bristled with a combative air. I could see he meant to have it out with Casimiro.

Why would a man who existed on Casimiro's charity plus the largesse of Lawrence (who was forever slipping him money) want to challenge his benefactors?

Pride. Pure, unadulterated, unreasonable Iberian pride. Pan con Chinches had awakened from a sound night's sleep in the doorway of Lodato's Pharmacy with a clear picture of how Casimiro had insulted him and trampled on his pride. He saw the insult as clearly as he saw the end of his reddened nose. The telescope on Mount Palomar was not needed to clearly define the insult

Butter. The problem was butter. It was bad enough that Casimiro would not put boiling milk in his expresso, but to withhold butter on bread tips! Clearly it was not an insult to take lightly. It called for confrontation. A clarification, and a righting of a wrong. A Spanish man is nothing if he is not given *respect.*

Casimiro was summoned from the kitchen where he was counting the heads of lettuce in a freshly delivered case. He greeted Pan con Chinches in his quiet, guarded way. Pan con Chinches launched into his prepared diatribe, informing Casimiro of his illustrious ancestors, going as far back as his ancestors Vasco da Gama, De Soto, Pizarro and Cortés. At the end of this wheezing rampage, Casimiro stood in quiet shock, picking his eyebrows. The silence was broken only by the accelerated pounding of Pan con Chinches' heart murmur.

"You are banned from the café forever. Throw the ungrateful bum out."

And so Pan con Chinches, the resident charity case, was banished, never to return. Entreaties by Lawrence, who found Pan con Chinches' revolt funny, fell on deaf ears. Casimiro was unmoved. He was fair but hard.

The butt ends of the Cuban bread piled up, employees chose sides, and hard feelings resulted. It's things like this that contributed to the beginning of the Spanish civil war.

The identity of Pan con Chinches was always a mystery to me. Where had he come from? Who was he? I could not find anyone who knew

Butter Rebellion. *1993.*
Ferdie Pacheco.

until I talked to the definitive Ybor City historian, Tony Pizzo. He, of course, knew.

Amazingly enough, Pan con Chinches had been a lector in a cigar factory, which explained his inordinate pride that caused the Butter Revolution. As to his nickname, Tony Pizzo related that one day while reading a text to the workers Pan con Chinches had come upon the phrase "pan con timbas." That was a name for a common sandwich that poor people ate when funds were low. It consisted of guava paste and a slice of the cheapest cheese on Cuban bread. It was also called Don Alonzo. On this unfortunate day the lector misread it, and it came out "pan con chinches," or bread and bedbugs. Great was the laughter and derision that followed, and the name stuck. Incensed at becoming the butt of their jokes, Pan con Chinches quit his job as a lector. What eventually became of Pan con Chinches no one knows, not even Tony Pizzo.

A different kind of character was Scags, the eccentric scion of a prominent Italian family. Scags had an active early life with the ladies of the demimonde of 15th street, the unfortunate sequela of which was that he developed a social disease as a permanent reminder of his good times. By the time I worked at the café, he was a fixture at a table which had a mirror next to it—for while he did not permit company, he did not like to eat alone. Scags was always on the lookout for the FBI, so when Lawrence decided to spruce up the bathrooms he ran head-on into Scag's worst fears. Lawrence put in a hot-air machine which dried wet hands. Scags watched warily for a few weeks before using the bathroom. No sooner had the new menace been accepted than Lawrence put in ultraviolet toilet seats. Now, *this* was a confirmation of FBI involvement. Ultraviolet rays were the advance test of the death ray that Scags was certain would follow.

One very crowded winter night Scags found that his table next to the mirror was taken. Frustrated by this, he decided to check on the ultraviolet toilet seats in the bathroom. He wormed his way through a crowd of tourists, some of whom had stopped by the water cooler to fill up their glasses with ice-cold water. Scags detested the human touch, and if by chance anyone touched him, he had to immediately touch him back. Without a neutralizing touch, Scags was certain the stranger had taken a part of him. He only had so many touches in him, so he figured that if he didn't get his balancing touch back, he was in danger of disappearing, an alternative to being zapped by the death ray that did not appeal to him.

As he slid by the water cooler, a huge Germanic tourist from Wisconsin touched him on the back. Scags reacted in a flash, but the corpulent man was out of range. Frantic, trying to fashion a touch of some sort, he filled a water glass and threw the cold water over two ladies and directly on the man's back. The bridge of freezing water made the required touch and Scags was saved.

Casimiro was furiously plucking at his eyebrow as he banished Scags from the sanctuary of the Columbia Café. From that day forward Scags had to take his chances on the outside. I never heard from him, assuming, as the other waiters did, that Scags had been zapped by the death rays coming out of the electric fly traps over Pardo's meat counter.

❦ My first payday brought a stunning surprise. After a full six days of man-killing work, I proudly opened my envelope. My paycheck was for the princely sum of twenty-eight dollars, just like the other waiters'.

J.B. was waiting, and when he saw the check he marched me into the liquor store and angrily confronted Lawrence with the evidence.

"What are you trying to do, corrupt this kid? He's a boy, he doesn't make a man's pay."

Lawrence and J.B. were the best of friends, but Lawrence knew better than to argue.

"Well, what should I pay him?"

"A dollar a day," J.B. said sternly.

Lawrence took back the paycheck, tore it up, and gave me six one-dollar bills. I said nothing. Actually, I would have paid him six dollars to work the café. I'd made thirty-five dollars in tips. If it made J.B. happy for me to work for six dollars, it was more than OK with me.

I reported for work Monday with a big smile on my face. I now knew I had the job. I would be a café waiter for the entire summer! At six bucks a week plus tips, in twelve weeks I would be rich! And well-fed, for I ate the heavenly food three times a day, and was not above ordering a steak (by mistake) and eating it myself.

Generosity was a word that brought Lawrence to mind. Once when he was a struggling newlywed, his wife, the beautiful Gloria, had worked and saved her money to buy him an expensive coat he had admired in the window of Wolf Brothers, a fancy clothing store. She was able to save up for a year and buy it and also a matching necktie for Lawrence's birthday.

A prouder man never went to work than Lawrence Hernandez dressed in his new clothes. He met a Cuban political refugee at the Columbia who had an important appointment with a government official but was unable to dress properly for it. Giving little if any thought to what he was doing, Lawrence took off his new coat, his new tie, and dressed the needy refugee. The repercussions were many, but the surest and most predictable one was from the long-suffering Gloria.

As the war progressed we had a steady stream of VIPs trooping through the café to visit Lawrence. His generosity was legendary. I routinely saw him give away the watch he was wearing if complimented about it. The rear of the liquor store became a warehouse for hard-to-get items. Chanel No. 5 in huge bottles, silk stockings, watches, and all manner of gifts flowed to generals, admirals, congressmen, and the other men who ran the war. The other side of the coin was that he could also pick up the phone and talk to the White House. His nephew Gonzalo wanted to go to West Point. It was done. Little Lawrence, his bully son, took an Annapolis appointment. I was also scheduled for West Point, but the war ended before this drastic measure was taken. I have often wondered how I would have reacted to West Point discipline at eighteen. Now, I'll never know.

§ My father, J.B., was known as The Philosopher because of his ability to patch up quarrels and his talents as a peacemaker. I used to ponder on why he always carried a .45 automatic tucked into his belt at the small of his back. Why would a pharmacist carry a gun? I never understood it until I was writing my Ybor City chronicles and was visited one night by one of my father's friends. He finally solved the mystery for me.

When El Patio was being built, it occurred to Lawrence and some men of the Italian gambling profession that the restaurant would be a

Little Lawrence at Annapolis, 1945. Courtesy of Casey Hernandez.

dandy front for a Vegas-style gambling room. The room was built upstairs with a private hidden entrance to the street.

The immediate result was violent. A hotheaded tough guy ran a gambling joint called the Lincoln Club in West Tampa. His partner was Charlie Wall, who had a finger in every pie. It was immediately apparent that if a real fancy gambling room opened in Ybor City, the Lincoln Club would shrivel up and die. No amount of negotiating would cool the young tough guy and it all came to a head one night.

The side entrance of the Columbia Café faced a dark alley. One murky night J.B. and Lawrence stepped out of the side door to be met by a shotgun blast. Pellets peppered Lawrence, who was small, but did not hit J.B., who was large. J.B. piled Lawrence in his car and drove him to Trelles Clinic to be patched up.

In the end, the federals paid everyone a visit, suggesting that the government did not want the thousands of airmen going through Tampa to be exposed to gambling in any form. Reasoning of this type, and that load of buckshot, brought order to the affair. The gambling hall never opened. The room is still there. It's now used as a banquet hall.

❦ The golden era of the Columbia Restaurant ended in the years immediately following World War II. Lawrence's hard-driving lifestyle and his three pack-a-day cigarette habit resulted in coronary difficulties, which he ignored. He swallowed nitro pills as if they were candy to ease the pain.

One day during the holidays, Lawrence's generous heart just stopped. He was in the center of the restaurant, surrounded by customers, employees, and relatives. He simply slumped forward and died. His funeral was the biggest ever held in Ybor City. Everyone had a story about how Lawrence had touched them, and they all spoke of his great generosity.

I remember my final talk with Lawrence. The war was over. I had worked two summers for him, and I was a surrogate son. He felt he had to send me off to college in style. New cars were hard to get, but Lawrence found me a Ford convertible. J.B. heard about it before I had laid eyes on it. He felt that going to the University of Tennessee with a car was out of the question. I was crushed. But every time I returned from school to visit, Lawrence found a way to present me with $500, with the solemn proviso that I would never tell J.B.

"I want you to spend this on clothes, shoes, girls, and having fun. You know why doctors are such jerks about money and life? They never get to know about life beyond the practice of medicine. I want you to spend every cent on *life*. J.B. will take care of school, books, and that stuff. You bring a beautiful girl to the restaurant and buy her the best dinner. Tip handsomely. Live fully. Then I'll have done you a great service, so you will know about *life*."

Four times he handed me $500, more money than the Ford was worth. I think I made him proud. When he died, I was still penniless, but I had earned a Ph.D. in the ways of the world.

❦ With the sudden, unexpected death of Big Lawrence, the Columbia entered a turbulent, unhappy period of change which culminated in a major tragedy.

Little Lawrence, the Lorencito of my Columbia days, graduated from Annapolis and was about to begin his tour of duty. Then the war ended and the navy had an excess of ensigns, so it was not difficult for him to wangle a hardship discharge.

Little Lawrence was a strapping, handsome naval officer who had done well at Annapolis and even won a boxing championship, which was no surprise to me. A title was not all he won in Annapolis. He met and married a beautiful blonde southern belle named Libby, and when he showed up at the Columbia in his spiffy blue naval uniform, with a golden blonde on his arm, he was the envy of every man in Ybor City.

Annapolis had taught Little Lawrence many things, had polished his rough edges and taught him how to be a gentleman. However, not even Annapolis could curb his hostility, and his propensity for violent solutions to annoying problems.

Libby, aside from her striking physical beauty, was Scarlett O'Hara come back to life. She was witty, strong-minded, stubborn, flirtatious, fun-loving, and above all contentious. She was a champion in her own right. It did not take long to deduce that this combination of a southern beauty who prized her independence and an Ybor City tough guy, who had his macho opinion of what a wife should be, would ignite and eventually blow up.

During the few years that elapsed before the explosion, there was an uneasy truce in the ownership of the Columbia. Casimiro, who had pioneered the expansion and was the supreme commander, tried in his noble way to act as if Little Lawrence was his partner, but clearly his new son-in-law Cesar Gonzmart was now a factor in the equation. Casimiro went out of his way to befriend Little Lawrence and Libby, going to an occasional banquet with them to show the public their unity.

The explosion between Libby and Lawrence came one night in their Davis Island mansion. Libby's fierce independent streak was more than Little Lawrence could handle. At wits' end, his only solution was always violence. His boxing skills made the struggle unequal. Libby had gotten him to buy her a gun, ostensibly to protect her from burglars since he worked late every night. The contest now became equal.

One hot night, after an argument and a few punches, Libby pulled out the equalizer and shot Little Lawrence in the back. He did not die, but he was paralyzed from the waist down.

*Libby: the Scarlett O'Hara of
La Septima, 1945. Courtesy of
Casey Hernandez.*

A rare photo: Casimiro
smiling, out for a night with
Lawrence and Libby, 1948.
Courtesy of Casey Hernandez.

The tragic family before the tragedy: left to right, Mother Gloria,
Lawrence, and Casey, 1946. Courtesy of Casey Hernandez.

Aside from his bully properties, Lawrence was a good man, honorable and decent. In his defense I must say he was all man, and in this bitter moment his best qualities came out. He refused to press charges, and admitted that everything that had happened was his fault.

By this time they had two beautiful daughters whom he loved a great deal, and in everything he did until his death he protected them and Libby with equal fierceness.

The end was not easy. Lawrence recuperated at home, attended lovingly twenty-four hours a day by his mother, Gloria, a strong pillar of strength. His younger brother Casey, a college student, helped in any way he could, for he adored and idolized his older brother.

Two years after the shooting, Little Lawrence died during a trip to Havana with Casey and his mother. The death of her beloved husband and son in such a brief period of time proved to be too much for Gloria, and a year later she died of a heart attack at a young age.

Casey, the remaining heir to the Columbia, was a good-hearted, good-natured, handsome kid with a great smile. He was a soft touch, and life was a picnic to him. Whatever the contractual agreements were, the end of his involvement came at this point. From this time on, the

Columbia Restaurant would belong to Casimiro alone. The era of Lawrence and Casimiro had ended.

❧ Casimiro had only one love greater than the restaurant, and that was his talented daughter, Adelita. She had not inherited his shy, moody reticence. She was her mother's daughter, full of fire, dash, and laughter, brimming over with an infectious love of life.

Such was Casimiro's protectiveness that he would not allow her to attend the Juilliard School of Music in New York unless her mother went with her and rented an apartment. Every chance he got, Casimiro would hop a train and spend a few days with his beloved family.

When Adelita graduated, Casimiro insisted she play piano in the Quixote Room at the Columbia. She was a concert pianist, but Casimiro's overprotectiveness kept her from pursuing a professional career. Instead she found her Prince Charming in Ybor City's Cesar

Adela, at Juilliard recital, 1944. Cía. Fotográfica, Fotográficas Commerciales. Courtesy of Adela Gonzmart.

Gonzmart, a tall, handsome violinist who led a society band. He was successful and had his own sources of income.

Gonzmart did not sit well with Casimiro, but it was obvious to everyone who knew Adelita that she had inherited Casimiro's stubborn streak. She wanted to marry Cesar, and she did.

Cesar was regarded with great suspicion by the people of Ybor City. He was considered a dandy and a fop, a man not to be taken seriously, an adventurer who had hooked a prize catch. Cesar set about proving everyone wrong.

His charm and easy ways hid an active and ambitious brain. What Ybor City could not see, and later would not admit, was that Cesar Gonzmart was a visionary. He had the heart of a dreamer and the brains of a hustler. With great guile and intelligence he disarmed people and then imposed his will.

He was determined to learn the restaurant business. Although he did play the violin and entertain, mainly Cesar was actively absorbing the business of running the Columbia. Waiters snickered behind his back and called him *melenita de oro* (golden mane) because of his long hair which curled up in the back and rolled over his collar. When he heard them he would turn on his dazzling smile and say, "I play the violin, what's your excuse?"

The code of behavior in Ybor City at that time was that self-promotion, self-serving publicity and self-aggrandizement were taboo. Actors and politicians did that sort of thing as part of their profession. Normal people were humble, modest, and avoided publicity. They did not brag about themselves or call attention to their accomplishments. It was not considered the macho thing to do.

Imagine the impact of this tall matinee idol type as he courted the press, tirelessly getting publicity for the Columbia in local, state, and national magazines. Many criticized him for riding the publicity for personal gain. Whenever a Columbia article appeared, Cesar and his violin were pictured. And why not? Could they feature a picture of Casimiro sitting on a box of lettuce, plucking his eyebrows, a homicidal look in his eyes? While the articles made Cesar well-known, they also got the Columbia nationwide publicity and annual prestigious awards as one of the best restaurants in the land.

Adela married Cesar Gonz-
mart in 1946. Studio Armand,
Havana, Cuba. Courtesy of
Adela Gonzmart.

Ybor City people were simply not used to dealing with a show business type. The closest thing the waiters of the Columbia had had to deal with was a waiter formerly known professionally as the Great Roshay, whose act consisted of dancing on stilts with his wife. At the drop of a garbanzo he would bring out his scrapbook. When I saw a *New York Times* ad announcing that the Great Roshays were appearing with Artie Shaw's band in the Radio City Music Hall, he won my vote. However, with the lowering of ceilings in nightclubs his act lost its charge. Acknowledging that people did not want to see a couple dance on three-foot stilts, the Great Roshays packed it in and he became a waiter at the Columbia. I remember he was looked on with grudging acceptance, although he still wore stage make-up and his soft dancing shoes on Saturday nights in the Quixote Room where Cesar was playing. The Great Roshay was probably the only man in Ybor City who understood Cesar and liked him for what he was, an artist.

Cesar called to mind the oft-used Ybor City word *plante*. This is a hard word to pin down, but roughly it means outward appearance, or the front that you present to the world. Cesar understood the word perfectly. The following story probably illustrates it best.

Once Cesar was solidly ensconced in the Columbia, he felt secure enough to begin to implement some of his advanced ideas. He knew he had to impart the impression of personal wealth to the bankers in order to get the loans he needed to do his work.

It was well-known in Ybor City that the flashy Cesar had big eyes and tight pockets. The restaurant was in Casimiro's name, and it was a hundred-to-one shot that he would let Cesar touch the money for his outlandish schemes. The highly practical Casimiro considered his son-in-law a dreamer of Quixotic proportions.

One bright morning Cesar dressed himself in his perfectly tailored sports coat, walked into the Ybor City Cadillac dealership, and went directly to a shiny new convertible. The sales manager, instantly recognizing Cesar, leaped to assist him. Cesar mused that it seemed time for him to be seen in a Caddy convertible. The sales manager couldn't have agreed more. At that time, just after the war, I do not remember ever *seeing* a convertible Cadillac, much less knowing anyone who would be splendid enough, rich enough, or silly enough to "show his ass" in such

Cesar, the master violinist, 1948. Courtesy of Adela Gonzmart.

a garish display of wealth. The height of nouveau riche opulence was Santo Trafficante Jr.'s new white Buick Roadmaster.

There were two convertibles on the floor, a red one and a royal blue. With the experienced eye of a poker player and the guile of a con man, Cesar got in the blue one. The sales manager began to drool and harbor a germ of an idea that it might be possible to stick the violinist with the blue dog. People willing to pay $3,500 for a convertible had accepted the fact that they were going to stand out, and most figured that as long as they were going to call attention to themselves they might as well go all the way and buy a red car. Convertibles are meant to be red, is a saying among the Hurons.

"I'd like to take her for a spin."

"Yes sir, Mr. Gonzmart. Tell you what, keep it for a couple of days or so."

Cesar looked dubious, pursed his lips, let his long, beautifully formed fingers play on the silvery push buttons in the radio.

"Well, let's see how my wife likes it. I'll drive it for a few days to get her used to the idea."

"Fine, fine, Mr. Gonzmart. Keep it as long as you like."

Cesar had made a lunch date with a prominent Anglo, old-money banker of the Tampa establishment. He appeared at the bank in the gleaming new Cadillac with top down, its boot in place, and the radio playing a soft Glenn Miller tune.

They drove down Franklin Street making small talk, as the banker assessed the young man and his aura of newly found wealth. The rich, dizzying aroma of new leather was having its effect.

"When did you get the car, Cesar?"

"Oh, I just picked it up, paid cash for it, and drove it off. I always wanted a convertible." Cesar coolly left off the fact that it was a Cadillac, but dropped the hook of having paid cash.

"What did a beauty like this set you back, Cesar?"

"Three thousand five hundred and change," Cesar said, adjusting the sun visor and changing the radio station by mashing a button in the floor. The banker blinked.

"You know you shouldn't pay cash for anything this expensive. Why, hell, son, you should have come to the bank, we'd have financed it entirely." The banker looked for a place to deposit the ashes of his cigar, and Cesar, not taking his eyes off the road, pulled out a hidden ashtray from the dashboard.

"Why should I finance it if I can pay cash?" Cesar asked innocently, baiting the trap with the con man's staple, the greed of his victim.

"Well, son, you use other people's money. O.P.M. You never use your own. Cash, boy, you save that."

Cesar, his shadow, and bongo, 1948. Cesar is the one in the foreground. Photo by Margaret Larsey. Courtesy of Adela Gonzmart.

They rode on in silence, Cesar letting the banker marinate his greedy thoughts. The banker was rapidly revising his estimate of Cesar Gonzmart.

The Columbia Restaurant had done big business during the war. He figured Lawrence and Casimiro must have socked away a lot of midnight money, under-the-table, tax-free, wartime profit money. Hell, everybody had. So now, with Lawrence gone, old Casimiro must have let his son-in-law have the keys to the safe. Cesar Gonzmart was a man sitting on a future.

The air on the Bayshore Boulevard was clean, fresh, and clear. Birds wheeled overhead, pelicans dove into the water, and fish were jumping. Cesar felt it was time for his solo.

"If I let you finance this car, how long would the paperwork take? I hate the delay. I own this car free and clear, I don't want to wait for a bank to go through all that red tape."

"No problem, Cesar. Get me the bill of sale and title and I'll take care of everything personally. You don't have to do a thing."

Lunch went well, but Cesar's brain was reeling. How was he to get a bill of sale? A title?

Returning to the salesroom, he went to the sales manager's office and closed the door.

"I want to buy the car for the full price."

The sales manager could not contain his amazement. He had figured on Cesar bickering on the price. Knowing the car was virtually unsalable, he was sure Cesar would chisel at least $500 off the list price.

"I'm going to finance it through the bank." He handed the sales manager the card of the bank president. "He'll take care of the details."

"Sure. Of course. No sweat."

"Now, I must ask a small favor. This is to go no further than this room." Cesar's voice dropped to a whisper.

"Anything, Mr. Gonzmart."

"I need a bill of sale marked two days ago."

"But why?"

"Question of moving funds. I don't like people to know my business, you understand?"

"Of course."

"And make it look like I paid cash."

"Cash?" the man was having a hard time following any of this.

"And apply for the license with the same date, etc." Cesar got up, straightened his tie, buttoned his plaid coat, ran his hand lightly over his long hair, and smiled his million-dollar smile.

"Pleasure to do business with you," he said, shaking the man's hand.

"Anytime. Is there anything else we can do for you?"

"Well, there is one thing. It's to your advantage for people to see me driving around town in your convertible. More people might want to buy one, when they see I have broken the barrier."

"That's certainly true." The manager began thinking about the red convertible in the sales room.

"Don't you think it would behoove you to give me free service and wax jobs on the car to keep it looking good?"

"Most certainly."

"Good. See you same time next year."

From that day on Cesar did not need to appeal to his father-in-law for funds. The downtown bank backed him in opening another restaurant in Rocky Point, and in many other successful ventures which slowly convinced the people of Tampa that the slick-looking violinist was a visionary with dreams which came true. In time, with the aid of two strapping, hard-working sons, he expanded the Columbia Restaurant to six locations statewide. With the personable Adelita at his side, he pioneered the restoration of Ybor City, and today his family can look back with pride on his accomplishments.

Oscar Wilde once said, "To love one's self is the beginning of a lifelong romance." Cesar is living proof of the epigram. Yes, he loved himself, but he loved his visions, his dreams, and his accomplishments more, for with Adelita and the boys, he saved the Columbia Restaurant and made it grow. It's only fitting that he named one of his sons Casimiro, and that the tradition of fine food in beautiful surroundings continues the love affair of the Hernandez family with the Columbia, the Gem of Spanish Restaurants.

Casimiro I, 1910.

Casimiro II, 1938.

Casimiro III, 1948.

Casimiro IV, 1988.

The four Casimiros.
Courtesy of Adela Gonzmart.

Chapter 6

My Cousin, My Brother

Cousin Gus Jimenez, called Junior by all of my immediate family, was an only child. By my own definition, so was I. Oh, I had a brother, but I thought he was visiting from another planet.

So in a strange and wonderful way I used to wait in gleeful anticipation for Junior to be brought over to my home on Columbus Drive to spend the day in play.

Until I was ten I lived at my grandfather's large house at 1019 Columbus Drive, which also served as the Spanish Consulate. The Jimenez family was very close, and each son would visit at least once a week. This brought me the joyful prospect of having an additional playmate.

If I had to settle on a word picture of what Junior looked like it would be "Shirley Temple." I mean this in the most complimentary way. He was the only child of a spectacularly beautiful woman, Aunt Maggie, and my rugged, fun-loving, adventurous Uncle Gus, one of my mother's brothers. Maggie's great beauty was enhanced by her reluctance to recognize that beauty, or to admit it gave her any advantage. She was sweet, sharp, smart, a good, loyal wife and a great mother.

To this day I look back on our great good fortune to have come from such a wonderful family. I think of Gus, Maggie, and Junior as the yuppies of the thirties. The times were hard, but this family bonded together and rode the depression out in high fashion.

Junior would appear dressed perfectly in a cute outfit, anxious to get his stuff dirty in the backyard frolics of my rough and tough neighborhood. Every once in a while Maggie would let him bring over his pedal

The silver beauty and pilot Junior, 1933. Courtesy of Gus Jimenez, Jr.

car. Only people with money had one. Junior's was in the shape of a silver one-wing airplane with a star on the wing. Oh, sweet heaven, to be able to put on my twenty-five-cent Kress's aviator helmet and fly a mission in that silvery beauty. All I had to trade for it was a tricycle with a side-seat contraption, unwieldy and lacking in speed. When I rode in the side seat I had to carry a brick with me to keep from tipping over. With a great application of imagination, the thing could look like a motorcycle with a side car like they used in the Great War. But you had to have a powerful imagination. Making it even harder to imagine that this unwieldy contraption was a war machine was its color. Uncle Paul, a singularly original thinker with a bizarre streak, in a spasm of colorist enthusiasm had mixed together some leftover paint and sprayed the tricycle a bilious slime green.

But a silver monoplane with a star on the wing . . . well, Junior was always a welcome sight at my house.

☙ Wartime loomed large, and unexpected changes started happening. First my beloved grandfather, the Consul, our cultural guide to art, opera, symphony, and film, expired in 1938, at about the same time as the Spanish Loyalist cause died. He was lucky in that he ran out of breath and a job at the same time.

My father, J.B., was progressing rapidly up the prosperity ladder, and we were able to move to the gentle shabbiness of Tampa Heights. Our home at 1806 Lamar Street was large and comfortable, and we were able to rent the upstairs to my bon vivant uncle, the handsome ladies' man Ferdie (also my mother's brother) and his gorgeous wife, Margaret.

With my grandfather gone, and the big house not needed as a consulate, my grandmother and Aunt Lola purchased a house next door to ours. After divorcing Margaret, Ferdie would marry again and move into the house next to Aunt Lola and Abuelita, thus moving amoeba-like relentlessly forward toward 7th Avenue. Only Dr. Angulo's house remained on the corner to stem the inexorable tide of the Jimenez-Pacheco invasion.

It is interesting to observe the impressions and record the conclusions one draws from a review of a family's history.

Ferdie and Gus were close as twins, doing everything in life in tandem. For one brief moment in their lives they were both married to beautiful women named Margaret. Ferdie was movie-star handsome and married an American girl who looked like Wallis Simpson, the woman for whom the Duke of Windsor traded in the throne of England.

Now, God had dealt out the good looks in the Jimenez clan to Guillermo, Paul, and handsome Ferdie. Gus, as they say in the South, was behind the door when the looks got passed out. Not that he was ugly. He wasn't. Let's put it this way, when compared to his handsome brothers, questions were raised as to the validity of genetic breeding theory. If Gus Jimenez stood alone, he was neither handsome nor ugly. He was average. If you stood next to him and heard his joyful, animated

The four Jimenez brothers.
Back row, Gus and Ferdie.
Front row, Paul and
Guillermo, 1925.

The saucy young Maggie (Uncle Gus's wife) as a bathing beauty, 1925.

talk, in time you wouldn't notice his looks. The longer he talked, the better-looking he got. It's a lesson I cherished.

So the two brothers married beauties. Ferdie's Margaret seemed fickle, flirty, vaguely dissatisfied. She was a beauty and she knew it. Her attitude was warm but distracted. With Ferdie's Margaret I always felt I had to ask permission to sit on her lap and get a hug and kiss. With Gus's Maggie you needed no invitation. She was always playing with us, always inventing new things to do. My recollections of birthday parties were the ones thrown for Junior. Gus, who had a mania for new things, was always discovering new attractions. One year it was a piñata, a leftover from the family's passage through Mexico. Another year he rented a pony. To this day a birthday party was a term synonymous with Junior's party. Neither my brother nor I ever had a party. In our case it was not paucity of purse but a paucity of imagination. My father had none.

To this day I have a horror of special events celebrated by parties. Birthdays terrify me so that when I turned sixty, in order to obviate an all-out party like my imaginative wife Luisita wanted, I took my family to spend a week in Paris with a plastic surgeon pal, Howard Gordon, and his family. Somehow, I have the feeling that the ghost of Gus Jimenez infuses the body of Luisita when birthday time rolls around. Terrified, I wake up in a cold sweat on the special day. What will it be this time? Piñatas? Mariachis? Ponies? Flamencos? All the old boxers I've known? Female impersonators in gorilla suits?

Still, I enjoyed Junior's birthday parties.

᳜ One benefit of the mass migration of the Jimenezes to Lamar Street was that we could count on regular visits from the irrepressible Uncle Gus. Gus was never a man to sit still. He moved around even while trying to sit still on the porch. He was a salesman. It was in his nature to move. So in short order his visits became a sojourn into outer space. We were earthbound on Lamar Street. We did not travel in any direction. My *abuelita* and my mother never left the house. Enter Gus, the Marco Polo of our family.

Possessed with a salesman's joy of life and avid curiosity, Uncle Gus would travel to whatever was happening. If there had been a fire, Uncle Gus would take us to see the ruins. Most of the time he would know the "inside" story. He could identify a fire by the technique used by the arsonist; this one had been set by Candelita, the other by Pastachuta.

He was a treasure trove of gossip. When the government started to build an expressway between Drew Field and McDill, the two air force bases, Uncle Gus was there at night checking the progress. He had an ability to convert himself into a devilish kid. He knew what tickled and titillated us. If he knew no one was allowed on the freshly laid concrete roadway, Uncle Gus would seek out an unguarded entrance and ease his car onto the gleaming white, unmarked virgin highway. Once on the road he stepped on the gas, and Junior and I watched the speedometer

My favorite uncle, Gus. Lee Wilson Photography Co. Courtesy of Gus Jimenez, Jr.

needle on the 1939 Plymouth move from safe green to cautionary yellow and finally, with a squeal of joy from us to blood red. Watch out! Pilot Gus was in a take-off mode. He'd let us steer the car at high speed. Oh, the joy of that! The man took chances, he was a gambler, he was a boy dressed up as a man. Maggie, the perfect mate, would sit tight-lipped, pinching him surreptitiously, and my mother, a born-again fatalist, would hold Abuelita's hand. Both had long since stopped trying to tame the fun-loving, thrill-seeking Gus.

It was this type of upbringing that had such a felicitous effect on young Junior. God smiled on him.

He got the best of both worlds. Junior looked like Maggie. That could have been a disaster, because she was so good-looking. Uncle Gus got in a few tempering genes and the result was that Junior was an adorable baby, a cute teen-ager, and an attractive man. He never mentioned his good luck nor acknowledged it. Perhaps he took a page from Maggie's book. He chose to overlook it.

Uncle Gus and Ferdie went to work for a food broker firm known as Bonacker Brothers. They had offices downtown by the railroad tracks. Ferdie became the main man in the office, and Gus easily became their top salesman. The beneficiary fallout for me was that I could park my car in the safety of their downtown lot during the war years when parking spaces were scarce.

Gus's ambition and drive could not be contained in one occupation alone. He used his free weekends to turn into a commercial fisherman. For me his weekend fishing trips were the next best things to the Bataan Death March. Once he went out, he never turned back. This was particularly hard on me since Uncle Gus believed that my seasickness was due to inexperience. The resulting cases of mal de mer were epic in proportion. Sometimes it took me a week on dry land for the earth to stop moving. Junior, champion fisherman that he was, weathered it all with a beaming smile.

Mercifully for me, Ferdie and Gus bought a motel on Indian Rocks Beach, and fishing was shelved for the duration. It was called the Casablanca, and that was where it looked like it belonged. The Jimenez family spent the war trying to improve the place. I always felt like I was at an abandoned Foreign Legion fort. The survivors of the epic weekend work sessions seemed happy to escape when the war ended in 1945 and Ferdie and Gus sold the motel.

Junior showed his Jimenez genes early. One Easter someone—I have to believe it was Uncle Gus—gave Junior a dozen chicks. They were cute, fluffy little things. Once before he had been given rabbits, and they had given Junior a whole encyclopedia of information on mating and the unwanted results therefrom.

In less time than you can say Checkerboard Chicken Feed, Junior became a chicken-and-egg tycoon. Trundling through the neighborhood dragging his red Union Flyer behind him, Junior serviced the entire neighborhood with chickens and eggs. When his outside hatcheries proved insufficient for the demand, he took over the family's two-car garage. Uncle Gus was busting his buttons with pride. The boy definitely had "it." (The only "it" that counted was the one that would make a profit.)

Junior in basic training for air raid warden's job to come, 1939. Courtesy of Gus Jimenez, Jr.

We were in the middle of a big war. Junior jumped in with both feet. He was put in charge of hopping on his bike, putting on a helmet, and running around alerting the air raid wardens that an air raid alarm was eminent. This was an important job, and we all looked on with open admiration.

I, on the other hand, chose a more prosaic approach to the avalanche of incendiaries that were about to fall from the skies. I found that the girl with the largest breasts in my class lived four blocks away, and I felt it incumbent upon me to be on her porch when the blackout alarm was sounded. It did not do the war effort much good, but it did a world of good for me.

Inevitably Junior's and my paths diverged. I went on a long happy journey which took me to five universities in twelve years. Junior, constrained by the demands of a thousand chickens laying eggs with dismal regularity, stayed at home, went to the University of Tampa, and—in the way of all boys who learned about the mating game from watching rabbits early in life—married and sired four children in short order.

Many years later our lives crisscrossed again, this time as we were divorcing our first wives. We both found happiness in the judicial process, and almost coincidentally found marital felicity in remarriage to exceptional women. Junior and I continued our parallel course. We had daughters. They were perfect. We were blessed.

A jarring note in this otherwise felicitous family history came when adventurous Uncle Gus decided to fly in a jet plane, a new mode of travel, to a convention, and met with disaster. A small private plane struck the jet over North Carolina, and Uncle Gus was dispatched off to a new adventure, life in the hereafter. Knowing him as well as I did, I felt it was an ending he would have liked. No nursing home for Gus, no senile old age. Gus went out with a bang, just the way he lived.

§ So now, at our present Junior and I stand open-mouthed at our good fortune in life, both blessed by outstanding parents and by our own families which have enriched our lives. Junior experienced the joy of professional achievement in his field of education, and I have skip-bombed five career fields. And, in the end, I came to recognize what I knew all along. Junior was more than a favorite cousin. He was the brother I had always longed to have.

⟨ *Chapter 7* ⟩

Ybor City's Last Intellectual

Don Victoriano Manteiga was a tall man in a city of small people. At least it seemed so to me, as I brought him a *café solo* at the Columbia Café. He always sat by the window so that the sunshine would illuminate material he had brought with him to read. He seldom wasted time in conversation. People so respected him that he just had to nod when addressed, and return to his reading. He was not aloof, but distant. He lived in his own world.

The *lectores* (readers) in the cigar factories were employed to read to the workers as they made cigars. They were thrown out by the owners after the Big Strike of 1931 because they had committed the outrage of reading tracts about workers' rights. The angry owners had responded by barring them from the factories. Many lectors returned to Cuba to read in the cigar factories there. Some opened cafés or other businesses, but only a very few remained as disseminators of information. Don Victoriano Manteiga was one of the most distinguished and respected of all the lectors. But he had several advantages. He was tall, handsome and distinguished. He had a full, rich voice which could be heard over the sound of 500 *chavetas* (knives) cutting tobacco leaves. From a high perch in the middle of the hall he read in his sonorous voice the works of Zola, Cervantes, and Molière. His command of the Spanish language was perfect. When he spoke extemporaneously he was mesmerizing. And he was the personification of truth as gospel. He was incapable of dishonesty. His opinions were arrived at only after careful study. He was Ybor City's resident intellectual.

Don Victoriano as a young lector, 1920. Courtesy of **La Gaceta.**

What constituted an intellectual in Ybor City? Don Victoriano did. An intellectual's work was his brain. No one ever saw him lift a finger at hard labor. His hands were soft and pink. He was always correctly dressed in a coat and tie. His clothes were immaculately clean and pressed, and his shoes shone to perfection. He never wasted time in coffee-shop *chisme* (gossip) because he utilized every moment reading to seek knowledge.

Don Victoriano was always available to speak at important functions: a birth, a baptism, a funeral, the dedication of a new building, a factory picnic. His presence lent importance to every event. He was much sought after to speak by crowds of admirers. And, lastly, he was *never* without his reading material. Whether riding in a streetcar, sitting at a café, or standing on a corner, he was always reading. Or so it seemed to me.

Don Victoriano had a characteristic tic, a jutting out of his jaw combined with a twisting of his neck to the side. He was always adjusting his tie and collar. He always sat bolt upright in his chair and never slouched. When he drank his *café solo* he held his cup with the small finger crooked, sipping delicately. He wiped his mouth after every sip. It seemed to me that he got more coffee out of that demitasse than anyone else. Either his sips were miniscule, or he continued to sip absentmindedly after his cup was empty.

When the lectors were barred from the factories, Don Victoriano found time to expand a small newspaper he had been printing for some time. Since his job as a lector involved translation of the daily news from the *Tampa Tribune*, Don Victoriano had begun to print these translations as well as local news. The newspaper was *La Gaceta*, which began publication in 1922 and continues to the present day.

With full time to improve the little paper, Don Victoriano made gigantic strides. He expanded every department of *La Gaceta*, and began printing it in Spanish, Italian, and English. The paper was the main source of information and news in Ybor City. It eventually outgrew and outlived *La Traducción-Prensa* and other Ybor City periodicals.

Don Victoriano was so removed from the social life of Ybor City that few people knew of his personal life. He seemed immune to gossip. He had a son named Roland, but I never met his wife. He was a solitary figure, accompanied only by his books.

The war came with great suddenness. Everyone was forced to adjust to gas and food rationing, housing problems, and shortages. We had moved into a new home on Lamar Street in Tampa Heights, the attraction of which was a separate upstairs two-bedroom apartment which we rented for precisely the same amount as our mortgage.

Two bachelors lived upstairs. They were both handsome, with plenty of money. One was my uncle Ferdie, recently divorced; the other was a

A Lector in Action. *1993.*
Ferdie Pacheco.

devil-may-care, ladies' man named Wilson Davis—strangely enough, my uncle's ex-brother-in-law. Their nights were never boring. They lived happy bachelor lives with lots of girls and parties.

When Pearl Harbor was attacked on Sunday, December 7, 1941, we tried to go about our lives as usual, as though only Ybor City represented the known world. That is, with the exception of Wilson Davis, who impulsively jumped into his new 1941 dark blue Mercury convertible and was first to enlist in the U.S. Marine Corps recruiting office. Before we could say goodbye to him, he was gone, shipped out, headed for the First Marine Division and eventually Guadalcanal.

Imagine my shock to see Don Victoriano in my parlor, giving my mother a deposit and accepting a key to Sin City upstairs. *The saint and the sinner,* I thought. *Now that is going to be interesting.*

Uncle Ferdie, who was a year over the draft age, was hale and hearty and subject to abuse because he wasn't in uniform. He took up a hermit existence and began a regimen of self-improvement. He bought a modest set of barbells from Charles Atlas and invited me to use them whenever I came home from school. I set my sights on becoming Mr. America.

The net result of this doomed-to-failure experiment was that although I was expanding my mind, my body remained pencil-thin. This was because I hadn't planned on the arrival of Don Victoriano in the apartment while I was working out. To work out in front of an intellectual who had work to do was unthinkable, so eventually I abandoned my Mr. America project.

I varied my time of arrival because I was curious to discover if Don Victoriano *ever* took off his stiff collar and tie. I hoped I could catch him in a bathrobe, or in his undershirt. I was sure the humid heat of a Tampa summer would keep him out of the front living room, which was mostly windows, and keep his collar buttoned.

On looking back at Don Victoriano's clothes, I understood their attraction. He was defined by what he wore. Today there are no such definitions. In those days you could tell what a man did by his uniform: a waiter, a streetcar conductor, an ice-cream man, a butcher, a mail carrier. Don Victoriano looked like what he was: an intellectual. I never saw him without a shirt and tie, sleeves fully rolled down, with his gold cufflinks in place.

*Note the solitary lector (upper right) reading to a vast assemblage of workers. 1930. Courtesy of **La Gaceta**.*

*Don Victoriano
at the height of
his fame and
popularity,
1939. Courtesy
of **La Gaceta**.*

Don Victoriano talked to me in a different way. He seemed eager to find out what a high school student thought about the war, social mores, and life in general. "Conversation" is probably too strong. a word for a one-way lecture, but he at least gave me the impression that I was having a one-on-one conversation with him.

When the war ended, Uncle Ferdie stopped his self-imposed exile from the social life. Wilson Davis returned from the war and married a Ford dealer's daughter. Ferdie married a cosmetologist from O'Falk's Department Store, and Don Victoriano welcomed back his son Roland from the Pacific War, beribboned and suffering from parasites unknown to Ybor City doctors.

My conversations with Don Victoriano influenced me deeply. I was already an avid reader, and the lector encouraged me to broaden my scope. He encouraged me to write and to express myself. He urged me to aspire to his lofty plan for me, to become an intellectual. He believed I could achieve this goal, yet deep down inside I knew I wouldn't. Ybor City summers were too hot to suffer the discomforts of a starched shirt and tie in order to gain the intellectual distinction.

Don Victoriano's son Roland slowly took over the reins of *La Gaceta*, substituting hard work and sweat for his father's facile intellectuality. As Don Victoriano grew older, he shrank and became wrinkled, his hands twisted by arthritis, yet his brain was always clear.

I last visited him at the end of his life. He received my wife Luisita and me with his Old World courtesy, leading us to his book-lined office.

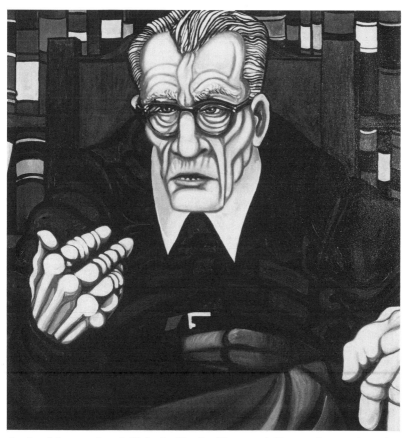

An Aged Lector Can Still Stoke Up the Fires and Give an Impassioned Speech. *1986. Ferdie Pacheco.*

*Roland Man-teiga, editor and publisher of **La Gaceta**, who carries on in Don Victoriano's noble footsteps, 1989. Courtesy of **La Gaceta**.*

For over two hours he held us spellbound, recounting his early days as a lector. With customary foresight, my wife brought her camera, and she caught the fire in his eyes, the eloquence of his gestures. Our visit inspired me to paint him not as he had once been, the tall, elegant lector, but as he now was, an old man, a survivor, an editor and battler, the voice of the people of Ybor City.

Our meeting led me to decide to write a long novel about the lectors and the immigrant experience in Ybor City. As I worked and reworked the chapters, I felt Don Victoriano was looking over my shoulder. When the writing was going well, I could sense his approving nod: "Yes, that's the way it was." When my writing wasn't true to the spirit of his time, I could almost see his frown: "No, no. That's not it. Do it again, do it over. Do it right!"

I consider it my good luck to have known El Lector, Don Victoriano Manteiga, the original intellectual of Ybor City.

Chapter 8

La Economica Drugstore
Free Deliveries

The world seemed full of promise, as once again I clipped on my black tie, walked down to Oak Street, and caught the trolley to the Columbia Restaurant to begin my third summer. While my less fortunate friends sweltered in the heat of a Tampa summer, I luxuriated in the cold air-conditioning of the café, eating sumptuous food, rubbing elbows with the rich and notorious of Ybor City. At the end of the first summer I worked at the Columbia, I had accumulated a tidy sum in the bank.

I should have known from the caterwauling in the front of the house that my plan was about to crash on the rocks of reality.

My father was the solid core upon which my family was founded, he had become serious about developing a source of income which was safe and would see both his sons through the expensive medical education costs to come. The only business J.B. knew was the drugstore business. This business he knew exceptionally well, coming as he had from a long line of pharmacists. His years in the wholesale business had introduced him to all of the doctors in Ybor City. He lived life rather recklessly and had not saved his money, so he had to set his sights rather low when it came time to buy a business.

He bought a small ethical pharmacy on Columbus Drive and 16th Street. It was a clapboard building which was so termite-ridden that it leaned right or left depending on how the wind was blowing. The old pharmacist who sold us the store lived next door with his wife and a

La Economica: Free Deliveries. Corner of 16th Street and Columbus Drive, 1945.

large son, Ernest Rubio, who was a Jesuit high school football hero. It seemed to me that his sole job was to keep the drugstore from collapsing on his home. Some days the store was one foot from the house, other days it was two feet away.

The first thing my father did was to change the name to La Economica, denoting an economic place to buy. The second thing he did was to hire two boys with bicycles to deliver purchases to customers' homes. He also traded in his massive black Buick for a modest 1941 two-door Chevrolet.

There were unwritten laws about place, class, and cars in Ybor City. Doctors owned Buicks, pharmacists owned Chevrolets. If a pharmacist was foolish enough to buy a Buick or, God forbid, a Cadillac, the doctors would resent it. More importantly, the patient would feel the pharmacist was getting rich off his misery. A doctor is supposed to become rich and show off his prosperity. A druggist is not. That is the way it was perceived in Ybor City.

My father's first plan was for my older brother, Joseph, to work in the drugstore. My brother disintegrated under the thought of going to work in Ybor City and had to be put to bed with *manzanilla* teas and *tilo* flower enemas. I didn't need to read the tea leaves to know what it meant to me. Goodbye Columbia Restaurant, hello La Economica Drugstore. To say I was dismayed at the possibility of going from the well-paid, star quality, air-conditioned, glamorous job of Columbia Cafe waiter to the hot, unpaid slavery of a drugstore is to put it mildly. I was crushed.

I hope you noticed I mentioned no pay. My father was a generous man but he had strong feelings about family finance. We were all to work hard for a common goal. This goal was to accumulate funds for our college educations; therefore, whatever salary we got would go towards this aim. J.B. maintained that I could count on his paying for my education for as long as it was needed. That was the deal. Work now, get rewarded later. Meanwhile, whatever small needs I had he would give me upon request. After all, a streetcar only cost a nickel, and a movie fare was just a dime, and I could take a Hershey bar from the drugstore. Fifteen cents a week was affordable. It does sound a bit Dickensian.

The other side of the coin made sense. It made me feel mature to work for J.B. Ever since I was young I always wanted him to be proud of me. I shined his shoes, even the black and white ones, which were tough to do well. I washed his car every week and waxed it once a month. I studied twice as hard to make top grades so he could brag about me. Now I was presented with the ultimate opportunity: a chance to help my father when he needed it most. The fact that it entailed sacrifice just made it sweeter.

I discovered that there is no business more demanding than owning a family ethical pharmacy. The hours were 8:00 in the morning until 11:00 at night, Sundays and holidays included. We hired another pharmacist to work on alternating days—morning and night one day and only the afternoon on the following day. Not bad, compared to a galley slave. No days off.

Pharmacists were scarce during the war. We were lucky to find a short Spaniard, who claimed he spoke English. He would spend the slow hours leaning against the counter reading the *Tampa Tribune*. His interpretation of what he read was rich in imagination, and his pronunciation was positively byzantine. "Eisenhower," for example, always came out "Chi-chin-howzer."

In those days a counter prescription was a necessary feature in Ybor

City drugstores. In tough economic times patients did not have the money to see a doctor, or, if they belonged to a clinic, did not have the time to sweat out a long waiting period. The answer was to be diagnosed and treated by your pharmacist. J.B. was considered an unofficial doctor. He was great at giving the patient exactly what he or she needed to make them well. It surprised me to discover that this was not only considered unethical but illegal by the state of Florida. University professors, while teaching you it shouldn't be done, also said after class that if you didn't do it you'd lose all your customers. Today, with the prohibitive costs of a doctor's visit, I note we're back to accepting a druggist's advice and treatment. Isn't it odd, how economics dictate ethics?

One morning J.B. was in the back making up a prescription when a patient with a heavy cold came into the store. Our Spanish pharmacist put down the *Tampa Tribune* for a moment, looked over his glasses, and put his cigarette down. He seemed deep in thought as the patient described the symptoms of common cold. Scratchy throat, rheumy eyes, runny nose, fevers, muscular aches, a productive cough.

"Do you have aspirin at home?"

"Yes," the patient sneezed into his soggy handkerchief.

"Do you have strong tea? Lemon? Honey? Rum?"

"Yes."

"Take two aspirin with the hot tea mixture every four hours. Get in bed and stay in bed for two days."

"That's all?"

"If you are not over it in four days come to see me. But remember. Stay in bed."

The patient left, a look of disappointment on his face, doubtlessly headed for Lodato's Pharmacy to buy a load of cold remedies.

J.B. stormed out of the back and towered over the small pharmacist.

"Listen, we're here to sell medicine not furniture."

Sure enough, by the end of the month we hired a man of infinite professional expertise and personal sweetness. Gus Moreno II was a handsome, well-groomed man with a charming disposition and a kind heart. His gentility was widely admired in Ybor City and his father, although in his eighties, was still a practicing pharmacist at Trelles Clinic. Dr. Moreno was a widower and much sought after by single ladies of the

Dr. Gus Moreno II, a gentle and courteous man who was an extraordinary pharmacist. 1947. Courtesy of Gus Moreno III.

community, but he kept a gentlemanly silence about his personal life. He was all business in the store. He became the glue that held the store together. When J.B. died, he bought the store. His only son, Gus Moreno III, became my roommate at Spring Hill College and graduated with an M.D. degree from Georgetown University. He is now a prominent gynecologist in Miami.

❧ My first impression of La Economica was not good. It was painted a dingy greyish-white with a waistcoat of dark green. A young blonde-headed boy was sweeping the sidewalk and gutter. This was Cecil, our drug clerk, a boy straight out of Charlie Dickens's *Oliver Twist*. He was the Artful Dodger come to life. He was to make the drudgery of drugstore life fun and engrossing.

Years later I sat at my first lecture in the Pharmacy College at the University of Florida. The course was called Drugstore Management. It

Cecil Arias, the
Artful Dodger,
1946. Courtesy of
Cecil Arias.

was a farce. It was taught by a tall, gaunt, thin man who had diplomas
in both law and pharmacy. He couldn't make a living in *either*. So he did
the only thing he could do. Taught school.

He opened the lecture with a question.

"What do you think is the first thing a store owner will ask you to do
on your first day as a graduate, registered pharmacist?"

My hand shot up. Others, too intimidated to venture a guess, sank in
their chairs. He nodded smugly in my direction, and pointed to me with
his No. 2 pencil.

"Sweep out the gutters and the sidewalk in front of the store."

A look of amazement and disappointment filled his Lincolnesque face
and told the shocked class I was correct. See, most of them had not met
J.B. or Cecil or even heard of La Economica Drug Store: Free Deliveries.

As J.B. went about the business of turning on the lights and putting the change in the cash register, Cecil took an empty R.C. Cola bottle and filled it with water. Applying his thumb to the open top, he began to sprinkle the old, unpainted wooden floors. When he was sure the dust wouldn't fly up, he swept out the store. This technique was important, for dust was a drug clerk's arch enemy. It was bad enough that it swirled through the open doors and landed on the counters and floors; infinitely worse, it landed on the thousands of bottles of medicines. On days when the dust was flying, Cecil's usually smiling face assumed a funereal expression. Dusting off bottles was no fun. When I came to work, Cecil's load was lightened. He was happy to have a partner. The mixture of boredom and two devilish minds proved to be incendiary, and a combustible symbiosis was formed between Cecil and myself.

The day started with manufacturing chores. This was the fun part. We were an ethical pharmacy in the days when the old homeopathic pharmaceuticals were in daily use. Modern medicine and modern manufacture and packaging had not yet taken place. To look at a modern shop today and compare it to our shop in the forties is to compare a Neanderthal man to an astronaut. Modern shops exhibit the mortar and pestle as a relic. We used them. We had four sizes.

Having witnessed the remarkable progress of medicine over the past fifty years, I look back and try to tell my children what it was like to manufacture and package a bewildering variety of natural drugs. Oddly enough, the pendulum is swinging back. My youngest daughter, Tina, is interested in natural remedies. For those of you who share this interest, let me tell you about some ancient remedies. Bear in mind, these items were sold daily over the counter. It took all Cecil and I could do to keep the shelves and drawers properly stocked.

To reduce the drudgery we concocted races to see who could package the fastest. We raced each other, and when that grew dull, we raced the clock. I can assure you that by the end of the summer Cecil and I could win the gold medal in the Drug-Packaging Olympics.

The most popular powders came first. These included boric acid, used as a cleaner and disinfectant, then Epsom salts, a killer laxative. To compound the packaging agony, each was dispensed in two sizes, five-cent and ten-cent blue cylindrical cardboard boxes. I must add that we had to put on labels and type each label on a rickety Underwood typewriter, which was rumored to be the first typewriter ever made.

We must have had a lot of nervous women in Ybor City because the quantity of "nerve" medicine we sold was amazing. *Tilo* (tilia flowers) and *manzanilla* (chamomile flowers) were far and away our best sellers. Somewhere in Central America there had to be a country whose trade depended on growing tilo and manzanilla for export to Ybor City.

In addition to leaves, flowers, and roots, the two best-selling remedies for "women's problems" were Miles Nervine and Lydia Pinkham's Tonic. A tablespoon of these products was the equivalent of a double dry martini. It's no wonder the women of Ybor City sat quietly on their porches to catch the late afternoon sun with a wide smile on their faces.

Stomach trouble was treated with paregoric, which is camphorated opium. In those days the patient did not need a prescription. The signing of the paregoric book by the patients was all the law required. It was curious to look at the book at the end of the year and see how many signatures got shakier and shakier.

We made elixir of terpin hydrate and codeine in big five-gallon jugs. You didn't even need to sign a book for this cough syrup. We did a big business on Saturday nights. You didn't hear many people coughing at a movie or dance.

Bottled medicine was more fun because we got to use a graduated cylinder. It was a point of pride to do a hundred bottles and not spill a drop. Funnels were disdained by Cecil and me as the mark of amateurs.

Whatever happened to the practice of swabbing the throat? We bottled a glycerine, iodine, and tannic acid combination which was guaranteed to make a raw throat vanish after a few swabs. When I had a sore throat, I looked forward to a good swab. It tasted "mediciny", as they are now fond of saying on the tube.

Buchu leaves, althea root, and senna leaves were given for various urological problems. Buchu leaves also seemed to help impotence. We sold a lot of buchu leaves.

One of the worst smells known to man was the odor that came from making tincture of asafetida. To put it as kindly as I can, it was as if you found yourself in the middle of Tokyo during a dysentery epidemic when the sewage system backed up. It was a sure sales killer that day.

Asafetida was one of the mystery drugs. We actually wrapped asafetida in spider webs to hang as an amulet around the neck. It was supposed to ward off "evil airs" and malignant curses. Getting the spider webs was not tough since we rented to a family of spiders living in our stock room. Eventually, with the coming of the GI Bill of Rights and higher education, the sale of asafetida dropped off. Thank God.

Black customers, of which there were few, used turpentine a great deal. They used it on cuts and abrasions. They drank it in combination with creosote for colds and coughs and combined it with croton oil for a laxative. I tried to taste it once and could never understand how they kept it down.

Copal was a sticky mess of a gummy ointment which we disliked, because it was hard to get off anything it touched, usually fingers and clothes. It was put under a foot, at the arch, to ward off airs to the lungs and muscles. Even our delivery boys wouldn't buy that concept.

Ointments were fun because we got to use spatulas and tin boxes, manipulated with a great deal of style. The covers had a blank label and only I was allowed to write on them because I printed in neat block letters. I considered it an advantage to have this ability. Boric acid and zinc oxide were white, ichthyol was a sticky, smelly black ointment used to "draw" pus, or bring a boil to a head. It was also used to shrink warts, but it didn't.

For a time we also had leeches in a jar, which stimulated Cecil and me to new heights of devilment. In time, La Economica discontinued leeches. Too bad, for they went well on the hands of traveling salesmen and the backs of innocent delivery boys.

Chest colds which might develop into pneumonia were treated very seriously. Antibiotics were unknown in the early forties and pneumonia could be a killer. The acceptable treatment was the placing of cataplasma, or plasters, on the chest. These commonly were made of mustard which burned like hell or flaxseed meal which smelled like hell. The torture of having a searing hot, smelly, muddy mess put on the anterior chest wall was absolutely medieval. Whether it had any therapeutic effect, I cannot say, yet I can attest to the fact that it kept a patient from complaining about having chest congestion. Seen in the dim light of such a rationalization, I suppose it might be justified.

For those who required pain to feel better, hot drinking glasses were placed on the back. The heat and the inverted glass were supposed to suck out the bad vapors. J.B. knew how to do it but fortunately he didn't have to do it very often.

Being sick in those days was not fun. Ipecac, an emetic, was always given to "clean you out." I've met few people who enjoy throwing up. Of course, this was before the age of bulimia.

If emetics didn't work, laxatives certainly would. The taking of a laxative was an almost daily occurrence in every Ybor City home. If a child came home from school looking "peaked," the mother would make the child stick out his tongue, would pull down his lower eye lids, look at the palm of the hand and the nail beds, and pronounce her diagnosis: "He sure is coming down with something."

The grandmother would then be consulted and invariably she would say, "Give him some working medicine."

I became an expert on laxatives by experimenting on our delivery boys. When a new boy signed on, he had to pass Cecil's Courage Test. We began easily enough by offering him a block of Hershey chocolate, which was, of course, Ex-Lax. If he survived a few days of this, we offered him a cold Seven-Up which we kept in the icebox. (Seven-Up and citrate of magnesia taste the same to the unsophisticated palate.) And so it went for a full week. Many an accident took place, but the drug deliveries to the homes never faltered. If the boy stood up well to this torture, we stopped after a week and he was never bothered again. Young boys, full of mischief, should never be put in an environment of boredom and left in charge of pharmaceuticals.

Laxatives started mildly with milk of magnesia, then to cascara sagrada, bitter and awful-tasting, to Pluto water, also awful, to citrate of magnesia (also called lemonade because it tastes like lemonade), to castor oil, the heavyweight, no-nonsense laxative, to the Big Bertha of all laxatives: croton oil. Ex-Lax was dessert in comparison.

Croton oil sounded sinister to me. I only heard it mentioned in hushed tones, whispered at the foot of the bed by the relatives convened there to decide on a course of therapy: "This means we must resort to . . . croton oil."

My young mind, steeped in Flash Gordon, would immediately flash to the dark and sinister Planet of Croton, inhabited by a race whose every living moment was spent contemplating some form of evacuation of the lower digestive tract.

Once my small daughter, Tina, heard me tell a veterinarian to give our cat croton oil. She was so happy, thinking the cat was going to be given croutons. I was struck by the enormity of difference that a letter could make to a word. It could mean a completely different thing. A simple *u* was the difference between the oral delight of a *crouton* and the exquisite anguish of the excretory explosion at the other end, caused by *croton*. Perhaps this is the sole factor which caused Tina to change her career from pharmacy to creative writing.

Laxatives, however unpleasant, were nothing compared with the terror of suppositories and enemas. When little, I would climb up a tree to avoid a suppository, and would have left home to sidestep an enema, except that my mother forbade me to cross the street alone. So I was without recourse.

The world of pharmaceuticals was largely based on French and German theories. I find their preoccupation with bodily functions typical of both nationalities, and the clearest cause for World War I.

The French like to eat long, rich meals with many courses, heavy with sauces, followed by high-calorie desserts. Quite naturally, they are a nation in desperate need of strong, moving medicines, and impatient as the French are they resort to suppositories. To be truly French is to carry a dozen suppositories. If a Frenchman is to be away from home any period of time, he carries the suppositories. At the opening of *Doctor Zhivago* in Paris, the theater sold suppositories during intermission.

The Germans, a militaristic race, concentrated their considerable genius on mayhem and ate foods which resembled construction materials. Forts, dugouts, and abutments could be constructed from the heavy foods they ate. To mix the bolus into a proper concrete consistency, they drank enormous quantities of beer.

Consequently, the remedy had to be harsh and explosive. This was in keeping with the Germanic solution of any problem. The Germans favored the enema, which was heavy artillery. They heated up a quart of hot, soapy water, added croton oil and let fly.

The English, victims of an inadequate cuisine, were conditioned by thin gruels, and never needed laxatives, suppositories, or enemas. The Irish, perpetually in a state of starvation, eschewed "working medicine." They hoped to keep as much as possible of what they had eaten in the system.

It was left to the Spaniards to take the easy route when presented with the choice of which method to use (laxatives, suppositories or enemas). The Spaniard decided to take all three! Not more than one at a time, mind you.

They made such a deep impression on me that I have never taken "working medicine" in all my adult life. And I never ordered any prescribed for my four children. To this day, Tina will neither forget nor forgive her mother and grandmother, who held her down at the age of four and gave her a mild enema. Bitter memories are never easily blocked out.

Besides mixing emulsions, tinctures, syrups, powders, ointments and suppositories, J.B. and Dr. Moreno also filled prescriptions, which in those days meant weighing out each ingredient and mixing them in the correct order. There was a famous pediatrician in Ybor City named Gavilla, and he had three types of baby formula, called, quite reasonably, Gavilla's Powder No. 1, No. 2, and No. 3. To mix a quantity of these in a gigantic mortar, weigh each in a powder pawner, fold them neatly, place them in a box, label them, wrap the boxes, and then label *them* took most of the day. After I returned as a registered pharmacist and had to make them, I found they were using only varying amounts of sugars: lactose, fructose, and sucrose.

Later still, when I came back to Ybor City as a doctor, I found that Gavilla was not even a doctor, much less a pediatrician. He was a naturopath who taught himself by continuous study and reading and, by dint of hard work, became Ybor City's main (if not only) pediatrician. Somehow the professionals of Ybor City managed to skip the education part. They learned as they went along. Certainly the best surgeon in town, Dr. Trelles, did not do a surgical residency nor was he board-certified. He just read his surgical manual and then operated. Later in life, it was a shock to me to find out that J.B., who was a superlative pharmacist, never went to school but had apprenticed himself at a young age to his father. When the state of Florida chose to stop recognizing such pharmacists but offered to register those so trained under a grandfather clause, J.B., in his hard-headed way, just refused to go get a license. This caused major problems at La Economica Drugstore. Only Gus Moreno had a license. Technically, J.B. could not dispense prescriptions. Ybor City is a unique place in many ways.

❧ We did a huge business in home deliveries. The answering of the phone took up a lot of time and required an accurate knowledge of our stock and its prices. Since part of our job was to replace stock and price it, Cecil and I were allowed to answer the phones. It was not a job for the faint of heart.

The prototype La Economica delivery boy arrived in the form of a mongrel-mutt named Montefoo. In those days there was a famous comic strip called Smokey Stover. The name Foo appeared everywhere in the strip, on clothes, walls, and fire trucks. It was a funny word. One of my classmates in high school refused to sign his correct name to test papers and instead signed Benny Foo. I wouldn't have been surprised if his high school diploma read Benny Foo.

Montefoo was a ragged kid from the Projects of Ybor City. In a way, he represented a certain class of kid in the best possible way. He doggedly refused to admit his shortcomings. He spoke doggerel "Spanglish" which was only understood by people living in the Projects. He could barely read or write and was only in school because the law required it. He knew nothing about the drugstore and was so inept that we would not allow him to help us in our packaging chores.

But if you've read Cervantes, Montefoo was like Sancho Panza. He had passed the Cecil Test of Courage, although Cecil had escalated it to the maximum level of croton oil. He knew the streets of Ybor City. He was a wizard bike rider. Nothing stopped him, not rain nor sleet, cold nor dark nights. He was a Hall of Fame delivery boy. But he coveted Cecil's job. What he wanted most was to answer the phone. To take an

Dr. Gavilla, the most highly regarded pediatrician in Ybor City, who did not possess an M.D. license. 1943. Courtesy of the University of South Florida. History Dept.

order. That was his dream. Naturally, it would never be. Not only was he unintelligible but he did not know the name nor the price of a single bottle of medicine.

One Sunday afternoon, as Ybor City lay sleeping quietly under the merciless summer sun and not a soul was stirring in the street, a woman called to order a three-cent stamp to be sent to the end of the known world. I was alone in the store, my father having fled our doldrums for the excitement of the card games at the Centro Asturiano cellar, where it was cool, and electric fans insured that it would remain so. I refused to send Montefoo pedaling miles to deliver a three-cent stamp. She called again, I refused again.

Montefoo sat reading a comic book, occasionally giving me a baleful look. I knew what that look meant. Montefoo wanted to answer the phone. Once, just once.

At this point the phone in the back rang. I answered and was delighted to find that it was a girl asking if I wanted to go to the beach. This request was not only exciting; I would have considered its possibility remote. I continued to talk, thrilled that I was talking to a real girl.

The front phone rang. The woman with the three cent stamp again, I was sure. Montefoo was on his feet. I was torn between duty and my amazing good fortune of having a girl call me. What to do? How badly could Montefoo screw it up? The worst he could do was take the order and then he would have to pay for the mistake of taking it miles and miles to this woman's house.

It was no contest. Faced with such a choice, any red-blooded teenage kid would do the same.

"Answer the phone," I yelled, keeping my eye on Montefoo as he darted to the phone, a seraphic look on his dirty face.

"La Eco . . . La Econ . . . La Enocom . . . La Coconomica . . . La . . ." Montefoo was sweating bullets. He realized he didn't know the name of the place where he had been working for a year.

"La Enocomm . . . La Ecomacki . . . La . . ." It was hopeless. "Oye, man, what the hell is the name of this place?" Montefoo yelled into the phone. A loud click sounded on the other end.

In desperation I bid my beautiful girl a quick good-bye. I ran to the phone, but it was too late. The line was dead.

"Was it a woman?" I asked in desperation, hoping against hope that it wasn't J.B.

Montefoo was crushed. He had blown his big chance. He would never ascend above the level of delivery boy. He would never become a drug clerk. He was doomed to a life of pedaling the red brick streets of Ybor City, eating Ex-Lax and drinking citrate of magnesia.

"Was it a woman?" I repeated.

"No. It was a guy."

"My father?" My voice rose two octaves.

Montefoo got a wild look in his eye and emitted a yowl which I took to mean "Maybe."

Several anxious moments later, the phone rang. I picked it up at the first ring. I heard the raspy voice of Dr. Angulo calling in a prescription. While I was writing, he cleared his throat, and said, "Who was that that answered the phone? It sounded like someone having an epileptic attack."

"Just a paregoric addict. He picked up the phone by mistake." I closed my eyes, thanking God for his infinite kindness and wisdom.

That was the beginning of an eventful day. Later that afternoon, as the sun passed overhead, I found myself on the outer edges of tedium. It was as hot as the insides of a Mexican's stomach after a chili glut. Not a breeze stirred. The flypaper hung motionless like obscene stalactites from the neon light fixtures. No self-respecting fly would land on one of these smelly strips of paper, and none had. I suspected they were all over at Lodato's drugstore, luxuriating in his air-conditioning.

J.B. disdained a soda fountain. No pharmacist worth his salt wanted a soda fountain. It was beneath their dignity. So my long imprisonment in this hot oven was accompanied by a gigantic thirst, which was unquenchable with plain water. I longed for a Grapette, a Delaware Punch, or, in a pinch, a Dr. Pepper. I had read every magazine on our rack. I had stocked the store, and even packaged everything that was needed. There was no one to phone. All my friends were at the beach. Even my mother was not at home. There was not a soul on the street. The only sign of life was a streetcar that passed every twenty minutes; the conductor, looking every bit as desperately bored as I was, would wave as he passed. We were shipmates on the SS *Ennui*.

Still, there was the girl. If my father finished his card game by five, or six at the latest, I could shame him into letting me take the car to Clearwater Beach, get in an hour's swim, watch the gorgeous sunset with this girl and get in a few kisses.

"Oye, man, you got ballooms?" A nasal voice much like Montefoo's spoke. I saw no one. I leaned over the counter. There was a ragged kid, face dirty, barefooted, staring at me with large eyes that looked like two Smith Brothers' Cough Drops.

"No, there's a war on, haven't you heard?"

"Ballooms." The boy thrust out his grimy hand, showing me a shiny penny. He was persistent.

"No ballooms." I walked around the counter and took him by the arm to the door. "No ballooms. Now, don't come back, understand? *No ballooms.*"

The afternoon dragged on. Streetcars came and went, time stopped. Nothing moved except the sun, which dropped relentlessly toward the horizon. I would stand in the door, fix my eyes on the distant point where the trolley tracks converged. I hoped that the dot I saw at that point would grow and grow, like a shimmering mirage, like Omar Shariff riding to the well in *Lawrence of Arabia*. It kept turning into my father's 1941 Chevrolet coming to my rescue.

"Balloom? Man, you got ballooms?"

"No, dammit. Get it straight. No balloom!"

Again I walked him out. This time, in my rising frustration, I hauled him by his dirty T-shirt. He looked back with tears in his gigantic black eyes. I felt bad.

I made a frantic phone call to assure my beauty that all was on schedule. Well, maybe a bit late, but we were flooded with prescriptions, and I might have to take care of the sick for a moment or two longer.

My mind flirted with the idea of calling J.B. at the Centro. Yeah, sure. If he was winning, he would kill me for calling him. If he was losing, he had to stay until he got even. Another streetcar went by, this time with a new conductor. My depression heightened when I saw him. Even the damned conductor had gotten off, and was probably surfing on an ironing board in the late afternoon Clearwater surf. Damn.

"Balloom?" The boy was back, now talking to me from the doorway. He looked like he was ready for a quick getaway. "Baloom, man?"

All of my frustrations and self-pity coalesced into a ball of unreasoned thought. I was screwed. I wasn't going to see my girl, I wasn't going to get to the beach, I wasn't going to kiss and hold her while the pounding surf drove saltwater up my nose.

But why shouldn't somebody be happy on this horrible Sunday?

"Come here, kid," I smiled my best disarming smile. The kid hung back.

"Baloom?"

"Sí, baloom, kid." I said, going to the prophylactic drawer and taking out a dime condom. I blew it up as big as I could. I tied a string to it. I took a pen and drew a face on it. It was a nice smiling face. The kid grinned widely and came to the counter. I handed him the balloom and refused to take his penny.

His smile was beatific as he ran out the door, triumphantly shouting to his friends who sat on the grey granite curbing across the street.

"Baloom! Baloom!"

God must look after well-meaning fools like me, for the child had no sooner got out of sight than J.B. appeared. He was in a great mood. He had won big, and he knew he was late, so he tossed me the keys, and a ten-spot, and told me to come back at eleven when the store closed.

The date at the beach was magnificent, beyond my imagination, and afterward I pulled up to La Economica Drugstore: Free Deliveries on a rare cloud of bliss.

Cecil was waiting at the door. He looked worried as he came to the car.

"Boy, are you in a load of trouble! The police were just here."

"The police?"

"Yeah. They were going to arrest J.B."

"For what?" My heart was pounding. My father in trouble with the police? Impossible.

The little kid had gone home crying when his baloom exploded. He told his mother he got it from Pacheco. His parents were furious when they saw the deflated condom. They wanted to beat up J.B. for selling a child a condom.

"But I *gave* him the balloon."

"Ferdie, the kid is just six years old." Cecil made a face that indicated that there are some limits of decency that even he wouldn't break.

My father had cooled down. The parents cooled down. The police cooled down. I was not available to be arrested so J.B. had promised parental punishment. The kid was given a handful of penny candy. It blew over. Much later, my father laughed about the incident.

❧ It is still a few minutes before eleven o'clock. My father is a stickler for the clock. Somewhere out there on the red brick streets of Ybor City, he figures, a man was no doubt racing in his car towards the drugstore at high speed. As the Regensberg Cigar Factory clock gongs the hour he would make a frantic rush for our door. Holding his melting pint of ice cream in his hand and his street edition of the *Tampa Tribune* under his arm, he would ask for a twenty-five-cent package of prophylactics and disappear into the night. Community service is what we're all about.

In the back, Cecil and I are finishing up wrapping a case of Kotex boxes in the Sunday *Tribune*. Now, the Kotex company has already taken into account the sensibilities of the ladies of Ybor City and has wrapped their well-designed boxes in plain paper. This is not good enough. We wrap them again in the Sunday *Tribune*. Who are we fooling? I don't know. I just know it's a lot of work and J.B's Victorian sense of decency demands it.

Outside, I hear J.B. sell a night watchman his nightly bottle of bay rum, which is either an aftershave lotion or after-dinner drink, depending on your disposition.

The night watchman is on his third bay rum and feeling frisky. In spite of the harrowing events of the night, J.B. is feeling devilish as well. The topic is hypnosis, which happens to be the watchman's area of expertise.

"Can you hypnotize Cecil?" My father winks at Cecil. Cecil understands. He is to let the old man think he has hypnotized him.

The old man tries mightily and Cecil, overacting badly, falls to the floor in a deep trance. The old man beams, J.B. shakes his head.

"Going under isn't hard. Getting him to come out of it is what's hard. Cecil looks like he might not wake up." J.B. has a worried look on his face. Cecil is motionless on the dusty wooden floor.

"No *problema*. Cecil, when I count to three you'll be out of it and you won't remember a thing. One, two, and . . ." he snaps his finger. "Three!"

Nothing. Cecil is a corpse on the floor.

The night watchman drinks down another bay rum in one mighty swig. J.B. looks at his watch. It's getting late.

"Cecil, wake up!" The old man yells in Cecil's ear. A miasma of bay rum envelops Cecil's tranquil face.

"Cecil, your mother is calling you." Now he turns away, cups his hands, and in a falsetto voice quavers a call for Cecil. Nothing. Cecil doesn't move although it *does* sound like Cecil's mother.

J.B. has gone to the icebox and brought a pail of ice-cold water which he hands to the old man. Understanding that the situation calls for desperate measures, the old man drenches Cecil with freezing water.

Cecil leaps up, a look of shocked disbelief on his face. J.B. treats the old man to another bay rum and another day ends as the doors close on La Economica Drugstore: Free Deliveries.

Chapter 9

Abuelita

My mother's mother was from La Coruña, Spain, of half-Spanish, half-French blood. She came here the wife of a diplomat, the Spanish consul to Mexico, and had seven children in the New World. The revolution of 1910 in Mexico resulted in the expulsion of all foreigners, including diplomats. They rode away from their opulent hacienda on a flatcar, their fortune sewn in the petticoats of the wife and the girl children.

She came to Mexico at the age of twenty. She died at ninety. She never learned how to speak English, although she insisted that all of her children be educated and excel in English.

My picture of my *abuelita* was so different from her children's. Where they knew her as a tough taskmaster, I knew her as a loving, benevolent, nurturing person. I loved her beyond loving for she never scolded or found fault, was quick to praise and encourage. I suppose tough mothers see the error of their ways and turn into sweet grandmothers. Mine did.

I was born in her large house, the Spanish Consulate in Tampa. All of her children had wed and fled. Only my old-maid aunt, Lola, lived with us. For ten years I lived as if I were in Spain, with the customs and diet of La Coruña. We traveled to visit neighboring towns and museums in a big Packard, and always stopped for picnic lunches along the way. It was heaven.

When my father moved up in the world, and we could afford to live in our own home, we moved to a wonderful house on Lamar Street, a shady Norman Rockwellian street. My grandfather died in 1938, and

Abuelita as a young woman in La Coruña, 1890.

Abuelita and Aunt Lola bought the house next door to us. It was a two story house. They chose to live upstairs and rent the downstairs. Next door to them my bachelor uncle Ferdie, the ladies' man, bought a similar house and married the most beautiful of his harem.

This clot of relatives gave a young boy growing up an incredible support group and a great way to make a living. There were always cars to wash, and shoes to shine.

But the best fallout of that gathering of relatives was that I had my *abuelita* right next door.

My day started by going to report to her before I went to school. I would burst into the house, noisily clamber up the wooden stairs, and run into the kitchen, her headquarters.

She was small then. Less than five feet. She had been taller, but arthritis and a life of hard work had shrunk her. By the age of ten, I was taller than her. She had grey hair combed back into a bun, a very Spanish look. After her husband died, she did not wear anything but black. For two months after his death she had neither read anything, nor listened to the radio. Old ways die hard. For every Sunday within my memory, my grandparents had taken me to the first-run movie emporium, the Tampa Theater. Not being able to understand English, Abuelita would write her own screenplay which she would tell us at a post-movie chocolate and *churros* snack at home. Frequently her plots were better.

The before-school inspection included reassurances, praise for good grades, a passing comment about how handsome I looked, a sip or two of her delicious hot chocolate, and on days when I was doing particularly well in school, an extra nickel to add to my dime lunch money, tied in my handkerchief so that it wouldn't get lost.

After school was even better. I would change from school clothes to play clothes, burst into Abuelita's house, bound up the stairs, and report the day's activities. Midafternoon was the time she darned the family socks. How this was possible with seventy-year-old eyes is now beyond me. Quietly she would lay down her thimble and wooden egg on a stick (which was inserted into the sock), and turn her full attention to me. She listened intently. She praised when deserved. Scolded when I reported a B instead of an A. Admired artwork. Reminded me that science was more important than art if I were to become a doctor.

Then we ate. It couldn't be too big a treat, for supper was at 6:00 sharp.

Mostly it was *sopitas,* or the morning *café con leche* put in a soup bowl over day-old cuban bread. Delicious. Or hot thick chocolate and *churros,* which are relatives of the doughnut, made at home. And she had a fantastic way of disguising Cream of Wheat with all sorts of cinnamon, sugars, peaches, and spices. When my classmates said they hated Cream of Wheat I thought they were crazy. Then one day I slept over at a friend's, and had a plain Cream of Wheat.

On festive days she made her specialty, *brazo gitano* (Gypsy arm). It is like a jelly roll, made with custard instead of jelly, with a sweet simple syrup poured on it. Suffice to say, it was the highlight of any week she made it.

When I became interested in history and began to question her on her family history, my afternoons took on a different quality. Initially she was reluctant to talk about it, as if by dredging up the past she was reliving it and making herself very sad. She missed her husband. Two of

Left to right: Grandfather, the Spanish ambassador and his wife, Aunt Maggie, Abuelita, Aunt Lola, 1930. Abuelita's hat was later used as a model for the steel helmets used in World War II.

her children had already died. "There is nothing sadder than to outlive your children," she used to say.

Winters in Tampa were sometimes cold, but they were short and never much below freezing. The problem was that the wooden houses were not very well insulated from the cold. Families used kerosene stoves in the rooms they wanted heated, and the rest of the house was frigid.

Abuelita heated the kitchen and adjoining bedroom. The afternoon sun would stream in the big windows, and we two would sit like puppies in the sun, warming ourselves in its rays, using its brightness to illuminate the photos which Abuelita would reluctantly take out and spin her stories about. Some were happy or funny stories, usually about the devilishly naughty Uncle Paul, the handsome black sheep who was always in trouble. Sometimes she became indescribably sad, looking at her strong oldest son who had died of a heart attack trying to be more successful than his father. The photos were in shoe boxes, and she never took them out unless I insisted. For some reason unapparent to me, her sons and daughters never asked to see them. In her way she nurtured and encouraged my insatiable curiosity about the past.

The one ritual which no son could wean her from was mowing her tiny lawn with a huge manual lawn mower and sweeping the sidewalk and the gutter in front of her house. When I got bigger and she got smaller, she would permit me to do the lawn mowing, but *not* the sweeping. Spanish women took pride in their homes which included a spotless house and a clean sidewalk. I did not find this unusual; my mother did the same in front of my house. But the sight of a tiny, bent-over eighty-year-old woman in black, energetically sweeping the gutter, took many people by surprise.

Much later, when I would come back from college and bound up the stairs to have my chocolate and *churros*, she still provided me with a receptive audience for my stories. She was a funny person, she liked to laugh, and I was always able to keep her laughing until nap time came.

I was lucky to be home when they took her to Trelles Clinic. There I could stay with her for long periods, and although she was unconscious and had no hope of recovery, I read to her when no one was looking. I always felt she heard.

When she was gone, when I realized that I had no one to go to who was going to be 100 percent supportive and love me without qualification, an overwhelming sadness enveloped me. It was the first time I understood the finality of death.

But, month by month, as I drove out with my Aunt Lola to trim my grandparents' graves and put fresh flowers on the tombstones, I felt her telling me to let go. She had always talked about the chain of life, the links that stretch back and go forward. She was saying, "Go on now, take care of your children and your grandchildren. That's how you can pay me back."

I have endeavored to live life as I learned it in her kitchen. I miss her to this day. Every time I see a bent-over grey-haired little lady I think of Abuelita, but now, I'm not sad. I'm happy I had her. I'm happy to have been the recipient of her life experience and the force of her quiet strength. And now, as my time approaches, I look forward to seeing her again. I will, I know it.

✤ Chapter 10 ✤

The Dream Merchant

There were people in Ybor City who were dreamers. They dreamed of making a fortune and returning to the Spanish villages they came from. They tried new ways to do things, even invent gadgets. They dreamed the everyday dreams of the Spanish immigrant in America.

And then there was Avellanal.

I never missed a chance to talk to the man who was so outlandish that his life seemed as though it could only be found in fiction. He lived a life of dreams. He created careers with puffs of air. Charismatic, entertaining, brilliant, and crooked as hell, Avellanal was the great character of Ybor City.

You can read books about a lawyer, a plastic surgeon, a gynecologist, a minister of God, a cryo-biologist, a free-thinking sociologist, and a lieutenant general in the Mexican Army.

Or you can read this chapter on the life of Avellanal, the dream merchant.

✤ A slim young man in a perfectly tailored white linen suit took off his straw boater and placed it on a small desk, next to a large .38 pistol. Carefully he hung his coat on a wooden hanger and placed it in the closet.

He hitched up his pants and took a seat at his desk. Unscrewing the top of a silver Parker pen and arranging a pad of lined legal-size paper, he paused, waiting for the first sentence to form in his distraught mind.

In his twenty-second year, fresh from graduating in law from Webster

Dr. J.R. Avellanal, honored physician and long-suffering father of the Dream Merchant, 1920. Courtesy of the University of South Florida History Department.

University in Georgia, José Luis Avellanal saw clearly that he had been betrayed and that his only solution was to commit suicide. He was planning a final irrevocable, melodramatic gesture to show the smaller minds of Ybor City what he thought of them.

The darkly handsome son of the most prominent doctor in Ybor City, his childhood had been turbulent. He was the only son of Dr. José Ramon Avellanal, who had founded El Bien Público Clinic, who had been decorated by the governments of Spain, Cuba, and the United States, and who was the leader of the Ybor City medical community. His son, José Luis, had grown up as his father's exact opposite.

His earliest outrage occurred when a neighborhood kid looked through a knothole in a fence at José Luis, who shot his BB gun through the hole. Fortunately it did not hit squarely, but did do ocular damage. This was long before the days of civil lawsuits, so the good doctor smoothed things over for his son with immediate medical attention and a generous application of cash.

No sooner was he out of that doghouse than José Luis's fertile mind developed a plan to build an electric chair. Yet what was the use of an electric chair without someone to electrocute? A convincing salesman, he talked a younger boy into getting strapped into the chair. Before the boy could say "Help!" he was zapped by a weak electrical current.

The boy was taken to El Bien Público with burns on his legs and arms. José Luis was crestfallen; the results had not lived up to his expectations. The victim was Anthony Grimaldi, who grew up to be a bank president and the head of the Draft Board during World War II. Today many speculate that his boyhood electrocution burned the conscience out of his brain, thereby uniquely qualifying him for both jobs.

The good doctor shut his son up in his big house on Nebraska Avenue, hoping solitude would excoriate the demons in his head. He should have known better. José Luis, inflamed by reading *The Prisoner of Zenda*, engineered an escape which included borrowing the doctor's huge Buick Phaeton. This well-conceived plan overlooked a single detail. He had not learned how to drive.

The ensuing automotive mishap in a ditch outside of Orlando led the doctor to adopt draconian measures. He banished his son to a military school in Georgia. This experience engendered in the young Avellanal's impressionable mind a lifelong love of uniforms and military paraphernalia.

José Luis returned to Tampa after an ill-conceived romance, during which he was charged with kidnapping a young woman for immoral purposes. The love affair ended when the young lady shot and slightly wounded her swain.

Avellanal took rooms at El Pasaje, a famous hotel and restaurant, where he brooded on life's injustices. One day, after being rebuffed by his peers, he sat down to write his final paper, an elaborate suicide note.

He began in a style worthy of Tolstoy. If this was to be his last document, it would be eloquent.

Dr. José Luis Avellanal, bon vivant, libertine, and man of science. 1937. Courtesy of the University of South Florida History Department.

This life no longer has an interest for me. Nothing surprises me. That which I thought was practically immutable, has become most changeable. Only in the promises of my father could I believe, for when he promised anything it was done exactly so. How different to the words of my uncle, who would promise anything, and then on the grounds that his action was for a person's good, he would not live up to it. How different! How different!

Finally I realized that the work required for what I wished was so enormous that I would die before completing it. But I was sure I would start the movement that at some time would bring about desired results. This was to be done by my becoming a *film director* after I finished *Law*.

I could earn money and with it I could employ a host of scientists, stenographers, etc. and following the methods, which have already been written in my notebooks, definite plans could be made for a campaign. I would merely supervise, and all the problems could be confronted by experts: confronted and solved. Therefore my ability would consist in selecting which experts would work for me.

Having set forth his goal, he now launched into his personal problems.

My being a director had another viewpoint besides making money, which was the solving of *sexual problems*. I need, absolutely *need* (see "Sexual Impotence" by Robinson, page 259) the opposite sex. I need to caress them, I need to kiss them. I need to love them. I become nervous, dissatisfied when I cannot obtain them; but when I do obtain them all the good that surrounds me turns to sunshine, and I am most happy.

Yet, he cannot find solace in promiscuity.

I am very hard to please, picky. I have been with over five hundred women, and not one has fully satisfied me. Only three could pass, just pass. And why? Because (1) They were not pretty. (2) They were all would-be parasites.

He left his problems with women aside with a sigh, and got on more solid philosophical ground:

My ideals have all been shattered. Little by little have they seemed harder and harder to solve. And now, they no longer are possible because my father's promises were false, at least, no longer to be lived up to.

And what promise could possibly be worth taking one's life? The anguished young man continued:

If I obtained a degree of law, I would be given an automobile of my choice, and $200 a month. And why should my worldly ideals be shattered because the latter was refused? Because the career (law) I am following is not one that I like. Every day it bores me more and more. I hate it. Law is crooked. Backward. Its theories are too far behind the knowledge of science. This can best be seen in how the law punishes criminals, and how they are left. The courts are all corrupt. Yes, corrupt. Dwarfs of incompetence reside there. How else to explain the crime of the "Sullivan Act," in prohibiting the right to bear arms, in direct contradiction of Article II of the amendments to the Constitution. Also the imprisonment of a man who fails to pay alimony is an outright abuse!

How can anyone with a sense of duty, morality, and injustice see these things without speaking out? How can they quietly let it be? It has always remained the same, only a few of us have been able to see what was right, while the majority persist in their erroneous concept of these things.

After two more pages of convoluted thoughts about the dangers of women who were after his money, and the desirability of movie stars because they were not only beautiful but earned their own

money, he returned to his program to better the world. He devised a
time table:

2 1/2 years to begin preparations.
5 years to make money through movie direction.
1 year to learn German.
1 year to be lost because of illness.
4 years to finish movie directing.
2 years of practical work.
2 years more to work as assistant to a great director in
America.
5 years to make $100,000 with which to further educate, and
receive titles.
2 years for sickness, etc. incurred in the years of hard work.
This gives me: 24 1/2 years of work.
I am now: 22.
I will be: 46 1/2: At this age I would begin to prepare.
To become perfect: *4 more years.*
I will be: 50 1/2 years. At this age I will begin my major work.
It is then too late to accomplish anything worthwhile.
What *could* have been accomplished in 28 years? My program
was in a word:
THE SCIENTIFIC TREATMENT OF ALL PROBLEMS:
1. Reform the Penal System.
2. Conversion of Prison to Psychiatric Units.
3. A more rational system. The one in Russia is ideal: a postcard marries you, and also divorces you.
4. More equal rights for women. Let them have equal duties,
and rights.
5. Scientific solutions for labor and economic problems according to the greatest minds and authorities on the subject, not
left to legislators and politicians.

He went on to further indict his father and his uncle and the
"system," leaving only a sincere apology to his mother. He formally fin-
ishes his suicide note: "I hereby make it known I commit suicide."

In a curious afterthought he decided to tidy up the mess his suicide would create. This he decided to write in Spanish: "P.S. I took this gun from Mingo by force. Please find the holster in my dresser drawer."

Having licked and propped up his folded eight-page suicide note against the inkstand, he took the pistol and shot himself.

In the shoulder. His ideals were noble, but his aim was poor.

Shortly thereafter the long-suffering heroic Dr. Avellanal died, doubtlessly breathing a long sigh of relief to be forever relieved of the tedium of having to put up with his son's bizarre way of life.

The thirties proved a fertile period for Avellanal experimentation. For a time Ybor City was in danger of a major rat infestation which was directly attributed to Avellanal's advanced theories of cryogenics. No cat was safe from Avellanal, who was busily freezing them.

"I'm attempting to bring them back to life," Avellanal would say in his serious way. Finally he abandoned his experiment when he realized that he would never be more than 50 percent successful. He had the freezing part down perfectly, but he had a 100 percent failure in reviving the cats. Laying low from inquiries of the Society for Prevention of Cruelty to Animals, Avellanal flooded legal and scientific journals with his well-written and nearly sensible articles.

Avellanal began to feel that it was time to make his move into politics. Surviving his suicide attempt had given him new energy to pursue his formulas for social reform. Aiming for the moon, he entered the race for the state senate. He aimed for the moon, but hit rock bottom instead. His advertisement in the *Tampa Tribune* was an unabashed listing of his qualifications, real or imagined, and his platform. At the end of the ad was this reassuring line:

"Due to being in litigation all of his life, he is now well-qualified as a fighter to defend people's rights." Perhaps reasoning of this type confused the voting public of Tampa, for he received a record low vote and a few subpoenas to end his political career.

Discovering that the simple people of Ybor City had little understanding or tolerance for an original thinker and free spirit, Avellanal decided to go to the intellectual capital of the Americas, Havana, where he believed he would be appreciated. He returned to Ybor City in 1940 with diplomas and boards in plastic surgery and gynecology. It was in keeping with the breadth of his interests that he trained in two medical disciplines which had virtually nothing in common. His licensing by a U.S. specialty board was never proven, but nonetheless he became Dr. Avellanal.

Now a fixture at El Pasaje Hotel, Dr. Avellanal began yet another career. In 1944 he announced that he had been ordained a Baptist minister, and began holding services in the hotel. Not since Rasputin has the world seen such a libertine ally himself with the Divinity.

Observing this man, one had to admire his variety of interests, if not his moral rectitude. You had only to step into Dr. Avellanal's rooms to get legal advice, a nose job, a gynecological examination, and pray to your Maker. He was a one-man professional building.

Avellanal finally went too far. In the 1940's, he established Southern University right there at El Pasaje. He obtained a charter, which was either a tribute to his salesmanship, or a commentary on the ease of bribing politicians in charge of such things. He offered no courses, only degrees. Eventually, the County offered jail.

A trial was held and Avellanal defended himself brilliantly, by saying

*Avellanal runs for the Senate! Courtesy of the **Tampa Tribune.***

El Pasaje Hotel, Avellanal's headquarters. Burgert Bros. Studio. Courtesy of La Gaceta.

he had done nothing wrong. He had provided a college education for the poor. A diploma in "chiropractic" studies cost $500. Considerably less than in any other university in the state, Avellanal maintained, looking the judge in the eye. An incorruptible judge, with a clearer eye for justice, revoked the charter of Southern University in 1947 and prohibited the further issuance of degrees.

Dr. Avellanal once again sought the solace of a new land where his multidimensional talents would be accepted and appreciated. Like Cortés he discovered Mexico.

He traveled to Mexico by way of Cuba, where he stopped over. Flourishing in the free and easy land of the *mordidas* (bribes) of Batista, he created the Legion of Honor of the Republic of Cuba. By the simple strategy of introducing the idea of an official ribbon to bestow on worthy recipients, he devised a way to enter the highest social levels and to make a handsome living. There's never a shortage of people willing to pay money for honors, especially if the medal is large, and affixed to a nice broad red sash.

Enter Fidel Castro, exit Dr. José Luis Avellanal.

Now armed with boxes of ribbons and medals to confer on gullible officials, he continued to Vera Cruz, Mexico. Before the Mexicans could say "Ai, guacamole!" Dr. Avellanal had bestowed his medal on the governor of the state of Morelos in front of a solemn joint session of Congress. He began to work his way to Mexico City, describing himself as a retired cancer specialist.

Somehow he talked the Mexican government into making him a lieutenant general. Pictures arrived in Ybor City, showing Dr. Avellanal in full uniform and medals, standing next to the U.S. ambassador to Mexico during a Fourth of July celebration in Mexico City. By this time his entry in the book *American Men in Medicine* had grown to an eighty-five-line biography, listing his many medical affiliations, including the Association of Military Surgeons.

Tiring of Mexican cuisine, Avellanal came back to El Pasaje, as he always did when a posse was closing in. He announced he was pro-

Cuban President Fulgencio Batista (second from right), Dr. Avellanal (third from right), and several other recipients of the Legion of Honor, 1940s. Courtesy of the University of South Florida History Department.

gressing in the discovery of a method to rejuvenate grey hair. His own hair was black, a cosmetic rather than a scientific cure.

In 1970, he volunteered for and, amazingly enough, when one considers his foregoing history, was accepted on the advisory committee for the Ybor City campus of Hillsborough Community College.

About this time, El Pasaje was in danger of destruction by the misguided urban renewal crowd. The good doctor was active in saving his old domicile—the home of his law office, plastic surgery and gynecology offices, Baptist church, and Southern University. For his efforts he was given a special preservation award by then U.S. Senator Richard Stone. Avellanal showed up in his handsome lieutenant general's tan uniform, with enough medals on his chest to embarrass a Soviet field marshall.

Almost every person in Ybor City took a perverse pride in the little man's fancy life. He was the most colorful of my father's friends. When he came to our drugstore, he created excitement. He was never short of stories, causes, new theories, and outlandish plans.

In the light of what I studied in medical school, and learned in my long life, he was marginally cracked, but what a wonderful bit of color he added to our lives. With Avellanal, anything was possible. He talked of rocketry and moon flights before anyone thought they would take place. Many visionaries who see ahead of their own time are considered crackpots by more earthbound, practical people living normal, sensible lives.

So the dapper, ebullient, kinetic José Luis Avellanal overcame his suicidal impulse and survived to provide Ybor City with a subject for wonder and nonstop gossip. He shone brightly at El Pasaje. If he had channeled his brilliant mind into socially acceptable endeavors, there's no telling what he could have accomplished.

To people who remember Dr. Avellanal, he is a legend who evokes smiles, and a good story or two. I am slightly embarrassed to admit it, but I loved the old guy, and the improbable adventures of his life, his crackpot visions, strange escapes, and stubborn values. I saw him last in 1980 when he came to an art show of mine at the Columbia Restaurant. Mercifully, he had left his tan Mexican Army suit at home and was nattily dressed in a Palm Beach suit, with only a modest ribbon in his lapel.

On the lam again. 1940ð. Courtesy of the University of South Florida History Department.

After a scholarly discourse on my art and its comparison to Daumier, he bid me farewell.

"Where are you going?"

"To take the bar in Georgia. I plan to practice law in Atlanta."

By this time he was in his seventies and I had a feeling that it would be the last time I would ever see him. So I took a moment to hug him and tell him that in some as-yet-unrevealed-to me way he had influenced my own life. He smiled, winked, patted me on the back and walked out.

I heard he passed the bar and died while practicing law in Georgia. I'm not surprised.

Chapter 11

Trelles Clinic

A Love Story

The first sensation I had when I walked into the operating room at Trelles Clinic was one of awe. I was fifteen years old. My father had arranged for me to observe Dr. Trelles operate. Being excused from my duties at La Economica Drugstore was exciting enough, and to be in the presence of a man so famous for his surgical skill was overwhelming.

Dr. Jorge Trelles was an impressive man in every way. He was in late middle age. His face, once handsome, was now padded with fat, which gave him a froglike appearance. His abdomen was protuberant and hung over the sink as he scrubbed his hands and arms preparing for surgery. He had a beguiling smile, twinkling eyes, and a brilliant wit. He'd published a few novels, and had an artist's eye. He was also a ladies' man, and had won Ybor City's greatest prize by marrying the beautiful Conchita.

The operating room was blinding white. In those days the surgical team wore white and the patient was draped in white as well.

Since I would only be observing, I was not required to scrub. Later, when I was allowed to assist Dr. Trelles, I experienced the thrill of scrubbing and being gowned.

The patient was already draped and prepped. A small portion of abdomen presented itself through the opening in the drapes. It was painted a strange orange color. The screen separating the operating field from the

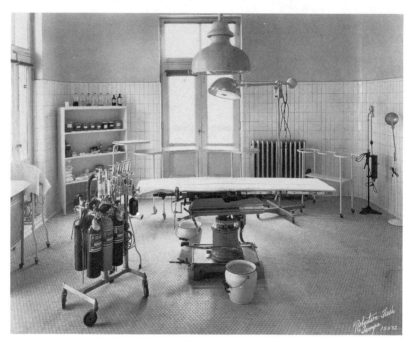

Operating suite, 1942. Robertson-Fresh Commercial Photographers. Courtesy of **La Gaceta**.

patient's head was in place. Over the top of the screen I saw a pair of luminous black eyes. They were the most beautiful eyes I'd ever seen, and they belonged to the fabled Conchita. People had told me bits and pieces of their turbulent romance, but aside from serving her supper when I was a waiter at the Columbia Restaurant, I had never been so close to her. Her breathtaking beauty was hidden by a surgical cap and a mask.

Dr. Trelles had taught Conchita to administer the anesthetic. She had become a master at it. These were the days when an ether or chloroform drip was hand-administered. In order to do it properly, Conchita sat at the head of the table, holding the patient's head. After the patient went under, her fingers maintained the angle of the jaw to insure an adequate airway. In order to do this, she had to hike her skirts, and virtually cradle the patient's head in her lap. The effect was not lost on the surgical team, who avoided looking at her beautiful legs when her skirt was at mid-thigh.

Conchita Trelles had known me since childhood and welcomed me warmly into the inner world of surgery. I could sense her radiant smile behind the mask. She placed me at an advantageous position to observe, and whispered that if I had any questions I should ask her and not disturb the surgeons. I noticed, gratefully, that she did not warn me about fainting. She gave me confidence by assuming I was too old to pass out at the sight of blood. She knew more than I did, because I wondered about that as I anticipated the surgery.

The surgery proceeded with deliberate speed. I was so engrossed by the procedure that I didn't have time to worry about fainting. I was enthralled by Trelles's mastery and, sensing this, he gave me a running narration. He was a born teacher and, as such, a born actor.

Dr. Jorge Trelles as a young surgeon. 1930ð. Courtesy of Tony Pizzo.

Midway through the operation, Conchita began to hyperventilate. Her eyes filled with tears and she looked wild. Trelles gave her an irritated look. She looked like a wild animal stuck in a trap. Finally Trelles said to me, "Take her in the other room and rub some alcohol on her chest."

Delighted that I was called upon to help, I eased Conchita toward the scrub room, my arm around her trim waist. She slumped against my thin body, and we left the clean world of surgery for a smelly space of domestic intrigue.

The longer I worked in Trelles Clinic, the more accustomed I became to the game they played. Trelles inflamed Conchita's jealousy by leaking stories of his sexual conquests. But on this day I was an innocent bystander, happily rubbing an alcohol sponge on Conchita's long, beautiful neck. She gasped, as the alcohol took her breath away. She ripped open her white blouse, revealing her perfect breasts. She pointed there, and I respectfully rubbed alcohol on her, attempting to keep my mind in neutral. It was impossible, of course. She soon recovered spontaneously, patted my cheek as though I were a five-year-old, smiled her dazzling smile, fixed her clothes, remasked herself, and went back to her duties fully restored. It took me considerably longer to return to the operating room, much to Trelles's amusement.

Much later, when I learned about their strange love story, I understood that jealousy was the crucial element in their incendiary relationship.

• Dr. Jorge Trelles came to Tampa and took Ybor City by storm. His talent was obvious but his wit and personality also made him successful. He was a complete doctor. He did not limit himself to surgery, but knew every aspect of medicine. He was a healer in every sense of the word. When he was unsure of procedures or diagnostics, he looked them up in his vast library. The town embraced him.

Trelles was a pillar of society. He was married to a thin, angelic, religious lady who was sweetness and decorum personified. She had to possess the patience of a saint, because Trelles was a confirmed ladies' man. He had an eye for the ladies and they had eyes for him. After all, he was a healer with a courtesan's flair for intrigue. His wife was an expert at

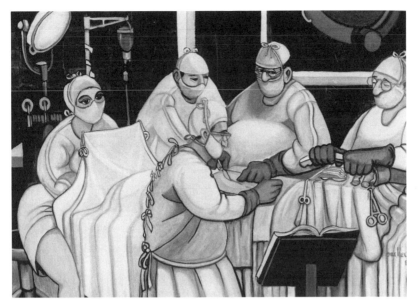

Surgical Distraction. 1986. Ferdie Pacheco.

looking the other way. This was called *la vista gorda* (the thick view) by Ybor City gossips. Many wives were expert at it. It was necessary, if they wanted to stay married.

In time, Mrs. Trelles gave the doctor five children, all girls. Some saw it as an ironic punishment for a man so consumed in chasing women. Far from settling him down, it made him even more restless and his sexual adventures became more frenetic. He needed a special woman to calm him down.

A few blocks from Trelles' large house on Nebraska Avenue was a house on Palm Avenue that he knew well. It was a house of joy. There, a hothouse flower was growing quietly, being groomed for big things by an ambitious mother. Her daughter was strictly supervised, and she grew into an astoundingly lovely teen-ager. The word spread that a beautiful young lady was waiting to be courted.

Conchita had two immediate suitors, both great connoisseurs of beauty, both wealthy. One was Trelles, who represented safety, goodness and the secure life of medicine. The other was a handsome gambler named Zarate, who represented the wild fast lane and the insecure life of a gambler. Both interested Conchita.

Both courted her assiduously, both became obsessed with her, and in the end the choice fell on Conchita. She did the only thing possible: she chose both. For several years the happy trio lived in contentment, then something clicked inside Trelles's head. As Conchita matured into full womanhood, she showed evidence of a brilliant mind. He became obsessed by the idea of marrying her. The thought of abandoning his angelic wife and five daughters did not seem to bother him. Getting rid of Zarate did not seem a problem. The world of glamour held nothing for Conchita. She had a big heart and found his world of medicine most desirable.

What did present a serious problem was the risk of total ostracism by important citizens of Ybor City. These were conservative times, rich in the hypocrisy of a moralistic society. If Trelles abandoned his family to marry his mistress, it would destroy his practice. No decent person would come to his office.

His friends begged him to reconsider. The lector Manteiga, the restauranteur Hernandez, the druggist J.B., and especially the gambler Zarate came to plead with Trelles.

But his infatuation with the lovely Conchita was so great that Trelles moved swiftly to get divorced and marry her. The town was stunned. They turned their backs on "Trelles and his whore."

Undaunted, Trelles rented the second floor of a coffee warehouse on 8th Avenue near 15th Street. He set up an office with a small surgical suite and two hospital beds at the rear.

"A man will boycott me until his wife has to have her gall bladder taken out. Then they will come running," he said. He was confident about himself, and so secure in his abilities that he set about teaching Conchita to be his nurse.

He was right. In addition to his assessment of the situation was people's curiosity. His office proved irresistible. Was Conchita really working there? Was she as lovely as the men said? Would she forget about being a kept woman and become a caring selfless nurse? The thin-lipped women gossips nodded smugly, "We'll see."

Before long, Trelles had outgrown his cramped quarters and bought the entire building. No longer would the aroma of coffee permeate his surgery. He remodeled so that the entire bottom floor was taken up

Conchita Trelles,
1930s. Courtesy
of **La Gaceta**.

with diagnostic and administrative suites, pharmacy, and radiology lab. The top floor became a fifteen-bed hospital including an ample surgical suite. Trelles was back, and Conchita was with him.

Zarate left town, as gamblers are wont to do. Trelles had Conchita, body and soul. Gradually, the town grudgingly confessed that this sloe-eyed beauty was serious about nursing, and about attending to their needs. She did have the healing touch. She cared.

Somewhere along the line, Trelles and Conchita turned his practice into a socialized medicine clinic. The Trelles Clinic gave you cradle-to-grave care for one dollar a week. This included X-rays, lab, pharmacy, surgery, and hospitalization. It might have been the medical bargain of the century, particularly as it combined the surgical expertise of Dr. Trelles with the loving care of the beautiful Conchita. The clinic prospered.

As the years flew by, Conchita expanded her area of responsibilities. She was both the administrator and the chief nurse. She soon took over the duties of the anesthetist from a barber who had been doing it between haircuts. As Trelles grew older and fatter, he was less able to get up in the middle of the night and deliver babies, so Conchita was taught to do it, adding obstetrics to the list of duties she performed, while continuing to exercise her healing charm on patients.

I learned a lot about the science of medicine from Dr. Trelles, yet I learned the *art* of medicine from Conchita. Patients listened respectfully to Dr. Trelles, but they didn't believe everything he said unless Conchita sat beside them on the bed, put her arm around them, and told them the truth. If Conchita said it was so, it was so. The art of medicine. It's gone today because now it's considered malpractice. In fact, viewed by today's yardstick, Conchita was a criminal. Thank God her patients didn't know that.

The years flew by, and Ybor City began to disappear. Old people died. Young people moved away. There were fewer patients.

The Cuban exodus provided a breather, new life for the Trelles Clinic. The clinic hired a cute new nineteen-year-old secretary. By this time, Conchita had accommodated herself to Trelles's ways and no longer needed alcohol rubs to diminish her jealous anxieties.

With great rapidity, the teenager caught the eye of Dr. Trelles. He would now play out the final chapter in the life of a Don Juan. He fell for her like a ton of black beans.

There were complications. She was married to a young Cuban and had a child. This proved no obstacle to Dr. Trelles, since, as we have seen, he could not listen to reason in matters of the heart.

The play moved through its dismal progression of stages until it reached its finale. The girl left her young husband, and informed the

Surgery by the Book. *1993.*
Ferdie Pacheco.

happy old doctor that she was pregnant. The oldest line in the world always works best on an old roué.

Ybor City was shocked and saddened to hear that Trelles was divorcing his loyal Conchita and marrying his young secretary. Conchita was evicted from the clinic she had helped build. She was trapped. She had spent her youth treating the sick and was now unable to even change a bandage. She did not have a nurse's license. She could not legally deliver a baby or administer a clinic. Conchita took her broken heart to her Davis Island home and went into seclusion.

The ecstatic old doctor built a new house and moved into it with his new baby. Yet another baby girl. The *mala lenguas* (gossips) brought the news to Conchita. The baby did not resemble the doctor at all. Conchita was too broken-hearted to care. Time would take care of the May-December couple, as indeed it did.

Dr. Trelles was old and exhausted. He hired three professionals to take Conchita's place. It was never the same. The heart had left the Trelles Clinic.

By the age of sixty-five, Dr. Trelles developed diabetes, which is what happens when you rub a sixty-three-year-old man up against a twenty-year-old girl.

Things disintegrated rapidly after that. The young girl left when it was discovered that Trelles would lose his leg. Now he was alone, sick, and dying. His clinic was in shambles.

For those of you who read novels of romance, it's not hard to guess the next step in our saga. Of course Conchita returned, took him to the Davis Island home, and nursed him until he died.

§ In 1986 I did a series of Ybor City paintings for the University of South Florida which were shown in the mezzanine gallery of a bank. The place was full of friends and interested buyers.

Suddenly a hush filled the gallery as they turned to see a vision of glamour ascending the escalator. She was serene and confident. Conchita had arrived. I was deliriously happy to see her. We fell into each other's arms, and I said, "Conchita, I thought we were both dead." She was still beautiful in her late seventies. She was the best looking older woman I'd ever seen.

Conchita in her late forties, with the rapidly aging Dr. Trelles. To her left is Paul Pizzo, father of Ybor City historian Tony Pizzo.

Conchita and me. Our sweet last meeting, 1986.

I had done a painting of Dr. Trelles operating while reading medical text. Conchita was present at the head of the operating table, her eyes accented by the white cap and mask. Her long well-formed leg extended to the side. The painting was called *Surgical Distraction*.

In one of those neat endings Hollywood uses in their films, Conchita was living with Zarate's nephew, who now owned four successful HMO's. He bought my painting for her, unaware that I would have gladly given it to her.

My wife and daughter met her and we went off to the Columbia Restaurant to have a big supper. We talked into the night and promised to meet again as soon as I could return.

Soon thereafter Conchita died. We never met again, but at least I had the chance to tell her how much she meant to me, and how deeply I had loved her all these years.

She smiled her glamorous smile. After all, she was used to being loved.

Chapter 12

The White Shadow

People walked into the Federal Building with their shoulders hunched, hands jammed into pockets, and their collars turned up against the late December cold. Old-timers couldn't remember a colder December than this one in 1950, when Senator Estes Kefauver had brought his crime-investigating committee to Tampa to sort out the crime and political corruption of Hillsborough County.

The crowd at the door parted as a tall man in a straw hat and well-pressed dark suit made his way to the door. He smiled as the crowd recognized him and called to him.

"Give 'em hell, Charlie."

"Don't tell 'em nothin', Charlie."

"God bless you, Mister Wall."

A bemused smile never left his face as he entered the meeting room and took his place facing his inquisitors. In Tampa, the Kefauver Committee was chaired by Senator Lester G. Hunt; Kefauver had opted to stay with his family during the Christmas holidays. It was common knowledge in the coffeehouses of Ybor City that Senator Hunt had volunteered to chair the Tampa meeting so that he could get a free ride to the Gator Bowl, where his college team was playing. To a Latin population used to noblesse oblige, it was an understandable reason.

I was on Christmas holiday from the University of Florida, and as a keen observer of the Ybor City crime scene, I was in daily attendance at the hearings. There was no play, no movie or book that could compete with the Kefauver investigation for pure entertainment value. It had an Alice-in-Wonderland quality. The evasive double talk used by politicians and crooks matched anything Alice found when she fell down the rabbit hole into Wonderland. There was an element of real pleasure in hearing the old sheriff, Hugh Culbreath, explain how he had amassed a huge fortune in several bay-area banks when his salary was a modest $7,500 a year.

For years I had heard stories about the legendary Charlie Wall, who lived in my neighborhood when I was a child living in my grandfather's house on Columbus Drive. Occasionally I would see him driving his big Cadillac, and he would always wave back at us sitting on the stoop. Sometimes a small man drove him. Everyone knew that was his bodyguard, who was named Baby. Charlie never sat in the back seat, but always next to Baby in the front seat.

In the coffeehouses the life of Charlie Wall was told and retold many times. He began life at the top, being the son of a prominent Tampa surgeon, Dr. John Wall, who had served as a Confederate Army surgeon and directed Richmond hospitals during the War Between the States. He accumulated further fame for his work on yellow fever. Charlie Wall's childhood was a happy one and his start in life boded a successful course.

His teen-age years saw a reversal of the family fortune. At thirteen, his mother died. His father remarried, and two years later he died unexpectedly at a medical meeting. This left the troubled teen-ager with only his stepmother, whom he heartily disliked. Charlie Wall promptly shot her. Fortunately she did not die. Charlie was sent to a juvenile detention center, where he learned all about how to circumvent the law. To further instill a healthy respect for law and order, he was then sent to Bingham Military School. He managed to get himself expelled by being caught in a whorehouse.

Charlie Wall returned to Tampa determined to make a success in gambling. By 1910, he had a reputation for both cleverness and toughness. His family was prominent in government at both the local and state levels and Charlie proved a nonstop embarrassment for them, so it was decided to back him in his ventures in Ybor City. At least an Anglo, backed by police and city politicians, could impose his will on the warring factions and turn a nice profit while he did.

Charlie Wall in
the 1930s. Cour-
tesy of the
Tampa Tribune.

This led to three decades of relative order as Charlie Wall rose to become the head crime figure in Ybor City. He was a peacemaker, an om-
budsman, a man who opposed violence. It was then that he became
known as the White Shadow. So in a city where arguments were often
settled at gunpoint, Charlie, backed by the establishment, brought the
city an uneasy peace.

Not that Charlie Wall was not a target of those who hated being told
what to do by an Anglo. The oddity was that Charlie chose to build a
big house on the corner of 17th Avenue and 13th Street, in full view of
his enemies. He did not pick the safety of Palma Ceia, the Anglo section, but built his castle in the heart of Ybor City.

*Charlie Wall before Kefauver Committee, 1950. Courtesy of the **Tampa Tribune**.*

I would often walk by his house hoping to catch a glimpse of the famous man. Every afternoon he would sit on his porch reading the *Tampa Times,* an easy target for an assassin. I could see his bodyguard waxing his big black car, while his two gigantic mastiffs slept peacefully next to his rocking chair, lifting their huge heads when anyone walked by the front of the house. How many days I had hoped he would notice me and talk. What a coup if I were to be invited to sit and drink a Coke with the crime overlord of Tampa.

❦ Charlie Wall put his straw hat on the table, pulled the hard chair back, and sat at the desk facing the senator. His face was wreathed with the beatific smile of a man who had survived three decades as the Top Man. At seventy years of age, retired from the rackets, he felt beyond danger. What he would be telling the senator was ancient history, well beyond the statute of limitations. Charlie Wall was sworn in.

After some testimony about his history and a description of the game of bolita, the senator got down to the number of times Charlie's life had been threatened.

SENATOR: When did the first one occur?

WALL: 1938. I imagine.

SENATOR: According to our records, it was in 1930.

WALL: It's possible. I don't remember.

SENATOR: You mean there have been so many times that you don't remember? It didn't make an impression on you anymore?

WALL: No, I wouldn't say that.

SENATOR: Well, the first time you remember . . . tell us about that. That certainly must have made an impression.

WALL: Oh, yes. First is when I came out of my garage. My wife was with me, a little in front, and I came out on the sidewalk to my front gate, and some folks came out in an automobile, and a fellow started shooting with a pistol.

SENATOR: Shooting at you . . .

WALL: But I didn't realize he was shooting until the thing hit me, and then, of course . . .

SENATOR: Hit you in the back?

WALL: (Laughing): Well, it kind of. As the negro says, it glimpsed me.

SENATOR: Glimpsed?

WALL: Then, I fell down, and somebody shot a shotgun, but of course, I was down when they shot the shotgun, and the buckshot didn't hit me. Then, as the car drove off, I shot at it. I think maybe I had a pistol too.

SENATOR: There were two men? One with a shotgun, one with a pistol?

WALL: I thought there were three.

SENATOR: After the investigation, was anyone ever arrested?

WALL: No, sir. Not that I ever heard of.

A tittering went through the courtroom. No one was ever arrested in gangland shootings. Everyone knew that Charlie Wall knew perfectly well who his assailants had been. Obviously, the score had long since been settled. The senator was amazed at the cool way Charlie Wall accepted being shot at as part of his life in Ybor City.

SENATOR: Have you done anything to remedy that situation out there between the garage and the main house?

WALL: Well, the *last* time they did it, a friend of mine, a businessman, came out and built an entrance from the garage to my bedroom. Now, I can drive into my garage, even in a driving rain storm and never get wet.

SENATOR: Even if it were a storm of bullets or whatnot?

WALL: (*smiling, as the crowd laughed out loud*) Well, it would help, Senator.

The Senator took a healthy drink from a coffee cup and continued.

SENATOR: When was the next time?

WALL: In '38 or maybe '39. I was going home in my car and a fellow with a shotgun shot out of the back of a truck. I saw the barrel of the gun sticking out of the back of the truck.

SENATOR: You were alone? You were driving?

Incredibly enough, assassins missed Charlie Wall again. 1930s. Courtesy of the **Tampa Tribune**.

WALL: I was driving and when I heard the shot, and didn't hear the sound when the pellets hit, why these things went around me . . . they didn't hurt much, just burned a little.

SENATOR: (*smiling*) Just *glimpsed* you again?

WALL: Yeah. So I began to dodge and try the best I could until I saw that thing go down in the back of the truck. So I started to go on by the truck.

SENATOR: And then?

WALL: Another gentleman climbed in on the front seat with a shotgun and I thought maybe he wanted to shoot me. (*Loud laughter from the crowd. Wall's eyes were twinkling.*) And I guess he did, too, because about the time he shot, I ducked down and he tore up my car pretty bad, so I took my foot off the accelerator, and the car was moving, and I don't know . . . I guess kind of outguessed him, and turned the wheel to the right and the car went up on the sidewalk and wobbled a bit. I heard the truck leave, and I was very glad to part company with them and drive on home.

SENATOR: Did you have any threats or warnings?

WALL: I wouldn't have been out on the street if I had had any warnings.

Once again the litany of a fruitless investigation. No arrest. No grand jury investigation. Another gangland shooting unsolved.

I was eager to hear about the most recent attempt because it entailed a bit of derring-do by Baby and a colossal bit of driving. A car had approached Charlie Wall's car on Nebraska Avenue and as Baby saw a man aim a pistol at them, he slammed on the brakes and threw his car in reverse. The traffic was heavy, and Baby's maneuvering as he backed up while firing in response was a feat told over and over again in the Ybor City coffeehouses. The pursuing car had crashed into another.

Charlie Wall claimed that these three attempts on his life were the only ones he could remember.

SENATOR: Just to clear things up, Mr. Wall, were there five or three attempts?

WALL: I don't think I remember the other two.

SENATOR: You probably would have remembered . . .?

WALL: Oh, yes sir!

SENATOR: Was there any reason anyone would want to make target practice out of you?

WALL: (*innocently*) No, sir.

SENATOR: The situation goes beyond coincidence when it occurs three times. Would you want to guess the reason why, or the identity of them?

WALL: No, sir.

SENATOR: Could it be because you are very influential in the gambling underworld?

WALL: I couldn't rightly say. Of course, it could be.

SENATOR: Is it perfectly all right with you for someone to take a shot at you every year or two?

WALL: Quite the contrary.

SENATOR: You haven't had adequate protection?

WALL: Well, there was nobody right there behind me looking after me, but every time this occurred, an officer would come and ask me if I wanted to cooperate and see if we could find the people. But it wasn't the easiest thing in the world. I wasn't much interested in finding who it was that was doing it. I was more interested in keeping from getting killed.

SENATOR: But when things settled down, you are interested in seeing that the person responsible wouldn't try it again, are you not?

WALL: Very much.

Rare photo of Charlie Wall in his bedroom, 1955. Courtesy of the **Tampa Tribune***.*

*Charlie Wall is taken for his last ride, 1955. Photo by Henry Rod. Courtesy of **La Gaceta**.*

SENATOR: And that situation has never been taken care of?

WALL: No, sir.

SENATOR: I think that is all.

The crowd smiled and nodded as the tall, dapper crime boss of Ybor City shook the hand of the bewildered senator. Once again the elusive Charlie Wall had done his slip, slide, and glide and passed another inquiry, providing his inquisitors with nothing more than a history lesson.

Charlie Wall had only one weakness. It was a big one. He had become addicted to morphine. In his last years, summoning his fierce will power, he broke himself of the habit, going cold turkey at home.

One night in April of 1955, after having a drink at his favorite spot on Franklin Street, he was offered a ride home by an Italian gambler he knew very well. Time and age had dulled his normal awareness of potential danger.

That was the last time anyone saw the affable, personable Charlie

Wall alive. He was found brutally beaten with a baseball bat. His throat had been cut.

The gambler reported dropping Charlie off early in the evening, and from then on, the gambler's whereabouts were meticulously proven. His alibi was air-tight, and Charlie Wall's name now heads a list of unsolved gangland murders. With the death of the White Shadow, one of Ybor City's most colorful chapters ended.

Chapter 13

Home Movies
An Album of Memories

Why did my mother always smell so clean and fresh? I guess because she used talcum powder and Palmolive soap.

Soap. Each family had its own favorite. People never varied their soaps. Why? We used Palmolive, my cousin Gus Jimenez's family used Camay, and the athletic Henry Angulo used red, octagonal Lifebuoy, which removed athletic sweat. Every jock used Lifebuoy Soap. Imagine their disillusionment when Lifebuoy got rid of the antiseptic smell after the war and advertised "A new and *improved* soap."

Hair tonic was by Fitch. A dime bought red or yellow Fitch hair tonic at Kress's 5 and 10. Fitch Shampoo was used by the better-offs, but regular folks washed their hair with the same soap they used to bathe in. I seem to remember castile soap, from Spain or Cuba, which my mother used for her hair. She had lovely hair.

We had mandatory haircuts every two weeks. My gang went to Gaspar, the partially deaf old barber at Nebraska and Palm. The shop was high-ceilinged and had a white octagonal tile floor, covered with trimmed hair. The noises were the sound of the ceiling fan and the constant clicking of the scissors. I loved it because I could read *Liberty, Saturday Evening Post,* and *Collier's* magazines there, and because Gasper put lilac talc on the nape of your neck. You not only appeared to have a fresh haircut but you smelled like it. My father got a daily shave by a barber in front of La Economica Drug, until one day the feds came and dragged the barber off to the rehab center at Lexington to take a cure for his morphine addiction. My father resorted to his two-sided Gillette Blue Blade razor with great relief. He never let a barber shave him again. Sitting on the edge of the bathtub and watching him shave was a morning highlight for me. That was when we talked. He appeared to enjoy it; I loved it.

One of the benefits of our immobile society was the fact that street vendors brought to our door everything my mother needed for running the house and feeding the family. In this day of fast-food chains, shopping centers, and high-mobility life, it seems impossible to realize that the housewife of Ybor City did not actually need a car. For that matter, most families in Ybor City didn't own a car. The few cigar workers who did drove the cheapest and easiest cars to maintain, two-door Model A Fords. These cars only saw the light of day on Sundays when the family went for a ride, usually down Bayshore Boulevard to Ballast Point. My static life drove me bonkers. I longed for movement, for change, for action. I was a typical teen-ager.

The parade of vendors began early in the morning even before we awoke. The Cuban bread man would hang a loaf of freshly baked bread on a nail in our door frame. The milkman was recognized by the clink of the glass bottles. He would pick up empties and replace them with filled bottles of milk, with cream at the top. The coffee man would follow, but not daily, with his half-pound of freshly ground Cuban coffee. By not buying a large amount, my mother made sure the coffee was always freshly roasted. It made a big difference.

Vegetable trucks came, followed by fruit vendors. The fruit was fresh, whatever was in season. Strawberries were a great treat because they were in season only once a year. Fishmongers appeared next. There was a repellent man who came by, selling live crabs in a burlap sack. I hated seeing him. First, he and his crabs smelled terrible. Second, the crabs were alive. Not only was I frightened of their gigantic claws, but my mother had to kill them. To this day I hate to see anything die, with the exception of grasshoppers, which are enemies of garden-lovers. I could not stand to see the food I loved so much being prepared. I didn't want to see a chicken or fish being gutted or cleaned. One of the best dishes my mother prepared was tongue in a tomato sauce. One day the butcher brought over an entire tongue. I took one good look at that big tongue and could never eat it again. To this day the thought of a tongue plate sends me fleeing to the men's room. (It's odd then that surgery appealed to me so much in my medical career.)

Toward mid-morning the bakery wagon pulled up, offering cakes, pies, and doughnuts. My mother, frugal and inventive, made all our cakes and pies, so this vendor was out of luck at our house.

El Encanto Cleaners arrived at mid-afternoon, followed by El Cobrador, the collector, once a week picking up a dollar for full care at one of the clinics. Ours was the Trelles Clinic, probably because he was one of my father's closest friends. And, of course, because beautiful Conchita worked there.

The walking candy hawkers included a solemn man dressed in white, with white gloves, a stainless steel hammer, and a mountain of rock candy and taffy. I never heard him speak a word. He must have been a German.

The other old reliable was the *piruli* man. This poor guy lugged a big round log with 150 *pirulis* stuck in it. A *piruli* was a cone-shaped lollipop; the top of the cone was lemon, the bottom was strawberry. They cost a penny apiece. At his slow pace it must have taken him all day to sell his 150 *pirulis*. Imagine $1.50 a day!

For years I asked everyone about the *piruli* man. How could he survive on such a meager amount of money? Who was he? What was his name? Where did he live? Finally, as I was ready to give up, an old man at the Tropical Sandwich Shop told me that the *piruli* man actually made a living selling bolita to housewives door to door. The candy was just a front. If true, I find it disquieting. He was born at the wrong time. Today he would be working for the state of Florida selling lotto. All of us would have been deprived of the succulent *pirulis,* and many hours' worth of a tasty treat for a penny.

The iceman would come late in the afternoon. For us thirsty kids, this was a moment we had been waiting for. He would drive to the back of the house and chip away at a big block of ice, carving out the amount ordered with a sharp ice pick. As soon as he was out of sight, carrying the ice wrapped in a burlap sack on his shoulder, we would jump on his truck, scoop up the slivers of ice, putting one piece in our mouth, carrying what we could in our hands, and escape before we were caught. Just why our iceman would begrudge us kids some shavings I have yet to fathom.

One day, I was deep inside the truck bed, under the tarp, when I heard the gruff iceman chasing my pals away. He started the truck, and before I could jump off, headed down 7th Avenue, picking up speed.

I pounded on the cab, asking him to stop and let me off. He laughed and said he was not stopping until we reached West Tampa. I was about eleven years of age and was allowed to leave our block only to walk to school. I was in a panic. I got to the back step of the truck, and without looking back, leaped off. I had not realized that you could not land on your feet from a moving truck and not take a nasty fall.

I also had not noticed how close the car behind us was. I landed, fell back, struck my head, saw stars, heard brakes, and was dimly aware I was *under* a car. If this had happened with today's low-slung cars, I would have been killed.

The worried motorist pulled me out. I was taught never to cry or complain, so manfully I brushed off my torn jeans, and wobbled my way home. The iceman never mentioned it, but I got scolded for tearing my jeans. I told no one about my narrow brush with death. I dug a deep hole in the path to the back of the house, covering it nicely with twigs and leaves. I can't say it wasn't a soul-satisfying pleasure seeing the big iceman disappear into the hole in the earth, ice block and all. Revenge is a wonderful plate, especially when eaten cold.

Nightfall produced the last vendor, a kindly old man with a worn-out horse pulling an ice cream wagon. There was a dim kerosene lamp by his side, illuminating his wrinkled old face. He looked like the personification of a sigh.

The game was for one of us to buy a nickel ice cream stick. While the old man was in the back getting the stick we would unhitch his horse. We would run into the darkness of the hedges to share our ice cream stick, holding our breath as he called out "Giddy-up." The horse went off, reins trailing, and the old man was left with his mouth ajar. It seems cruel to do that to an old man at the end of the day, and I assure you, I have learned my lesson. I wouldn't do that now. I swear I now give all men of great age proper respect.

The Olfactory Life

Speaking of horse-drawn wagons brings me to the smells of Ybor City, which have stayed firmly affixed to my olfactory memory. Here are a few.

Fresh bread being baked at La Central early in the morning, the smell of early-morning fog, the afternoon grinding of coffee beans at La Rosita, the inky smell of *La Gaceta* newspaper delivered in the afternoon. Freshly mowed lawn after a rain. Gardenias in bloom. Orange blossom time in the groves. The stale cigar smell commingled with the smell of fresh coffee in the cool cellar clubhouse of the Centro Asturiano. The smell of a roasting cuban sandwich in the front oven of the Columbia Café. The sawdust and garbanzo soup smell of Las Novedades. The smell of popcorn at the Ritz Theater Saturday matinees. New clothes at Fernandez and Garcia. The perspiration mingled with perfume and freshly cleaned suits at the Sunday tea dances. The smell of fresh lipstick and rouge when dancing cheek to cheek. The boozy smell of beer in the joints along lower Franklin Street.

The musty odor of old books at Edwards' Bookstore. The joyful odor of airplane glue signaling a new project or a finished model airplane. The smell of a locker room in Jefferson High School. The machine oil smell while cleaning a rifle in ROTC in high school. The sweet talcum smell of Abuelita as she fixed an after-school snack for me. The new-car smell of Aunt Lola's new 1939 Plymouth. The heavenly smell of new leather in Wilson Davis's 1941 Mercury convertible. The whiskey and cigarette smell of the Columbia Liquor Store when Big Lawrence was boss. The clean pharmaceutical smells of La Economica Drugstore when J.B. was manufacturing. The antiseptic smells of Trelles Clinic. When did drugstores stop smelling like drugstores? When did hospitals stop smelling clean?

The University of Tampa's ancient and musty odor. The Max Argintar Haberdashery smelled like new straw hats. Jefferson High School smelled as though the janitor had just swept the halls. Buster Agliano's, like freshly caught fish. El Encanto Cleaners, like steam and benzene. Manuel Arñiella's Latin American Garage, the smell of new rubber tires and gasoline. Uncle Paul's garage, the scent of oil. My step-grandmother Pennsylvania's piano room with odors of mahogany, chamomile tea, and geranium talcum. The Tampa Theater, cool as marble. The Garden Theater, stale air blown by rotary fans. My father's cool blue '41 Plymouth dark blue delivery truck, when he managed the Sharpe and Dohme pharmaceutical company, mixed new car aroma with the pharmaceutical smells of Sucrets and ST 37, a mouthwash. Dr. Meyers, the one-armed dentist, who reeked of cigars as he leaned over the patient. Our maid, Nana, who smelled of the asafetida pouch she carried around her neck. The awful stink of cheap sneakers after a hard game of football on the street. The stench of socks worn so long that the bottoms turned to stone. The lovely odor of sun-dried bedsheets.

Pillows smelled of feathers. A chamber pot under every bed, left over from the days before indoor plumbing. New undershirts and BVD's from the department store. My uncle John Pacheco's roses in bloom. The stench of hundreds of chickens in the garage of my cousin Gus Jimenez, Jr., the ten-year-old hustler. The lovely aroma of a woolen bathing suit, especially when worn by my uncle Ferdie's beautiful wife Margaret; getting my head pressed to her ample chest might have something to do with the heavenly association. Wet woolly bathing suits were itchy, and the rented woolen suits at Clearwater's pavilion always came with the dread question about who had worn them before you. Steeling yourself against the thought of the alien crotch, you hurried to dive into the first wave. The smell of saltwater. The sensation of saltwater up the nose. The water of Sulphur Springs was ice-cold and smelled differently. In Pass-a-Grille the city water smelled of rotten eggs—hydrogen sulfide, ugh! City water tasted great when put in a clean milk bottle and stored next to the ice in the ice box. The tap water from a garden hose smelled different from cold water in the ice box. The smell of the first bite of a fresh tomato. Oranges and grapefruit smells. Why don't avocados have a strong smell? Perhaps because we had two huge trees in the backyard and were desensitized by hundreds of avocados bombarding our roof.

Why did black grasshoppers smell awful when stepped on, but not yellow grasshoppers? Roaches and spiders had no smell. Black ants didn't hurt you but red ants stung like hell. The lingering smell of chloroform or ether years after surgery. The horrid pungency of black ichthyol ointment placed on warts to remove them. (It didn't.) The fresh taste and smell of throat swabs. The repellent stench of a flaxseed meal plaster on the chest. Castor oil's smell could not be disguised, to say nothing of its taste.

The unique smell of cordite, gunpowder, in the Gasparilla parade. Stage makeup on a beautiful girl on a float. The clean electrical scent of streetcars. The mud flat stink of Tampa Bay. The smell of bait on the piers in Palmetto Beach. The fish odors at the Ballast Point Pier.

And, in Ybor City, one aroma common to all establishments: cigar smoke.

The Sports Life

Every kid in Ybor City played sports of some kind. Those lucky enough to live close to Cuscaden Park could play baseball, football, and basketball since the facility was ample enough to accommodate these games. For the rest of us, the street was our athletic field. It seems hard to imagine we were stupid enough to play tackle football on the red brick streets, especially since the boundaries were the sharp granite curbstones. Or we played in the grass driveways by the house.

We bought mock-leather football helmets at Kress for fifty cents and decided to do one-on-one tackling drills. Byron Dawkins carried the ball, I tackled him, he fell on a sawhorse. It cut the top half of his ear off. So much for Kress's protective helmets. The aftermath was more impressive than the injury. Byron's father was a tough-as-nails railway engineer. First he poured turpentine on the cut edges, then he lined the two halves up and bound them tightly with a cloth. Then he whipped Byron with a leather strap for being so stupid as to get his ear chopped off playing football. With basic training like this, it's not surprising to find out that Byron survived World War II after serving with distinction in the Marines. Yes, his ear healed.

The big baseball hero in Ybor City was Al Lopez, an Ybor City native. My father was very friendly with him, but my Uncle Ferdie was closer because his gorgeous wife Margaret and Al's wife were close friends. He was always around if he was in town. One day Al gave my father a baseball signed by all of the New York Yankees. Murderers'

Al Lopez, Ybor City's first major leaguer, 1930s. Courtesy of Al Lopez.

Row. A team that boasted Babe Ruth, Lou Gehrig, King Kong Keller, and that gang.

My father, who was not one for souvenirs, gave me the ball with the explanation that these signatures were very important. I recognized only Babe Ruth. We all knew the Sultan of Swat. The Bambino. Later, during the war, I saw him at the Columbia, his slouch hat and camel's hair overcoat over his shoulder, looking like a news photograph of himself. He was big and fat, with a bulbous nose. I could not bring myself to confess to him what had happened to his autographed ball.

One rainy day we were playing baseball in an empty lot and the older Alvarez boy hit a home run and lost the only ball we had. The game was tied and appeared over. Then it occurred to me that I had a ball at home. By the time we finished the game, the autographs were long gone, obliterated. What would it be worth today? Don't ask.

The most famous boxer I ever met was Jack Dempsey. When I was ten years old my father came home at mid-afternoon, which was unusual, got me bathed and dressed in a suit, and rushed me to the Columbia Restaurant. The great Dempsey was finishing his *café solo*. His smile was blinding. He took my small hand in his huge hard bear paw and called me Champ. I was speechless! He put me on his lap and went on talking to Lawrence until it was time to go. Then he pulled a small pair of gold boxing gloves from his pocket. They were tied together by a yellow string with yellow tassels. They carried the initials J.D. on each glove. Having now been around the insensitive louts that have called themselves Champion, I can tell you that it took a big-hearted man to carry around these trinkets to give out to kids and fans. I wore it on my key chain through college and the service and into middle age, when I lost it. I still regret losing that small trinket. It was priceless.

And now, years after the long, happy ride with the Ali Circus, I have even lost my Ali championship ring. Imagine my luck. In one lifetime I have lost meaningful mementos of Babe Ruth, Jack Dempsey, and Muhammad Ali. It's a good thing Joe Louis never gave me anything but a firm handshake and warm smile.

Fights were held at Benjamin Field, and Ybor City fans followed their fighters with great fervor. Of all the kids who tried to get to the big time only Chino Alvarez and Ulysses Valles showed enough promise to

Tommy Gomez meets Jersey Joe Walcott, 1944. Courtesy of **Tampa Tribune**.

be considered real fighters. Later, as the war approached, a tough heavyweight, Tommy Gomez, crawled into contention via the KO route. He was crude, but could punch like Joe Louis. He was drafted into the army, and just before he was sent into combat, the kind gentlemen of Madison Square Garden in New York gave him a chance to get into top contention. All he had to do was knock out an old, over-the-hill, unemployed longshoreman. A black man with broad shoulders, a barrel chest, and bird legs. His name was Jersey Joe Walcott. Tommy Gomez went off to fight the Germans with a king-size headache and a blind spot in his memory about a tough night at the Garden. Tommy came back, shot up by German bullets, and was never in contention again. When asked what he might have done differently in his life, he stated that he would have liked to have gone a year earlier to face the Germans. He still can't remember what happened to him after he was introduced to Jersey Joe.

My first experience watching a fighter train was with Ybor City's Danny Nardico, the Fighting Mailman. I fell in love with the dusty wooden floor, the swishing sound of the jump rope, the rat-a-tat of the speed bag, and the thump of the heavy bag. I loved the look of the equipment, the ritual of wrapping hands, gloving, and taping; the big head gear as it slipped over the greased face, pressing the facial tissues together, and the Neanderthal look that a big mouthpiece gave a fighter.

Boxing. I was hooked. Then Nardico went out and did the impossible. He beat Jake Lamotta, the Raging Bull. He was a pure puncher and their fight was an epic of brutality. Danny Nardico did not make it to the championship, but in Ybor City he was treated like a champion. Later in life he was dealt a bad hand. He contracted Hansens's Disease—leprosy—and was condemned to a sad end, a true tragedy. We all loved Danny Nardico, who seemed to exemplify the never-give-up spirit of Ybor City kids.

Sports in Ybor City were an integral part of everyday life. We rooted for teams that had Ybor City boys playing for them. The Brooklyn Dodgers were our team because Al Lopez caught for them. When he switched to managing, we switched with him. First we rooted for the Cleveland Indians, then the Chicago White Sox. Gentleman Al Lopez. Even today he is spoken of with reverence.

Pro football did not count with us until Rick Casares made it big with the Chicago Bears. We rooted for the University of Florida for masochistic reasons and for Notre Dame because we needed to have a winner now and then.

Local football focused on Hillsborough and Plant High School games. The annual Thanksgiving game between those two had the importance of today's Super Bowl. We took the game to heart in Ybor City. Names stick to my mind from that era: Benny Fernandez playing for one quarter with a homemade nose guard, then playing without a helmet for the rest of the game. Linemen: Chelo Huerta, small but with a heart big enough to make All-Southern, Frank Lorenzo, Eddie Diaz, and a number of kids out of Cuscaden. Bob Tramontana comes to mind. One isolated play, seen in slow motion, as if in a fog: Guy Tompkins kicking a field goal from an impossible angle to win a close

Thanksgiving Day game. Talk to anyone who was there, and chances are no other play has stuck in his memory, but he can clearly remember Guy Tompkins' kick.

Movie Theaters

The best movie theater ever constructed in Tampa was part of a series of theaters built by the Loew's chain. It was a replica of a Venetian doge's palace. It had a high ceiling painted dark blue with twinkling stars and clouds. People from Ruskin, a nearby farming community, thought they were outdoors and wouldn't go to the theater if it looked like it might rain that night. I'm sure Loew never thought of that when he put in the twinkling stars.

In the thirties, the Tampa Theater played first-run films which changed every week. Mostly they were MGM pictures, which boasted modestly in their advertisements, "More Stars than in the Heavens." When the picture was popular, the theater management dressed the ushers in appropriate uniforms. *Gone with the Wind,* for example, had ushers in Union as well as Confederate uniforms. More Rebels than Yankees, of course. Snappy Hussar uniforms for *Charge of the Light Brigade.* And so on. Guys fought for the job of ushering at the Tampa Theater.

Wilson Davis got his Don Juan start in the balcony of the Tampa Theater. His stories of the action to be found in the balcony during a hot afternoon were the stuff of great erotic literature. In fact, I saw some of the same stuff in Peter Lawford's book, only instead of Wilson's Plant High cheerleaders, Lawford's afternoon dalliance was with seventeen-year-old Lana Turner. Today somewhere in America, theater ushers of the thirties meet, high in a cool dark balcony, and swap pelvic stories while on the screen *The March of Time* drones on interminably.

I would have sold La Economica Drugstore to get a job as an usher at the Tampa Theater. Ushers there looked like forwards for the L.A. Lakers. They were tall, blonde, with perfect Ipana teeth. Aspiring ushers who were Ybor City guys got jobs at the Ritz where every Saturday they placed their life on the line. Or they worked at the

Tampa Theater interior, 1940 Courtesy of the University of South Florida History Department.

Garden Theater where the only action they saw was Chicken Cacciatore writing bolita tickets in the men's room.

The program at the Tampa Theater was simple and direct. Coming attractions, a Pathé newsreel, *The March of Time* (once a month), a cartoon, then the dread organ of Eddie Ford, rising up from the orchestra pit in a spotlight, playing a popular upbeat song, smiling through the booing. Soon he swung into the "Beer Barrel Polka," with the words on the screen, a bouncing ball to tell the people from Ruskin what words to sing. If you made it through this without fleeing to the all-marble men's room on the basement floor, the feature would follow.

I had criteria for going to the men's room. Foremost was the organist Eddie Ford, second was *any* song by Nelson Eddy. Third, any really mushy love scene. Fourth, any crying scenes featuring a kid in a wheelchair or hospital bed. Fifth, cruelty-to-animal scenes, whether Rin Tin Tin or Lassie. All horror scenes, starting with King Kong, the lurid ape undressing Fay Wray, or Dracula flossing his teeth, or Franken-stein—especially when he took a bride. I spent a lot of time in the basement, as you can figure out. It was especially tough because I didn't smoke. There were no transistor radios and no reading material.

Many years later it was my unpleasant fate to be taken to a Miami nightclub where the star act was Nelson Eddy. I was wild-eyed by the time the old man launched into "Shortening Bread," a mind-killing old southern black song. As he reached the end of the song, with applause welling up in the mentally defective audience, Nelson Eddy did a strange thing. He died. As sometimes but not often happens, he remained upright with his eyes opened, and the band played two overtures. It remains the longest ovation I've ever seen accorded a corpse. Years later, I found out his co-star Jeannette McDonald loathed him, and somehow it made me feel better about Nelson Eddy.

During the war years you had to line up to get into the Tampa Theater. If you wanted to get a seat for the eight o'clock movie, you had to get there for the six o'clock to get in line. The lobby would fill, then spill out into Franklin Street, which wasn't air-conditioned.

Across the street was a cheesy little theater called the Franklin whose main attraction was that they would play second-run films in a double feature. Usually an A film at least a month old, like a *Thin Man*. The

*The dismal Rialto Theater, 1950s. Photo by Henry Rod. Courtesy of **La Gaceta**.*

second feature was a current B film, such as *Boston Blackie's Revenge*. Included were the coming attractions, two cartoons, a month-old newsreel showing Hitler taking Austria—when you read in the newspaper he had just taken Czechoslovakia. The Franklin boasted two major attractions for me. First, Eddie Ford could not appear here. Two, the ticket cashier was my long-suppressed secret love, Joyce Brantley. Of all the people I knew, or have met since, only one family went there every Sunday intentionally. They were Italians who couldn't speak English. They went there because they could stay in air-conditioned splendor twice as long, for half the price. They also brought their own pizza.

During the war a small new theater opened at the bend of Franklin Street at the mouth of Sin City. It was called the State Theater. Warner Bros. felt they were putting out enough films to have their own first-rate house. It was clean, fresh, and smelled of recent construction. The seats were new and soft. The floors were not covered with the slime of two generations of Coke, popcorn, and gum chewers. It was here I saw *Casablanca* and all the other Bogart classics. Errol Flynn, Ann Sheridan, Dennis Morgan, George Tobias, Gary Cooper, Bette Davis, and loads of great stars appeared in the Warner's movies. I was so taken, I applied for the job of usher. The manager took me to the bathroom and offered me a stick of Juicy Fruit if I would show him my "thing." First of all, I chewed spearmint gum, and second, he was in the wrong ball park. I was looking for Wilson Davis country, he offered me Oscar Wilde.

Down at the foot of Franklin Street was the Rialto, an old ruin of a theater that had been used by the WPA to put on sad plays about depression life. The plays were all staged in grays and browns. Not surprisingly, they all failed. It was rumored that the director had contemplated suicide by jumping off the Davis Island bridge, but the tide was out and he rejected diving head first onto the Tampa Bay muck and thereby covering himself with worse-smelling excrement than he already had with his plays.

Still, at the Rialto I saw Orson Welles' *Citizen Kane,* one of the greatest movies ever made. It was a resounding failure when it played there. The Rialto had its own aura of theatrical disaster.

On Tampa Street, one block from Franklin, there was a cavernous old movie house that was reopened in time to take advantage of the war fever. In what was to rank with the most bizarre bits of programming, the Victory Theater chose to play *All Quiet on the Western Front,* a bitter, terrifying antiwar film made in the early thirties when it was fashionable to decry the war, and to expect that we had seen the end of wars.

I went to see it in a spate of patriotic fervor. I had just seen *The Fighting Sixty-Ninth,* a rousing drum-beater with Cagney, George Brent, Alan Hale, Pat O'Brien, and the entire Irish Mafia of the Warner's lot. I was sure I wanted to enlist in the infantry when my time came. I wanted a trench coat like George Brent wore. It never got dirty, while all the regular guys looked liked giant clots of mud with legs sticking out.

I left the Victory Theater in a cold sweat. I took my World War I German spike helmet and hid it under the bed, with all of my American Legion magazines. I decided that when my time came I would follow the lead of Lew Ayres, the young actor who played Paul in the film. I would file as a conscientious objector. If it had scared hell out of him, and he *knew* it was make believe, imagine me, an impressionable four-teen-year-old.

When the time came to enlist, I signed up with the air force—which, looked at philosophically, is practically the same thing.

By the university, on Lafayette Street, there was a modest theater called the Park. It was kind of a schizophrenic theater. Sometimes it played first-run films, sometimes double features. My only memory of it is one of keen disappointment.

My favorite band was Artie Shaw. We never saw live bands in person in Tampa. Suddenly, the WDAE and WFLA radio stations announced stunning news. Artie Shaw's eighteen-piece orchestra was playing at the Park Theater. Incredible! I couldn't wait for Friday.

I went to the first show, prepared to stay until midnight. The band's theme, an eerie tune called "Nightmare," started with the tom-toms beating, then instead of the distinctive clear clarinet, I heard a tenor sax. Not good.

The curtain opened, and the band was there. All except for Artie Shaw. Tony Pastor, Shaw's pal, tenor man, and vocalist, came to the front to announce that Shaw had been seized by an ailment, later diagnosed as nuttiness, and had given up the band business. Before the packed house could attack him, Pastor swung into *Begin the Beguine*.

Artie Shaw is now eighty-two. I have had many opportunities to meet him, but I will not. The Spaniards harbor and nurture their grudges.

Ybor City had one main, if dinky, movie house. The Ritz Theater was well-known because it was where all Ybor City kids would pack in to see a series of cowboy movies, serials, cartoons, newsreels, *and* hang around for a spin of the roulette wheel. The prize was a red Schwinn bicycle. I went there until I was eligible for a senior citizen pass, and I swear they were still raffling off that red Schwinn. It remains the best entertainment bargain I ever had. For a dime my senses were satiated, my stomach filled on my neighbor's popcorn, and my gambling sense was honed. All that for a dime.

The Casino Theater at the Centro Español could hardly qualify as a movie theater. It played Spanish-language films, and when I wasn't fast enough to duck and dodge, my grandmother made me go with her. As far as I could see they played the same Libertad Lamarque film over and over,

The Broadway Theater in the 1930s. I never met anyone who went there. Courtesy of **La Gaceta**.

changing the costumes but not the plot or dialogue. The only intriguing part for me was watching roaches travel across the backs of the seats in front of us. Once a small mouse had the temerity to get between the screen and my grandmother. She slew it with one swipe of her brogan.

Once, in Mexico, I met Libertad and told her of my grandmother's fixation with her. Libertad spoke charmingly and knowingly about my grandmother although their only connection had been at the Casino. She was still telling me about my grandmother when they led her away.

The other movie theater was called the Broadway, and was so bad even I never went in to see a movie there.

The only theater without some form of air-conditioning was the Garden Theater at Nebraska and 20th Avenue. From my house on Columbus Drive we could walk there. By night the theater was musty but cool, with the hum of giant fans adding to the film in a strangely comforting way. Here we saw *Magnificent Obsession*, a weeper, *It Happened One Night*, a comedy, and *Showboat*, with Irene Dunne, Alan Jones, and a real Broadway cast—all in all, one of my favorite musicals.

Of course, we also had to see *Oil for the Lamps of China* and—the only time I remember my mother coming with us—a dog of a picture called *Trail of the Lonesome Pine*. That did it for my mom. She never went to another film, and even the news that they had air-conditioned the Garden did not dislodge her from the parlor, the Havana radio station CMQ and *The Adventures of Chan Lee Po*, or was it Charlie Poe? When Chinamen speak Spanish in a Cuban dialect, things get confused.

The only meaningful breakthrough that came along was the discovery of a gold mine known as a drive-in theater. At first, it was date heaven. I had to wait until videotape was invented to see how all the movies I went to turned out. Usually my ending was superior to theirs. I believe I can lay claim to starting the van idea when I would rent a panel truck, put a mattress in the back, and take my date to a double-header at the drive-in.

After the war, families started to come to the drive-in and bring their children, and dogs, and in-laws, and tubular lawn chairs; and things changed.

I quit the drive-ins in the early fifties, and, of course, they folded soon after for lack of business.

The Mystery of the Vanishing Courthouse

One of the most interesting aspects of my travels throughout this country was the variety of town squares to be found. In the South most had some dedicatory statue to the Lost Cause. All had their own individuality which seemed to define the town. There was no town

The Tampa Courthouse and the Confederate monument. 1934. Burgert Bros. Studio.

square that was more unusual than the one we had in Tampa. What made it unique was a Moroccan courthouse, beautiful and exotic.

The impression I always had was that the architect that planned the Tampa Bay Hotel had made it too long. At some point Mr. H.B. Plant took a pair of scissors and simply cut off one end of the building plans.

"Well, what are we going to do with it?"

"Build it on the town square, and give the damned thing to the city for a courthouse."

And so they did.

After reading *Gone with the Wind* in 1939, I became totally immersed in the Civil War. I had heard of it in history class, but it didn't become real until I got involved with Scarlett, Rhett, Ashley and Aunt Pittypat. It was then that I discovered the Confederate monument in front of the courthouse. At every opportunity I would go and sit on the benches and stare at the statue. It made the story on the pages real. It was about actual people, and they looked exactly like the monument.

There were two Confederate soldiers. One faced Franklin Street, one Lafayette. The one facing Franklin Street was marching, shouldering his long Springfield rifle, his roll blanket crossing his chest, his pants legs tucked into his shoe tops. He wore a slouch hat, not a kepi. The other rebel was hatless, his head bowed in defeat, an indescribable sadness on his face. It was made of white marble and had a tall obelisk which rose to the height of the surrounding palmetto trees. Later, when I learned to sketch, I spent many days drawing both men. When I started doing oil paintings of Civil War scenes, the two men found their way into many paintings.

As if these two weren't enough to whet my appetite for Civil War artifacts, there was also a Napoleon cannon on display. This trim, neat instrument of death sat peacefully on its concrete pad. It was available and accessible. A boy could scramble all over it, aim it, load it, and fire an imaginary load of canister at a passing trolley. With a little imagination, that artillery piece could furnish an hour of exciting play.

To balance things out, on the other side of the lawn was a heavy German cannon from the First World War. It was thick and cruel-looking. It did not have the romantic air of the Napoleon. But it was interesting in its massiveness and detail.

It always seemed to me that we were very fortunate to have such a unique courthouse square. Every town had a Civil War monument, or a cannon, but we were the only ones to have an ornate Moroccan building for a courthouse. It was the height of distinctiveness, and perhaps this very delightful quality was it undoing. Politicians are an unimaginative lot, without flights of fancy, always seeking to please the masses, to blend in, to homogenize. The exceptions are few, and the bunch that decided to tear down our precious jewel, our distinctive trademark building, had no such exceptional politician among them.

What could they have been thinking? Was there not one man among them with a sense of history? A love of antiquity and beauty? Was it an eyesore to be razed as soon as funds were available? Certainly not. It was the only distinctive thing of beauty in the entire downtown area. The question still bothers me these many years later. Why?

To get a better perspective I asked Harris Mullen, a retired newspaperman who covered the story for the *Tampa Tribune*. He replied, "I don't remember that there were any objections to it. Not in the Tribune editorial section, and not from the people. It was just an old building that was being torn down to make way for the future. No big deal."

The future, it turned out, was a parking lot, an ugly gash of concrete bereft of greenery, serenity, or memory.

Had they waited a decade, it might have been saved by the preservationists. It was certainly a historical site. What an abysmal commentary on the shortsightedness of an entire community. To this day I cannot pass Lafayette (now Kennedy Boulevard) without feeling a sense of loss and, yes, shame.

Drive-in Restaurants

Apart from the superlative restaurants and cafés of Ybor City, eating was haphazard at best in Tampa in the thirties.

The best eatery downtown was Morrison's Cafeteria. The O'Falk's only attraction was its manager, Wilson Davis. The food was leftovers from the Jefferson High School cafeteria. The major hotels—the Tampa Terrace, Jefferson, Floridan, and such—featured hotel food, and in the thirties that was condemnation enough. During my growing up there were no Chinese restaurants, pizza parlors, or established Italian restaurants. None. Why, I wonder?

Outside of Ybor City the best eating was at the drive-ins. There were four major drive-ins, each with their own flavor.

Downtown there was the Goody-Goody for business folks, married people, and other serious types. It was small, the girls decently dressed and respectful. I loved the name until I saw it on the gateway to a bordello in Nevada, and that killed it for me.

On Bayshore Boulevard there was the Colonnade. You had to be a student at Plant High School or the Academy of Holy Names to eat there. Its back parking lot was deep and dark and the waitresses were sharp and sassy. The food, especially the seafood, was superlative. The proximity of Bayshore Boulevard was very desirable for dating couples who wanted to park.

Falor's was the hangout for the Hillsborough, Jefferson, and Jesuit crowd. It was raucous, wild on many nights, with an occasional punch-out, but the waitresses were friendly, and the hamburgers were world-class. No matter how far away Tampa guys went during the war, when they met the subject turned to a Falor's hamburgers as the thing they missed most. The sauce made it so different. Of course, I never found out what it was. Actually, I *knew* what it was. What it was, was delicious.

The Big Orange on Lafayette by the railroad tracks was the place you went when you graduated from juvenile delinquent to adult delinquent. It was open all night and attracted the all-nighters. It was shaped like a big, round, orange. Honestly, it was. The waitresses were pretty, bright, jazzy, and available. It was a great way to prolong adolescence after high school and forestall maturity. I saw some of my pals there after they reached forty-five, still wearing their Hillsborough sweaters.

Social Clubs

Life in Ybor City, from cradle to grave, was irretrievably enmeshed in its social clubs. My life from birth revolved around the Centro Español and the Centro Asturiano, but the other clubs were well-known to me.

The most important one in my life was the Centro Español on 7th Avenue and 16th Street. When I was small its members were always at

Centro Español, home of the Matinees, 1940. Courtesy of Tony Pizzo.

my grandfather's home, which was the Spanish Consulate. It was when I swung into the teen years that the Centro Español took on a new meaning. On Sunday from three to seven o'clock, a tea dance was held. Anyone who could walk, let alone dance, would be there. It was the swinging, dancing equivalent of the singles' bars of the eighties. The Matinee, as it was called, was the place to be if you were breathing on Sunday afternoons. It took place on the top floor of the Centro Español building. The admission was nominal and guys that were broke snuck in. There was a bar which served mostly beer and Cokes although many a well-heeled citizen smuggled in a pint of firewater to lubricate his dancing parts.

Dancing was taken seriously. It was the best fun you could have, and it served the very real purpose of being able to crush a lively girl to your body who ordinarily wouldn't let you hold her hand in a movie theater.

The Don Francisco Orchestra was well-rehearsed and depended heavily on Glenn Miller stock arrangements. It would also whip into a Latin piece in a minute, and bring forth a delighted roar when it would play a pasodoble. The pasodoble, a traditional Spanish dance, became a

The Matinee Dancers . 1986.

Ferdie Pacheco.

contest in no time. This dance became a combination dance-a-thon, Kentucky Derby, and Roller Derby. The entire floor would be filled with swirling, twirling couples. The dance is a basic promenade with fancy spins at each corner of the dance floor. It was up to the expertise and ingenuity of the dancers to embellish what was already a joyous dance. If a girl had not been asked out she would dance with her girl-friend or alone. Even the chaperons, the *dueñas,* would momentarily lose their composure and fling themselves among the spirited dancers. If you weren't out on the floor when a pasodoble came around, you were either in a full-length body cast or dead-drunk.

The balance of the pieces Don Francisco chose were masterful. A set consisted of three slow pieces, such as "At Last," "Serenade in Blue," and "What's New," mostly Glenn Miller arrangements. A Latin piece was next, a rhumba or danson, "Amapola," "Perfidia," or "Yours," all of which were Latin favorites with English lyrics. The lesser dancers then cleared off the floor because the last piece of the set was a killer-diller, an up-tempo Big Band jazz arrangement which could vary from a medium-tempo jump tune, "In the Mood" or "Chattanooga Choo-Choo," to Benny Goodman's "Sing, Sing, Sing" at a wild tempo.

The dancers were so good that unless one was lucky enough to have a great partner it was better to watch than to dance. Every dance hall had a big fat guy with light feet, and he was the best. Armando El Gordo was a man with a John Candy body and Fred Astaire feet, and he was easily the finest dancer at the Matinee. When the war was in full swing, dancers like Macaco would bring new steps and styles from the Palladium or Roseland in New York. The pace was frenetic, and it was the most fun a teen-ager could ever have for a quarter.

When the dance was over, and the last tune, "Adios," played for the lovers and stags, the crowd would disperse. Those boys lucky enough to link up with a girl, and to have a car and a dollar, would head for the drive-in to sit in their cars, eat a hamburger and drink a shake, and park. Park was a euphemism for neck which was a nice word for make out which really meant . . . oh, you get the picture.

It was probably because I was so young and inexperienced, but the Matinees filled me with an excitement and anticipation I have not felt since. Oh, maybe the first Ali-Frazier fight matched it, but the Matinee

Centro Asturiano, 1920s. Burgert Bros. Studio. Courtesy of Tony Pizzo.

happened every Sunday. The girls felt the same, although they acted blasé. They spent the week making new dresses on their Singer sewing machines, thinking of new ways to disguise old dresses, and curling their hair. The boys could only make sure their old shoes were shined and their hair neatly cut, and if their fathers weren't looking, show up with a new tie.

When I revisit the Centro Español, my heart sinks to see it in disrepair. I want them to start the Matinees again, but then I realize that disco music and hard rock do not belong in this beautiful building. That teen-agers are no longer in need of cheap entertainment. Affluence brings about too many choices. "All good things in their time," my father always said.

Well, thank God, the Matinees were a good thing, and thank God, they were in my time.

The other club which played a big part in my growing up was the Centro Asturiano on Palm and Nebraska. It was an opulent building, boasting a theater, dance hall, banquet room, bowling alley, billiard hall, a café and gaming room. It was the most popular club in Ybor City and the only one named for a province of Spain, Asturias. Across the street was a good restaurant, El Boulevard, and next to it Gaspar's Barber Shop. In front was popular Henry Garcia's gas station.

What I am describing is a compact little world. Within a few square yards there were sufficient diversions and services to keep a man from wandering. And this was my undoing, for my father J.B. never saw the need to go elsewhere. It was here that I learned a personality trait that was to serve me well in life. I learned to be patient.

My father was a demon card-player. He loved gin rummy, and favored the game hearts. With a great capacity to retain numbers and a gambler's sharp instincts, he loved to lose himself for hours in the cool cellar of the club sipping expresso coffee, smoking Old Golds, and playing cards. It was my unfortunate lot in life to wait for him to decide when to quit playing so I could drive him to La Economica, and then keep the car. I was late to almost every appointment and date. My father did not judge being late by the hour but by the day. Many a hot Sunday I missed going to the beach because my father played through sunset.

Círculo Cubano, 1960s. Courtesy of **La Gaceta**.

His other undying passion was playing dominoes. While researching this book I ran into Pendas the foreman. He is now ninety-three, and did not seem surprised to find that he was pictured in the painting which serves as the cover of this book. When he found out that I was J.B.'s son he chuckled compassionately.

"It was your father who helped me pass the nights during the Big Strike."

"How so?"

"He would play until two or three in the morning. I'd have to throw him out of the house. He was a man who was never in a hurry to go home."

"Or to get to work," I added, thinking of those painfully long waits at La Economica.

The Círculo Cubano building was unquestionably the biggest and best. I went to dances there on Saturday nights, and saw many a prize-fight, but somehow it did not have the cachet of the Centro Español. Once they even staged a bullfight there, but it was not a success. The bull lived.

The Unione Italiano on 7th Avenue was called the Italian Club. I know nothing about it except I was never inside the place. Italians were great men of commerce, and understood business. Italians learned Spanish and spoke it well. They ate in Spanish restaurants, and generally got along very well with the Spaniards. They came to our dances, and integrated smoothly. We did not go to their clubs, spoke no Italian, and I can't remember a first-class Italian restaurant. When I was dating on a budget, the place to go eat was a small Italian restaurant, because they were the cheapest, and because I never met a human being who didn't like spaghetti. Italians soon became the economic backbone of Ybor City. By 1945, Tony Grimaldi owned the Columbia Bank; Nick Geraci and Valenti had organized the produce dealers into a wildly successful cooperative; the Italian Mob dominated the lucrative bolita business, and, in general, were in command.

The Italian Club also ran the Broadway Theater but it was every bit as awful as the Casino at the Centro Español, and I didn't go in there either.

In view of the fact that one of my closest friends, Frankie Accurso,

Unione Italiano, 1920s. Burgert Bros. Studio. Courtesy of the University of South Florida History Department.

was Italian, and my next-door neighbors, the Spanos, were Italian, I wonder why we never went into the Italian Club.

I blame it on Benito Mussolini.

Street Characters

Ybor City had more than its share of characters. There was a man nicknamed *Pepelolo* who adopted a sensible attitude about staying out late at night. On returning home he always threw a handful of pebbles on his tin roof. His reasoning was sound. If there were burglars in the house, it would scare them away by warning them the owner was coming in. If his wife's lover was still there, it would avoid a confrontation in which he was sure to lose a punch-out.

A familiar sight was a miser with a turn-of-the-century bicycle who roamed the alleys scavenging garbage cans for bits of cloth, buttons, metal, or discarded appliances. He frequented La Economica Drugstore, always buying in minimal quantities, making sure no purchase ever exceeded fifteen cents. His only son was a spendthrift. When the son graduated from high school the miser shocked everyone by buying him a new Ford convertible. When I asked him why he permitted his son to waste his hard-earned money, he smiled his gap-toothed smile and said, "He'll never have as much fun spending it, as I did saving it." And the wise old men of the Latin clubs smiled and said, as one: *"Cada loco con su tema"* (Each nut with his own nuttiness).

The first time I ever saw a dead man was in the Columbia Restaurant. The janitors there were two black men and a small, round Jewish man who looked like S.Z. Sakall, the character actor. Harry the Porter was the main janitor; you'll recall his neurological disorder that caused him to fling whatever he was holding in the air upon hearing the kissing sound. He was the ongoing target of many practical jokers. Ralph was a shucking-jiving playboy type, who chronically disappeared every Friday after payday and limped back Mondays covered with Band-aids. He was prone to razor cuts.

The little old fat man had a European accent. His face was pink, his hair white, and he dressed in shirt and tie even though he was only the morning mop-up man. He was very short and had a sweet face, and was always bowing and smiling when addressed by Casimiro or Lawrence. His job was to mop the floors of the patio and the Quixote Room, and prepare the *fonda* for the lunch business.

Besides a meager salary, his reward seemed to consist of a bowl of vermicelli soup, a good-sized piece of Cuban bread and butter, and a tall glass of ice-cold milk. When I wasn't busy I would serve him on the patio after his chores were completed. Sweetly he would thank me, and tell me what a good waiter I was.

The rumor was that he was an Austrian Jew, and one of the few of his family to escape the Nazi persecution of the Jews. He wouldn't talk to me about it, but would raise his eyes to the sky and lift his hands, palms up, and say, "Don't ask."

One day, when he looked especially tired, I took the opportunity to give him a little supportive therapy in the form of a cup of expresso, which he accepted. In a while, not having seen him leave, I went back to see if he needed anything else. Imagine my shock to find him lying on the tile floor, his arms outstretched, his eyes wide open, and his color gone. I had never seen a dead man before, and yet I was absolutely sure he was dead. I called some older waiters, who placed a tablecloth over his body. Soon, a hearse came, put him on a gurney, still covered by the tablecloth, and took him away.

I went back to work serving *café solo* to my customers, pondering on the frail string that holds us to this life. One minute you are drinking *café solo,* the next minute you're dead. It gave me new perspective on life, I can tell you that. I quit drinking expresso.

Tonsillectomy was a fad operation when I was growing up in Ybor City, and everyone has his own memory of that terrifying moment when your family took you to the clinic to have your tonsils and adenoids removed. I only remember mine because I was playing soldier in the yard when I heard my brother yowling. He had to have his tonsils removed, but he wouldn't go unless I went with him. That's how I got mine removed.

The best of the tonsil horror stories happened to Barney Waters, the writer and newspaperman. In spite of the name Waters, Barney was a Hispanic kid from Central Avenue, and was a tough kid, a street fighter and hard-nosed football player.

Most parents had a thing about their kids crying. My dad promised me a quarter if I didn't cry, and all the ice cream I could eat post-op. I felt borderline cheated when I found out that I couldn't swallow post-op, so the promise had an empty ring.

Barney's dad took an opposite approach. Rather than use bribery, he used threats. If Barney cried, then the doctor would be told he could go ahead and cut off his wee-wee, as penises were then called. Barney went into surgery determined not to say a word.

Sometime during surgery the doctor remarked that he noticed that Barney had not been circumcised. Since he was already under anesthesia, they might as well do that procedure as well. The father agreed.

Barney came to in a private room, his throat on fire, sick to his stomach from the ether. As he bent over to throw up, he noticed a stabbing pain in his groin. Pulling back the sheet gingerly, he beheld a huge bandage on his wee-wee! He tried to yell, but his throat was full of flames and phlegm. There he was, just nine years old, and already he was a eunuch.

Barney Waters,
1935. A nasty
surprise awaited
him. Courtesy of
Barney Waters.

It's days like this that build character. Barney pulled through but vowed never to go to surgery again, no matter what the reason, and he hasn't.

Nicknames

One of the reasons a plastic surgeon or a psychiatrist would have starved in Ybor City was because of nicknames.

The native of Ybor City who had any anatomical differences or strange habits or in any way differed from the norm was immediately tagged, and—no matter how long he lived—remained forever known by that nickname. I know many of my father's friends by nicknames but cannot give you their proper names. One of his best friends was named Tomate, yet I never saw him eat a tomato.

A man with a large head was called Cabezón, and one with the biggest head, Cabeza Mundo (World-size Head). A famous local coach who had a large head on a small body, Mundo en un Barquillo (World on an Ice Cream Cone), shortened to *Barquillo* in conversation. Two men who were known for their mean faces were Cara de Hueso (Bone Face, for his skinny face) and Cara de Cuchillo (Knife Face). Cuatro Pelos meant Four Hairs, and was a sarcastic way to say the man was bald. If a man had abundant hair, as in the case of Cesar Gonzmart, the violinist, he was called Melenita de Oro (Golden Mane). Pasita (Little Raisin) was a completely bald man whose wrinkled pate resembled a raisin.

A man with a large mouth was called Boca Buzón (Mailbox Mouth). The headwaiter at the Columbia known for his loud hailing of heavy-tipping customers was called Boca Vozina (Loudspeaker Mouth). Boca Cherna was a man whose lips resembled the mouth of a fish; Culito de Pollo, a man whose mouth resembled the back end of a chicken.

A boy who had lips like a goat was known as Bemba Chivo. Bombillo (Light Bulb) had a prominent nose. Buck teeth were not uncommon because no one had thought up the larceny of braces, and no one had the money to put them on if they had. Therefore, two common nicknames were Diente Frio (Cold Teeth) and Chavete, which was the sharp knife cigar makers used to cut the ends of the cigars. If you'd ever gotten bitten by a buck-toothed person you'd understand the name.

Cabeza Pendejo was a man with kinky hair which resembled pubic hair. Understandably, this was not mentioned in his presence, but everyone in Ybor City knew him by this name.

Of course, any illness, defect, or deformity gave you a permanent and clearly defining nickname. So El Cojo was a lame man; El Ciego, the blind one; El Sordo, the deaf; El Tuerto or El Bizco, the cross-eyed one.

There was a kid who had gotten a hand cut off in an accident who was called Mocho (Stump). In a strangely related way, his neighbor was a poor kid who was forced to wear his big brother's hand-me-down shirts. Since the sleeves were always far too long, his mother would cut them off, making a short-sleeved shirt. Consequently no one ever saw the boy in anything but short sleeve shirts, hence his nickname Manga-Mocha (Stump Sleeves).

The mixing of the races in Latin America produced kids of many hues. One who was half and half and sort of dark was called cortadito, after the color of expresso when a dollop of milk is added. A kid who was a few shades darker was called Technicolor. A jet-black baseball player was called El Indio (the Indian), and his brother who was a deathly white was called El Albino. Both were great athletes for Jefferson High School. They were also called the Chocolate and Vanilla Brothers.

Among the boys in the locker room the nomenclature was rich and varied when they chose a name to classify the size of a boy's manhood. The range was from Manguera (Garden Hose) to Malanga (Cassava Dick) to the lesser Canaria (Pipe) to the absolutely ignominious Tubito (Test Tube).

Girls were mostly exempt from nicknames, although I've never been able to figure out why. One particularly accurate feminine nickname stands out both for its descriptiveness and its rarity. A young, beautiful Cuban girl had a tiny waist and a well-rounded, protuberant rear end. She was called Culo de Valentine for obvious reasons.

Men were commonly nicknamed after the geographic location they came from: El Gallego (Galicia), El Andaluz (Andalucia), El Sevillano (Seville), El Madrileno (Madrid), El Valenciano (Valencia), El Cubanito, Borinquen (Puerto Rico). When a man took a fancy to a certain type of food it also became his name—for example, Tomate, Aguacate (Avacado), Chili, Croqueta, and Bon-Bon.

More obscure were the origins of names attached to the street characters. There was an indescribably dirty derelict whose name was Bolita de Churri (Ball of Dirt). Another liked to invoke a curse—crossing his fingers and chanting *"Foo foo de gato"* (cat dung)—over and over, so that became his name. A man who was always annoying everyone was called Rompe Nabo (Turnip Breaker), although the connotation was much more anatomically descriptive.

A boy who walked to school on cold Tampa mornings with small mincing steps, as if stepping on eggs, was called Pisa Huevos (Egg Stepper) or worse. A boy whose family owned goats was given the name

Cagalata (He Who Defecates Tin Cans). It probably comes as no shock to learn that he ended up as a psychiatrist.

I've mentioned Pan con Chinches (Bread with Bedbugs), Pepe Lu Babo (the Idiot) and the miser Bicicleta who rode his bicycle down alleyways. But the most famous of these was a man named Paracaidas (Parachute) who was unique in that he got that sobriquet from *not* wearing a parachute while going for hot-air balloon rides. He would take people up for rides at the factory picnics and fairs. One fine sunny day at a Pass-a-Grille picnic he decided to set a high-altitude record with his balloon. When last seen he was headed in the direction of Mexico, at a high altitude, waving furiously. Alas, he was never seen again. I feel that thorough research would probably reveal an ancient man tending bar in a Spanish restaurant in Tampico. Maybe, if things work out like they should, they'd find Amelia Earhart waiting tables alongside Paracaidas.

While I admire the accuracy of those nicknames, I feel absolutely furious about calling the hard-crusted bread that can only be made in Ybor City *Cuban bread*. I've traveled the world looking for bread as good as the bread made there, and have never found its equal, certainly not in Havana, Buenos Aires, Paris, Madrid, or Barcelona. Once and for all, let me get this straight, this bread should be called *Ybor City* bread, not Cuban bread. There's nothing Cuban about it. Let's call a crumb a crumb.

Mother's Day in Ybor City

Most of my friends had exemplary mothers and most showed their affection in the usual ways. One of my wildest, rowdiest friends was absolutely devoted to his mother, and maintained her in a comfortable manner until her death a few years ago at an advanced age.

The son whose devotion to his mother outdid all of us was an unusual man. He started in the cigar factories, soon learned that being a waiter was a better way to make a living, and adopted that way of life to this very day.

His name was Tony Garcia, but everyone knew him by his nickname Macaco. How he got that name even he doesn't know. He was

Tony "Macaco" Garcia, 1942. No greater love has a son for his mother. Courtesy of Tony Garcia.

good-looking, always well-dressed, a great dancer, and a superb story-teller. Macaco was also well-read, so his opinions covered a broad spectrum; he had a thought on everything. What made him unique in Ybor City was that he was fluent in English as well as Spanish and had a humorist's way with a story. Macaco took very few things seriously, and time spent around him usually brought a laugh or two.

Perhaps what made him a Hall of Fame waiter was his ability to carry on six different conversations simultaneously, and still give exceptional service. He knew and was friendly with all levels of citizens. He was as at home kibitzing with Congressman Sam Gibbons as talking with Roland Manteiga the *La Gaceta* editor, or Cacciatore the bolita man, or

Speedy Brown the cuban sandwich king. For each and all, Macaco had an observation, a story, or unsolicited advice. Macaco's station was not a quiet one. I always felt that an entertainment tax should be charged at his table.

What also made Macaco an unusual Tampa Banana was that he had traveled the world. Sometime during the war he joined the merchant marine, liked the view, liked the money more, and stuck with it after the war. His favorite port of call was New York. It was here that he found the mambo and the fast life of the Palladium Ballroom.

Macaco was the first white guy I ever saw in zoot clothes: pegged pants, high waist, broad lapels and ties. He stood out at the Matinees because he was an outstanding dancer and because of his clothes.

He was the only one of my friends who was as close to my father, J.B., as he was to me. Macaco was a man who didn't recognize social, professional or age lines. He was the only friend of mine who would go with me to the Central Avenue black district to hear the great jazz bands of Count Basie, Duke Ellington, and Louis Armstrong. He was truly a believer in the brotherhood of man.

Macaco carried a card case type of wallet in his chest pocket which showed his driver's license on one side and his mother's picture on the other. So in one of those rare moments of opportunity, I got the chance of a lifetime to pull a fast one on my pal Macaco. This opportunity germinated in a completely unrelated incident.

In the postwar world of Ybor City we still had censorship of sorts. At La Economica Drugstore we were not allowed to accept rolls of film that might contain nudity. In every population, however, there are those few who want nude photos of their girlfriends, wives, or mistresses. Why they do has never been satisfactorily explained, even by Freud. Maybe it has something to do with wanting to get caught. Now we have videotape which really nails it down.

At our drugstore we did an occasional favor for a good customer from time to time. Usually, the customer, acting furtive and guilty as hell, asked to talk to J.B. in private. J.B. would send the word to the developer, who would print the pictures himself and mark them *Personal*. So that no one else would see them he would staple them shut. These are the things they don't teach at pharmacy school.

I was stuck at the store on a long hot Sunday afternoon, bored out of my mind, praying for the arrival of J.B., when a fat little cigar maker came to the counter looking shifty and guilty. I perked up. Things were improving. I knew this customer's story.

For years this fifty-year-old Spaniard had been carrying on a clandestine love affair with a co-worker. Both were fifty, fat, and married. They fooled no one with their exaggerated pretense of not talking to one another. Everyone at El Reloj Factory knew they were lovers.

Absolutely mortified to find out that J.B. wasn't in, the man was stuck in a hard place. Out in the car, in the hot sun, were his wife and kids, dying to get to the beach. He couldn't go back without getting rid of the roll of film he carried. I decided to make it easy for him, for I was sorry for the old sinner.

"Leave it with me. I'll see J.B. gets it and sends it personal," I winked.

"Are you sure. . ." His face was red and covered with sweat.

"Go and swim easy. I know what you need." I smiled my best teenage smile and patted his back reassuringly. He was so relieved he almost forgot to buy suntan oil, which was his cover story for coming into La Economica.

I couldn't wait to call the photography shop and order two of each. After all, something good could come of having a roll of pictures of a fifty-year-old fat hoyden.

These were the days before *Playboy* and *Penthouse,* so the only nudes were found in *National Geographic* spreads on Pacific natives, or, on a more reliable and appetizing basis, in *Health* and *Fun in the Sun* magazines. The shot that appeared with the greatest frequency was the beach ball held over the head of a nude lass. The effect was to elevate the naked breasts, thereby giving them the look of perfection.

When the pictures arrived I was sure I would be rewarded by finding one of these over-the-head poses. Surely, I would.

Of course, I was right. One picture in particular was a gem of its kind. This small, fat woman stood in a sylvan glade, chubby arms holding a big beach ball over her head. To say she was hairy is an understatement. The rest I leave to your imagination out of deference to the feminist who may fire-bomb my home.

Well, what to do with this treasure? I put it in the secret compartment of my Amity wallet, for future use. I showed it to no one, not even my co-conspirator, the devilish drug clerk Cecil.

A few years later I found myself invited to an elegant engagement party at the Davis Island home of Casey Hernandez, the son of the owner of the Columbia Restaurant.

Casey had been matriculating through various educational establishments of the East and South, and had, by dint of sheer luck, found a beautiful western belle willing to marry him. She was very well educated and impeccably brought up in the manner of all well-to-do western families. In addition to looks, education, position, and wealth she also had a great sense of humor and understanding. These last two she would have to have to stay married to the fun-loving Casey. I thought I could test those qualities on this festive and very proper occasion.

As my guest I brought Macaco, who I felt might brighten up things a bit by relating his adventures in Morocco. I found his wallet within easy grasp of my fingers, and promptly lifted it. Disappearing to the solitude of the bathroom, I replaced his mother's picture with the nude Planet-of-the-Apes photo of the fifty-year-old concubine.

At last we found ourselves talking to the prospective in-laws, a nice, well-educated couple, struggling to make sense of the strange evening. I brought Macaco to their attention.

"Here is a man who truly loves and is devoted to his mother."

"How nice," the mother fluttered.

"Admirable, I must say," the father nodded happily.

"He is so devoted that he never has married, just so she wouldn't be left alone."

"That is devotion," the mother beamed.

"I've seldom seen such sacrifice. Why, the only photograph he carries in his wallet is his mother's. Show the folks the photo of your mom."

Without looking, Macaco displayed the picture in the wallet, unaware that the shocked couple were looking at the fat, nude cigar maker.

They turned and left in a huff, leaving Macaco in a quandary. Later, at the Big Orange, he took a look at the wallet picture. He laughed louder than me.

Macaco is now in semiretirement, dispensing his all-encompassing advice and philosophy from his station in Café Pepe. The service is flawless as usual, the observations on the national and international scene more acute, and the advice more bittersweet.

In a final bit of observation he commented on still being single and playing around.

"It's still the same game, only now I'm the one that insists that all lights are out and curtains drawn." Macaco takes another pull on his ever-present cigarette. "After all, who can stand seeing a nude, wrinkled sixty-year-old body? I even shave with two bathrobes on."

Visitor from Outer Space

By 1940 it was pretty clear that a major problem had arisen in Europe in the form of a dictator who had an uncanny resemblance to Charlie Chaplin. For years the citizens of Ybor City had known about him because of his involvement in the Spanish civil war, and so it came as no surprise that this power-hungry dictator could not be appeased, and that a war in Europe was inevitable. The rest of the United States felt that while this was distressing, it really had little to do with us. We hid behind a huge body of water known as the Atlantic Ocean, and the power of the U.S. Navy. They had a word for it. It was called isolationism.

The first indication of the seriousness of the war came in the fall of 1940. On a chilly October day our homeroom teacher, the thin, dignified Mrs. Wilson, brought a young boy into our class and introduced him. His name was Kevin, and he was English. We gawked at him as if he had come from outer space. He had a fierce look on his face, as if challenging the lot of us.

Kevin was short by our standards, though our standards after a few depression years were not much higher than his. He carried a small round ball under his arm, holding onto it as if he expected the entire class to jump on him and steal it away. It was smaller than a basketball, and a tad bigger than a volleyball. He called it a football, and we all snickered at his ignorance.

Kevin had a mass of red curly hair parted on one side and piled up on the other, giving the impression that he was wearing an RAF cap. In a school of sun-tanned Latin children he was a deathly white. Faded freckles covered his face. His eyes were a clear light blue and his eyebrows and eyelids were so light as to be almost invisible. This gave him an odd effect, as if he had stood in front of an explosion and had the front of his face burned off. When he smiled, which wasn't often, he showed carious front teeth which were crooked and twisted. It was not an agreeable sight.

In tropical Tampa his clothes appeared singularly out of place. The pants were made of a thick wool and looked as if they felt itchy. The white shirt had a stained collar and he wore the overly long sleeves rolled up to his elbow.

The pants were not long but reached to just below the knee. There a small expanse of deadly white faded freckled skin was seen. Heavy woolen socks had fallen in a roll around his thick-soled shoes. The shoes were high-tops, and made to last as long as the British Empire from the look of them.

A few days went by and Kevin remained isolated from the class, either by design or his own reluctance to venture forth and make new friends. He seemed truculent, and spoke little. When he did speak, we could not make out what language he was speaking. It did not seem to be English. Our English, mixed as it was with Spanish words and mispronunciations, was equally incomprehensible to him. An impasse.

To humor him, one day a bunch of us decided to play soccer with him. This seemed to please him, and placing his ball in front of him he proceeded to run rings around us, as we made clumsy attempts to stop him. The recess bell put a merciful end to the unequal match between one English boy and five American lads who had never heard of English football.

I told my mother about this strange visitor from across the sea, and she suggested I bring him home to play and stay for supper. I told her I didn't think he would come, for there was a problem of communication. "He'll come," she said in her matter-of-fact way. She was always right.

When I shyly broached the subject to Kevin he eyed me for a long moment, then he flashed his carious smile.

"Right. Jolly good."

"And you can stay for supper."

His eyes clouded over. This seemed a bit forward to him. In England, food was rationed. You might invite a chum for tea, but certainly not for supper. It took some doing to convince him it was all right. He seemed suspicious but happy.

A bright October sun beat down on us as we walked down the tracks of the Highland streetcar. I tied my sweater around my waist and undid my shirt. Kevin remained in uniform. I never saw him dressed in any other clothes except the ones he wore when we met him. His pale face flushed a deep red, but he did not voice a complaint. We got to the park, where a penny candy store was our objective.

Poor Kevin never had any spending money so he waited at the door as I went to the counter. The old man peered over his bifocals at me. I pointed to penny bubble-gum war cards and made a sign of two with my fingers. I looked at Kevin, who averted his eyes in embarrassment. I paid my two copper pennies and walked out of the store, handing one to Kevin as I went.

"What's yours?" I was looking at a card which showed a gigantic Chinese soldier with a sword over his head about to decapitate a cringing Japanese officer. It looked bloody. I loved it. I showed it to Kevin.

"Bloody good!" Kevin said, busily unwrapping his card and looking at it. "A bit of all right, that." His was a picture of a Spitfire shooting down an ME 109.

We swapped cards as we doubled up the flat sheet of red bubble gum and put it in our mouths. The streetcar bell rang as it stopped by the gazebo in the middle of the small park. I ran toward the back of the trolley, bent over as if I were a Huron warrior in *Drums Along the Mohawk*. Kevin followed, juggling his book with his precious football.

We arrived at the back end of the streetcar and I showed Kevin how to tuck his books in his belt and hold on with one hand. In this way we stole a ride to Tampa Heights, where I lived, and avoided a long walk.

Kevin appeared genuinely impressed when he saw the big two-story house on Lamar street. I heard a "Cor'blummey" said under his breath as we bounded into the back room, which was used as a breakfast den.

There on the table were plates which held pieces of cuban bread upon which had been spread delicious guava paste, covered with cream cheese. Beside the plates were two barrel glasses filled with cold milk. Kevin's eyes grew large as his mouth watered.

"Dig in." I reached for the biggest piece and stuffed a bit in my mouth.

"Aren't we waiting for the others?" Kevin stood uncertainly by the table.

"What others?" I pushed his chair with my foot under the table.

When we had finished our *merienda* (snack) I explained that it was our equivalent to their tea time. My mother came in and smiled sweetly at us and reminded me to change from street clothes to play clothes. Kevin took a long hard look at my closet. He especially noticed the different shoes.

One pair for school. Well-scuffed. One pair for going out. New and shined. One pair of basketball sneakers.

It was a small closet, and I shared it with my brother, who was hiding next door at my grandmother's, not wanting to meet a stranger from across the sea. The effect was that Kevin thought I had twice as many clothes and shoes as I had.

"Are you rich then?" Kevin gulped.

"Nah. Not that I know of," I said as I struggled out of my school clothes and into my well-worn jeans.

I sat on the linoleum floor to tie my shoes and motioned Kevin to sit by me as I flicked on my tiny Arvin radio. "Daniel Boone, Frontier Scout" was just coming on, and we stretched out on the cool linoleum to hear the exciting radio serial.

Kevin seemed to be electrified as his eyes turned to look under my bed. There were my treasures, my air fleet. My war trophies, a German spike helmet and a coal scuttle iron helmet.

Gingerly I rolled out a Fokker triplane, painted a bright red.

"The Red Baron," Kevin said.

I rolled out a Sopwith Camel with RAF rondels. His eyes lit up as if he were seeing old friends he had not seen in a long time.

"Billy Bishop. Albert Ball. Me grandfather was in the Royal Flying Corps, but he flew an SE-5."

It was my turn to be amazed. My curiosity was aroused. Here was a chance to talk to someone who talked to someone who had flown in the Great War.

"What did he say? How was it? Did he fight against the Flying Circus? How many kills did he have?" The questions came tumbling out.

Kevin looked unhappy. He very much wanted to tell me stories of the Great War, but he came up empty.

"My granddad was shot down his first week in the line. Went down in flames, he did. They called it Bloody April, me mom says."

Disappointed but happy to at least know someone who lost a relative in the Great War, I reached further under the bed and pulled out my two latest beauties.

"I seen a lot of them," Kevin picked up the Spitfire and did several swooping maneuvers. "And I saw what was left of an ME 109 like that one. Not much left, I can tell you." Kevin's eyes were wide and his voice hushed.

"Gosh. What about the pilot?"

Kevin made a terrible face and shuddered at the image forming in his mind.

"Like burnt toast with strawberry jam all over. Pieces of him, I mean. He almost wasn't recognizable, I mean, as a man. It was awful."

We both shuddered happily.

"Let's go fly some grasshoppers," I said.

"What's that?" He was running out the back door behind me.

The hedge that separated my house from my grandmother's had a shoulder-high hedge, and in that hedge hundreds of big yellow grasshoppers lived, eating happily away, unaware that they were about to become the pilots of my squadron.

I took my red Fokker and gave Kevin the Sopwith Camel. Taking twine from the Singer sewing machine drawer, I tied a grasshopper into each cockpit, then put one each on the wings. We crawled up to the second-story roof of my grandmother's house. We wound up the rubber bands which turned the propellers and at a signal let them go.

We watched in awe the glorious flight of our two planes. When the power ran out, the two planes glided beautifully on the air currents taking them over the trees and phone wires into the next block. Kevin stood speechless, watching the beautiful sight.

"My Camel went further," he exulted. "England forever!"

We shinned down the drainpipe, running full steam down the alley behind the house in order to rescue our fallen aircraft.

Kevin seemed genuinely surprised that the grasshoppers were alive. I hated grasshoppers and wished they would die on my flights, but the best I could do was to turn them loose on foreign soil, a block away.

The day ended with Kevin trying to tell my father J.B. why he was in Tampa while his parents were off in London fighting Hitler's gang. He kept us enthralled reciting what it felt like to dig a bomb shelter in the back yard and stay in it all night waiting for German bombers which never came. He talked to us about being given a box with a string to go around his neck. In it was a gas mask, and he and his little brother were told that there were terrible men called Nazis, which Prime Minister Churchill pronounced Naw-sies, who were trying to kill the children of England.

"But why?" Kevin's little brother would ask, his voice muffled by the gas mask.

"Never you mind, dear, try to sleep."

Eventually, when sirens sounded every night and searchlights crisscrossed the harbor skies, and guns fired skyward and bombs fell, Kevin was told he was to be moved to safety. He was separated from his mom, and once out in the country, from his kid brother, and then he found himself on a boat headed for a place called America.

"And here I am," Kevin ended his story. My brother and I sat enthralled, my mother busied herself with the dishes, and my father smiled kindly at the snaggle-tooth English refugee and patted his head, as if that made everything all right. J.B. stretched, looked at his watch, and announced to one and all that it was time to get back to work.

"Is your dad really going to work or is he going to the pub like me dad?"

"Work, I think," I said, it never entering my head to doubt anything J.B. said. If J.B. wanted to go to the pub, he just damn well would, and announce it boldly on top of that.

One day, just after we had gotten to spend this time together, Kevin vanished. Disappeared. No one had an explanation. Kevin just went back. Given his age, he probably got into the tail end of the war. Had he survived? Had he and his family made it through the blitz? What became of Kevin? What made him seem so different to us, why was he a foreigner?

Kevin was odd to all of us because he was the first authentic foreigner we had ever seen. But, considering we were all foreigners in this land, where I met newly arrived Spaniards, Cubans, Italians, Puerto Ricans, and South Americans every day, how could I be amazed by this whey-faced, freckled, redheaded boy from England? Why was he more of a foreigner that the others?

The answer was simple. The foreigners I met daily were "us." They spoke Spanish, and dressed as all of us did. The very fact that Kevin spoke differently, dressed in a strange way, and was separated from us by his "awkwardness" and his unique qualities, made him a foreigner.

I was thrilled to have met someone from a foreign land, and to hear firsthand what preparing for the war was like. It was a privilege to talk to a boy who had a relative who not only fought in the Great War, but who died fighting for his country.

I missed Kevin. He had not had time to say goodbye. Who had brought him? Who had taken him away? What became of Kevin?

I wonder to this day.

Chapter 14

War Years

The play was simple. I centered the ball to Marvin Dawkins, who had a good arm. I brush-blocked his brother Byron and outran my brother Joseph to where Dr. Angulo's blue 1940 Buick was parked. The oak tree beyond it was the goal. We were behind 14–0.

Byron tripped me. I pushed him into Frank Spano's four-door Ford. I scrambled up from the red brick street, noticing that my knee was bleeding. I sped by my brother, who was having trouble keeping his glasses on and running at the same time.

The ball was in the air. It was round and fat like a watermelon and it hung like a balloon in the clear blue sky. As if in slow motion, it came to me, it landed in my hands with a pleasant sting, and I caught it, bounced off the side of the Buick and ran to the imaginary goal line of the oak tree. I noticed a man standing by the tree. He was yelling. In the excitement of the moment I had not heard him, but he continued to yell. Triumphantly I put the ball down, and then I heard him clearly.

"The Japs just bombed Pearl Harbor! The Japs just bombed Pearl Harbor!"

I yelled at the Dawkins boys, relaying the news, and headed for my parlor. We huddled around the Philco console, trying to hear the announcer. It was not a drill. It was real. The nervous voice on the radio made us feel like the Japs were in Sulphur Springs.

"Somebody better go tell Frank," one of us said, and the Dawkins boys dashed out into the cold December afternoon to tell the regular army man, who was home on leave, that he'd better get back to the army because war had come to Ybor City.

I knew things were too good to last. The depression was ending. People had money. You could feel the excitement. After years of hard times, of strangers at the backyard gate waiting for leftovers, there was a feeling that happy days were here again. A song said that. FDR said that. Hell, everybody was saying it. It was great to have a buck in your jeans.

The hard times of labor strife, the head-busting strikes and the bitterness they left, were over. There were more jobs than people. The shipyards had opened up in Palmetto Beach. Two of them. One to make concrete boats. Would they really float? The government had decided to build a fighter base in Drew Field, and make a bomber base at the end of Bayshore Boulevard and call it MacDill Field. More jobs. Someone decided to connect the two fields with a newfangled wide divided strip of highway called an expressway, patterned after Hitler's autobahn. It was wide and straight as an arrow. More jobs.

Ybor City was jumping. The Columbia, Las Novedades, the Spanish Park, the Valencia, the Barcelona, and the many cafés overflowed. The dances were packed. Merchants sold out of clothes, shoes, and luxury items.

The war was coming, and new money found its way into circulation. Cars would not be made again until the war ended, so the streets were filled with new cars. J.B. got a new '41 Chevrolet, Uncle Ferdie a bullet-shaped '41 Pontiac, Wilson Davis, his brother-in-law, bought a spectacular '41 Mercury convertible, deep royal blue with red leather. Dr Angulo got a new Buick, and even the poorest family on our street got a Willis four-door, which may have been the ugliest car made in America.

Quietly, families bought big sacks of sugar. Fifty-gallon drums of gasoline and kerosene were hidden in the garages. Because of their close observation of the Spanish civil war which had just ended, the people of Ybor City were more aware of what a long war meant. And this was going to be a long war.

For the kids it was a time of excitement. Gone was the monotonous sameness of the poverty days when nothing happened in Ybor City but the same old thing. Oh, once in a while the bolita wars erupted, someone got killed, and then peace would descend. Elections were exciting as a pitched battle, but they only lasted a day. But now, the radio crackled with exciting news! The movie theaters were jam-packed, and the crowds ate up the war flicks. It was a war with well-defined villains. No trouble knowing that the Nazis were evil and the little Japs were out to enslave us all. The issues were clear-cut. We were right and they were wrong. Now, let's get together, go out there, and kick their butts.

We pre-Army-age kids lived a high wonderful life. All the excitement of war and none of the dangers or inconveniences.

Our older schoolmates began to enlist. Bobby Mendez shipped out in the merchant marine. His first ship was torpedoed outside New York Harbor, within sight of the Jersey shore. He was lucky. That convoy went to Murmansk and sustained 80 percent casualties. Bob Reed, our quarterback at Jefferson, enlisted in the Army Air Corps, destined to fly B-17's over Europe. Ybor City's All-American hero, Chelo Huerta, joined his teammate Augustine "Chunchi" Fernandez, and took the star of the Cuscaden Baseball League, Joe Benito, with them into the Army Air Corps. Wilson Davis gave up the playboy life and joined the marines on Pearl Harbor Day. He was in Guadalcanal before he learned how to spell it.

It was exciting and we younger kids couldn't wait to go. I was less excited than the rest because I had lived through the day-to-day agony of the Spanish civil war when I lived with my grandfather, the Spanish consul. We entertained many a returning hero, particularly a major who had been shot through both cheeks and had not healed yet. To see him eat would dampen anyone's enthusiasm to get to the front.

Our stay-at-home lives changed in subtle ways. We quit making Spads, Neuports, and Fokker models. Spitfires, ME 109's and Hawker Hurricanes were the ticket now. No longer did we read our pulp magazines like *Flying Aces,* and the variety of World War I stories. We weren't interested in Billy Bishop, René Fronck, Udet or Baron von Richthofen. Old stuff, that. Now we hungered for details of Sailor Malan, Sanford Tuck, Marseilles, and Galland.

We knew about Colin P. Kelly and how he dove his burning B-17 into a Jap battleship and sunk it. We celebrated his Congressional Medal of Honor and oohed and aahed over the fact that his son, then an infant, would automatically be given a place in West Point. What luck. How cool.

Later, in another war, a Tampa native would win a posthumous Congressional Medal of Honor: he was Baldomero Lopez, an Annapolis marine.

War brought rationing, and with rationing the black market. Ybor City thrived as never before. Downtown became a flourishing, booming, rollicking place. North Franklin Street, which had been a ghost street of empty storefronts, blossomed with beer joints. Servicemen jammed in from early afternoon to late nights. Girls appeared from all over the state. A great time was in the making: a party which went on for four years.

We who walked home from the Tampa Theater would dawdle for a moment at Edwards' Bookstore and Model Airplane Shop, then walk slowly by the pawn shops, so we could ogle at real guns in the window, then walk by the beer joints, hoping we could see a good fight or the MPs arrest a drunken soldier. Boy, was that different from the dull sameness of the old peacetime Ybor City days.

In 1942, I was working at the Columbia as a waiter when the movie crew for a Warner Bros. film arrived. The excitement in the town was great. No one had seen a movie being made since *Hell's Harbor* at Rocky Point in the twenties.

The film was *Air Force,* and it was to be a first-rate film. John Garfield and Harry Carey were the established stars, and the new crop, Arthur Kennedy, Gig Young, and George Tobias, were in supporting roles. It was the story of a B-17 in the early days of the war, and it was filmed at Drew Field. The public was not allowed on the base and so it was doubly exciting to find that the Columbia would be catering the meals, and that Casey, the owner's son, and I would work as servers. Casey, who seemed forever doomed to work in the hot kitchen, looked at the job as if it were a parole.

What a great feeling to be admitted to Drew Field by a helmeted MP holding a Thompson submachine gun, grim-faced, as he checked the contents of the truck and gave all the workers a thorough once-over. After all, the Fifth Column was in everyone's mind. Everyone was suspect. One never knew if a Jap had infiltrated the Columbia Restaurant kitchen and placed a hand grenade in the paella.

However severe the military visage of the MP, he was still just a young kid masquerading as a combat-hardened GI. When Gus, the bartender, handed the MP a cuban sandwich, he broke into a wide grin and waved us on.

We set up in front of a P-39 and I was in heaven. It was the closest I'd ever come to a real fighter since the Air Force flew into Tampa in the mid-thirties in a show of force. On that day I had wandered around Drew Field, actually touching the highly lacquered surfaces of the wings of the beautiful blue and yellow Curtiss P-6E Hawks. The peashooters—Boeing P-26's, ugly, single-wing, fat fighters—were the most modern, but I could not pull myself from the beautiful bi-wing Curtiss fighters. The bombers were big, fat, ugly Martin B-10's, the precursors of the B-17, the greatest bomber of the Second World War. Still, they were impressive to a kid in love with war planes.

On the movie set we were allowed to look at the planes, but we were kept at a safe distance by the MPs. To me the P-39 seemed beautifully designed with graceful lines; it was almost delicate. In flight, those features were a positive; in combat, the delicacy proved a disaster. The Japanese aces, in postwar books, reported licking their lips when they saw P-39 Airacobras. But at this time, with the patriotic fervor at its highest, we were told the P-39 would outfly the pathetic tin can airplane the Japs called a Zero. Some tin can.

It was exciting to see how a film was shot, and doubly so because we were so near to the real air base. Real P-39's were crashing on take-off and landing. The excitement at the base was high. I made a solemn observation that any fighter plane as hard to fly as the P-39 could not possibly be as great as our Air Force was telling us. It was the first of many such realizations regarding our military's flirtation with the truth.

The picture dealt with the adventures of one crew of an early B-17 bomber in the Pacific War. It was a potboiler plot with a formula crew. Hollywood war movies had to have a cross-section of America in every picture. We had handsome WASP officers, Gig Young and Arthur Kennedy; a tough big-city guy from the streets of Brooklyn, John Garfield; an old-timer from cavalry days but a heck of a mechanic, Harry Carey; and the comic Jew, George Tobias. We had not been liberalized enough to include a black in the cast, for blacks were only in menial positions in the

Air Force in the early days of the war. The obligatory female was played by the young Faye Emerson, and she was a dazzler!

Two problems arose at the end of the picture. One, Harry Carey, the old cowboy hero of a hundred films, was terrified of flying and had it in his contract that he didn't have to fly. The script called for him to be in the B-17 as it took off from a smoking, bombed-out airport. No amount of pleading would get him up in the B-17. Finally the director, Howard Hawks, a tough bird himself, got him to consent to be filmed in the B-17 as it rolled down the runway, gaining speed for take-off.

The shot was set up, the cameras rolling, Harry Carey looking green at the side gun window, and the signal was given. The director's face looked demonic in his glee as he signaled to the pilot. The plane gained speed, Carey looked sick, then terrified, and finally as the wheels of the big four-motored bomber left the tarmac, Harry Carey disappeared from view.

The plane banked once around the field; fake ack-ack bursting close by created turbulence which made the B-17 bounce crazily. Mercifully, it landed and with it came a raging Harry Carey. The director smiled at the crusty old cowboy. Carey was not in any further scenes, so he could yell all he wanted. The director had his shot. It was my introduction to film making, and I learned a lesson I pass on now to any young film actor: "Never, but never, believe anything a director tells you!"

The other problem was that the young actors were so well-fed, rested, and robust that even makeup couldn't convince an audience that they hadn't slept or eaten for two weeks and were desperately trying to leave Bataan.

One Friday I was at the Columbia Café bar, when I saw Garfield leading Young, Kennedy, and Tobias to the bar. Garfield ordered double Cuban Manhattans and started telling jokes and laughing. Howard Hawks had gotten them a company car, scrounged up the gasoline at Sardina's station, and suggested they take a weekend off. Take the Tamiami Trail to Miami and have some fun. Girls, gambling, booze, and eternal heaven.

John Garfield was a tiny guy. He was well-built in the manner of a bulldog, and he had a nice-looking face. Common, but nice. Tobias was a character actor, the poor man's Alan Hale, and a great comic. But nothing I had ever seen in Ybor City had prepared me for the astounding handsomeness of Gig Young. He went past handsome to pretty. Arthur Kennedy was WASP, Yale-Harvard good-looking. Gig Young was Robert-Taylor, Tyrone-Power pretty. At the time the conventional wisdom in Ybor City was that the studio had subjected them to substantial plastic surgery. Makeup, lighting, and a terrific cameraman made them look so great that they did not seem real.

Well, here was living evidence that there lived a species of man on this planet so good-looking as to not seem real. To make it worse, Gig Young, overcompensating wildly for his good looks, was a hell-raising man's man. The crew loved him, and he was, in fact, on the way to the war himself. With Gig Young to troll with, they must have had half of the Miami beauties in their suite in record time.

I was stunned to be in their presence. I did everything but ask for their autographs. I was envious. How could one get into this glamorous business? How could one ever be part of them?

Monday, early in the morning, Hawks called for the bedraggled crew to take their positions for the final shots. The actors stumbled into the B-17, eyes puffy and red-rimmed from lack of sleep, a scrubby three-day growth of beard on their chins, walking like zombies. Howard Hawks beamed. Nothing like a little realism to make a movie seem like actual combat. And it taught me that actors will go through hell to make their roles genuine.

When they packed up and left their corner of Drew Field, I wanted to go with them. Movie making looked like fun, and where could one go to find a beauty like Faye Emerson in Tampa?

Hollywood taught us what the air war was like in the land of make-believe, but in the skies over Europe three Ybor City heroes were finding out that the real thing was a far different thing. The three men had exciting adventures, but it took fifty years to find out what had happened to them. When the war was finally over and they returned, they responded to our questions with nonchalance: "Oh nothing. We got up, we went to work, we got back and sacked out." Then they ordered another double shot of scotch, terminating the conversation.

Perhaps this is the time to pay tribute to them by telling their stories.

Cadet Chelo Huerta, 1943: "Off We Go Into the Wild Blue Yonder." Courtesy of Marcelino Huerta III.

Before we are all gone, we should record some examples of what the boys of Ybor City did in the Big War. At least, these five.

The Ybor City Flying Aces

The rush to join the Air Force was great in the first days of the war. First we had gone through an era where all our heroes were aviators—from Rickenbacker and the war aces to Lindbergh, Doolittle in the air races, Wiley Post, Amelia Earhart, and Howard Hughes pioneering aircraft advancement and glorifying pilots in films like *Hell's Angels*. Most boys who had the confidence and desire to fly were athletes, used to competition and possessing great coordination.

So it was not hard to see why Chelo Huerta and Chunchi Fernandez, star footballers at Hillsborough High, were accepted into air cadets school immediately. They were tough and built like fireplugs. They looked like fighter pilots. They were pugnacious, rough, and aggressive. Just the stuff a fighter pilot needs.

Their contemporary and childhood pal was a tiny, thin boy named Joe Benito. His size had never interfered with his athletic prowess. He was the best shortstop in Ybor City, played in high school and in all the Intersocial League games at Cuscaden Park. But he was small and angelic-looking. To add to his image of being an academic scholar and far from a jock, was his shy, kind, quiet manner. No one could guess that inside that wimp exterior beat a warrior's heart. He was so frail that the Air Force must not have been paying attention when they inducted him into their flight program.

Chelo Huerta and Chunchi Fernandez would surely be fighter pilot hotshots. Joe Benito, if he made it through training, would probably fly safe transport or recon flights. The Air Force was ruthlessly accurate in assigning men to jobs they were most qualified for.

The ways of the military are hard to fathom, as I have said, and the

Capt. Chelo Huerta and his B-24 crew, Italy, 1944. Courtesy of Marcelino Huerta III.

Air Force certainly did things in a strange way. Chelo Huerta, the hot-blooded, quick-tempered, aggressive footballer, was assigned to a heavy bombardment group flying lumbering B-24's. Not exactly what the dashing Chelo had in mind.

Chunchi Fernandez was transferred to bombardier's school following a training school foul-up and ended up in B-17's in the Eighth Air Corps in England.

Joe Benito, the peaceful, nonaggressive tiny man, ended up flying the biggest fighter plane of World War II, the P-47 Thunderbolt fighter.

So much for Air Force predictability.

Of the three, Chelo Huerta had the most normal combat experience. The B-24 was a lumbering boxcar with a thin wing and four huge engines. Its landing gear was a tripod, its front wheel made the body come perilously close to the ground. On concrete runways the B-24 took off well. On wire-grid airstrips, it was touch-and-go if it took off at all. On mud, it was a life-threatening adventure. Chelo was stuck in Bari, Italy, in the mud. It was not surprising to hear he cracked up several B-24's and at one point was one short of being an ace. A Luftwaffe ace.

Chelo's big adventure came when he was shot down in Yugoslavia, broke his foot, and still had to walk his way out of the mountains to Allied lines. He was rescued by partisans and it took him a month to get back. When he got back to his base he was put in the hospital.

He had been laid up for a few days when he saw a small captain coming down the aisle reading the names on the charts, obviously looking for one of his men. Imagine Chelo's shock to see the baby-faced Joe Benito, his boyhood pal. The chances of Benito, a fighter pilot, being on a bomber base in Bari, far from his own base, were remote at best.

Chelo was not shy like Joe, or reserved like Chunchi. He was proud of his athletic accomplishments, proud of his obvious leadership abilities, and very aware of his movie-star good looks, and consequent prowess with the ladies.

After the war, he returned immediately to the playing fields at the University of Florida, and went on to coach an undefeated collegiate team at Wichita University, made up primarily of retired players from the Green Bay Packers. Chelo was a winner at all costs. Immensely popular and beloved by the community he so assiduously served, he died before I could ferret out the details of his war service. But, in doing research for a World War II novel I asked for his personal records, log books, etc. Joe Benito had given me his own combat log. It was a treasure trove of combat detail, the kind he was unable to relate in conversation, either because of his natural reticence or modesty, or because he had blocked out the nightmare of those years.

Chelo's son, Chelo Huerta, Jr., a prominent attorney, found his records and sent them to me to study. Placed side by side with Benito's war log, I was struck at how they so correctly reflected the personalities of each man. Joe Benito's were spare, sparse, and stuck to hard facts without personal comment, no matter how tragic or hard the facts were. It was a no-nonsense, no bragging, no self-revealing narrative of the air war of a P-47 pilot.

I read through Chelo's record with a growing smile on my face. Confident Chelo burst out on every page. "Piece of cake," he would write. RAF-type swagger showed a guy used to success, used to winning, used to taking hard knocks and turning them to his advantage. By the end, I was laughing out loud, as I realized that there were more pictures of babes, parties, and famous nightclubs than there was hard information on what his life was as a B-24 pilot. Handsome Chelo, the party animal, recorded his war as one long party, from babe to babe, not mission to mission.

Joe Benito flew ninety-three close-support tactical missions in his theater of operations. He was promoted to captain, won medals, and flew with distinction until the end of the war. In short, he had a heroic war. In addition to his combat achievements he was also fortunate to fly the entire war without injury.

The plane he flew was so large and fat in shape that it was called the Jug. It was primarily designed as a fighter; its mission, long-range escort for the B-17's of the daylight bombardment of Europe. As other fighters came along that were better suited to dog-fighting, the P-51 and P-38, the Thunderbolt took on a different mission. Air Force designers had made a rugged airframe to hold a huge radial engine. They found that they could hang much hardware on the wings. With droppable wing tanks they could range deep into Germany, disrupting rail

Citation for Distinguished Flying Cross, 1944

Joe M. Benito, 0826367, 1st Lt, 87th Ftr Sq, 79th Ftr Gp. For extraordinary achievement while participating in aerial flight as a pilot of a P-47 type aircraft. On 23 November 1944, Lt. Benito flew in a six-plane formation of fighter bombers in an attack upon emergency military bridges near Cassetta, Italy. Upon the approach to the target mechanical failure forced three of the aircraft to return to base. Immediately assuming command of the flight, Lt. Benito continued on the mission. Courageously pressing his attack in the face of intense anti-aircraft fire which heavily damaged his airplane, Lt. Benito enabled his P-47's to release their bombs with devastating effect upon these vital bridges. Then skillfully maintaining his crippled plane airborne, Lt. Benito returned to base and effected a perfect emergency land. His outstanding proficiency in combat and steadfast devotion to duty reflect great credit upon himself and the Armed Forces of the United States. Tampa, Fla.

Joe Benito and his P-47, "Sack Time," 1944. Courtesy of Joe Benito.

Joe had a girl friend nicknamed Baby, so he added "Baby" to "Sack Time." Courtesy of Joe Benito.

and highway traffic, shooting up air bases, ammo dumps, fuel dumps, and military targets. The P-47 carried two 500-pound bombs, rockets, machine guns, and disposable gas tanks. A fast fighter plane had been converted into a slow, accurate dive bomber.

The first hint in the log of the anxiety of the combat experience is the name of Joe's plane: "Sack Time Baby." When not flying combat, Joe curled up in a fetal position and got in premium sack time. He reveals a fighter pilot's superstition. Joe had a favorite pair of lucky gloves. One morning, his roommate, in great haste and unable to find his own gloves, borrowed Joe's lucky gloves. The pilot cracked up a fully loaded P-47 on the end of the runway and left a big empty crater as his marker. Joe never wore gloves again.

In a professional's cool note, he writes of the difficulty of bombing a bridge which had a village at one end. It was between steep mountains, and his flight was so intent on pulling out that they continuously missed the bridge and hit the village, which might have been inhabited by many people. The young pilot notes, "Village taking a hell of a beating," and the fact that they were briefed to be on the lookout for funerals sure to be going on.

Asked about this fifty years later, the quiet old man just shook his head, as if, on proper consideration, it would have been a regrettable thing if innocent civilians had died because of their misses. At the time, the young pilot was intent on the technical aspect of bombing a bridge and the common-sense aspect of escaping with his life; the other was not even a thought.

Another entry notes that he had come back to base with a 1,000-pound bomb attached to the wing. Attempts to dislodge it had proven unsuccessful. His flight leader flew beside him, looking at the dangerous bomb, and ordered him to fly out to the Mediterranean Sea.

One last attempt to shake it free would be made. If not, Joe was to bail out over the sea. Joe notes in his laconic manner that this possibility didn't thrill him since he had never learned to swim. Considering he was the pool boy at the Cuscaden Park pool, this was an astounding notation.

Joe was commanded to stall his P-47 in a steep climb. At the moment the plane reached its highest point, about to stall, he would fire all eight 50-caliber machine guns and pray the bomb would drop off.

In the cool manner of a surgeon writing a surgical note, Joe wrote that the bomb was shaken loose by the vibrations of the P-47 in a stall and the recoil of the eight machine guns. Period. No comment. No "Whew! That was close!" No further observation.

Shortly thereafter, the war coming to an end, Joe records an intense personal disaster in his same detached professional manner.

He was returning home with a captain who had been with him since they got to Europe. On a foggy day they had successfully completed their mission and were landing in formation on their muddy fighter base in Italy. They had used up all of their ammunition, their gas tanks were virtually empty, and they were headed for a no-danger landing.

Suddenly, the captain's landing gear collapsed, which on the muddy field was not dangerous. He switched off the engine to avoid fire and slid down the muddy field, careening slightly toward a stand of medium-sized trees.

With Joe riding alongside in his undamaged plane, the captain was smiling at this free playful slide. His P-47 stopped as it hit a tree at the point where the wing root meets the fuselage. The tree broke cleanly, fell across the cockpit, hit the captain on the head, broke his neck, and killed him.

This is recorded in a clear hand, without further comment or observation. Just the facts, ma'am.

I spent a night discussing this cool record of emotional events with Joe Benito last year. He had not dwelled on his war. He had not relived the moments of terror in the sky. He commented intelligently on my question about the events recorded in the log.

He had not really thought a lot about whether the village was inhabited. He had not been scared out of his wits by the possibility that the 1,000-pound bomb would not drop off. He was saddened by the captain's death, but in a time when life hung by a thread, it was nothing that required commentary or deep thought. Joe seemed emotion-proof.

It is relevant to note that Joe Benito came back to Tampa, graduated from the University of Florida, took a job at the tax assessor's office, and has never left his desk since. He also doesn't wear gloves.

It is perhaps the most characteristic example of this endearing man to relate what my probing of his war experience did to him. While talking to me about my novel, *Renegade Lightning*, he suddenly said, "You know, Ferdie, this morning I drove to work along the Bayshore Boulevard and for the first time I took notice of the beauty of where we live. The water was green, the sky a clear blue, there were sailboats out there, and pelicans diving for fish. It is great to be alive! And I said to myself, *Jeepers, I could have been killed in that war and missed all this.*"

Awareness comes to those who wait. Fifty years after the war ended, Joe Benito came up with the emotion that was missing in his combat log book. He might have died but he didn't really consider it a serious possibility until fifty years later.

Augustine Fernandez was known to all Ybor City as Chunchi. He was a second-string Chelo Huerta. He was a good-looking kid, but not as handsome as Chelo. He was a gritty quarterback for Hillsborough High School, but not All-State or All-Southern. He was built like a Basque stone-lifter, all thick trunk and heavy arms. He was in better proportion than Chelo, whose large head gave rise to his Ybor City nicknames, Cabeza Barquillo (Ice Cream Cone Head) and Mundo en un Barquillo (World on a Cone). They were similar in temperament. Great, friendly personalities masked their furious, aggressive, competitive natures. On the playing field they were fierce. They did not accept defeat easily.

Chunchi seemed destined to be a great fighter pilot, but his luck ran bad before he had a chance to prove it. He had soloed and was about to receive his wings when his instructor took him to practice touch-and-go's. These were take-offs, and after a circle around the field, touch-downs which continued into take-offs again. He was at a grassy part of the side of the field where there was no traffic.

On that end of the field there was a stand of trees and a shed where thirsty pilots, waiting to practice, would drink cold Coca-Colas. It was fed by an access road which ran by the field.

In one of the many quirks of fate that awaited Chunchi, a Coca-Cola truck driver in a lapse of sanity decided to take a shortcut

Cadet Bombardier Augustine "Chunchi" Fernandez, 1942. Courtesy of Augustine Fernandez.

across the field to the shed rather than drive the longer way down the access road.

Chunchi, in the rear seat of a Stearman Kaydet bi-wing, had his view blocked by the bottom wing. He landed on top of the truck. At his low landing speed he did not get injured, but he totaled the airplane and demolished the Coca-Cola truck.

Graduation was days away, yet Cadet Augustine Fernandez was washed out. No wings. Only the strong intervention of his flight instructor saved Chunchi from the infantry. He was transferred to bombardier school, which was a gigantic letdown, but better than humping it in the boonies.

By the time Lieutenant Fernandez made it to England, the Eighth Air Force under tough General Curtis LeMay was pounding Europe in a daylight bombardment campaign. The theory that the Americans could bomb by day had not been proven. The RAF had tried it with disastrous results, and had abandoned daylight precision bombardment for night-time area bombing of cities. The American theory was also proving a disaster; the Luftwaffe (ace general Adolf Galland) was using new fighter tactics and combining them with radar-directed, antiaircraft, rapid-fire eighty-eight cannons to inflict unbearable casualties.

The number of missions to be flown before being relieved was twenty-five. So far, no crew had made it to twenty-five. When Chunchi arrived in England, the average life of a crew was five missions. Times were hard.

When Chunchi had survived six missions, he felt he was living on borrowed time. His brother was an NCO in the U.S. Air Force Headquarters in London and wrangled Chunchi a three-day pass after his sixth mission. Chunchi met his brother with a letter written to his mother in case he didn't make it. He also entrusted his brother with his next most valuable possession, his Hillsborough High School graduation ring.

In order to make Chunchi's stay memorable, his brother had gotten him first-class accommodations at the BOQ (Bachelor Officers' Quarters), a bottle of twelve-year-old scotch, and a date with a tall showgirl. No sooner had he put down his A-2 bag than he had a visit from two burly MPs from his base. He was to report back instantly for an important mission, an all-out effort.

Chunchi tried to explain that his B-17 had been so severely damaged in the last raid that it was not flyable. The MPs explained that one of the B-17 crews was short a bombardier and Chunchi was the only bombardier available.

There it was! Bad luck any way you could look at it. A tough all-out effort with a crew of strangers. Bad news!

Chunchi tried everything from invoking the name of General Tooey Spaatz to his brother's position on the HQ staff. The MPs motioned for him to hurry up. Chunchi went to his last gambit: he told them about the showgirl and offered them the scotch if they'd just say they hadn't

Captain Fernandez and his B-17 crew, England, 1943. Courtesy of Augustine Fernandez.

found him. They took the scotch, telling Chunchi that with his chances of surviving, there wasn't much point in wasting it. They escorted him to the waiting jeep.

The MP jeep drove up to the Fort and delivered Chunchi in his best Class A snappy greens and pinks. The pilot tossed him the missing bombardier's flight suit and took his dog tags and gave them to the MP's. In those early days our Air Force intelligence men felt that the flyers should not carry dog tags so the Germans couldn't take them and use them. So, in a move straight out of *Flying Aces*, they had the flyers sew their dog tags in the lining of their flying suits. That must have fooled the Germans for at least twenty-four hours. This would seriously impact on Chunchi's well-being and general health.

The mission was a rough one. Flying Forts were dropping like leaves over Europe, and Chunchi's plane was hit hard by fighters but made it to the target and dropped its entire load on what they thought was the target. They missed it by several miles and obliterated a village near the target. On the wheeling turn to return to base, they were hit hard by eighty-eight fire. Casualties were high.

The navigator got his leg shot off at the knee but it was still attached by strong tendons. The officer was in shock, clinging doggedly to his navigator's desk. The pilot and co-pilot were in bad shape. It seemed a matter of seconds before the Fort would go into a spin which would make bailing out impossible. It also seemed a good possibility that the Fort would blow up.

The pilot pressed the abandon-ship button. Some of the gunners made it out. Chunchi was stuck trying to save the navigator, who was still frozen at his desk, his leg dangling by a tendon. Chunchi realized that he had to do something drastic, so he took the Cuscaden Park Solution. He clipped him as hard as he could. This seemed to get his attention and Chunchi was able to carry him to the open bomb bay and throw him out, praying he had enough strength to pull the cord which Chunchi had wrapped around his hand. Not waiting for the results, Chunchi dove head-first out the wildly careening, stricken Fort.

After the terror and loud noises of the past few minutes, Chunchi suddenly found himself alone in a grey sky. He looked for the navigator and saw no sign of him. He realized for the first time that he did not even know his name. They had shared an excruciating moment of horror, yet they had not even been introduced. He looked below to see a patchwork of green and brown farm plots. No sign of the Fort. Had it crashed? Had it straightened out and made it back to England?

Now he was close enough to earth to see irate farmers with pitchforks waiting for him. He was aware that he had just obliterated their village. They seemed very upset. Off to the right he saw the dust of a military truck speeding to the site of his landing. Would they get there in time to save him? Would the irate villagers pitchfork him to death?

At this point in the narrative, I stopped him to ask a question: "You're a nineteen-year-old kid who just wiped out a village, and you are about to land among the villagers. What were you thinking about?"

"I was wondering if that showgirl would be waiting for me when I got back to London."

Spoken like a true Tampa Banana! No wonder wars are fought by teen-agers.

Chunchi's landing coincided with the arrival of the military. He was taken to their camp, whereupon they began a program of savage beatings that lasted two weeks.

Chunchi was trained to give name, rank, and serial number, and every time he did that, they beat him harder. He was happy to tell them anything they wanted to know, and he was down to ratting out every bolita operation he ever knew when he found out what was making the krauts so sore.

Remember the dog-tags-in-the-uniform gambit? Well, since Chunchi was wearing another officer's flight suit, he was also carrying his dog tags. Unfortunately for Chunchi, the officer's name was Goldberg. To compound his difficulties, his captors were SS troops.

Fortunately for Chunchi, a Luftwaffe colonel showed up to claim the airman. He had confirmation that this was not Goldberg, and so Chunchi was released to spend several months in a Luftwaffe hospital, and several years as a prisoner of war in a stalag.

Aside from his adventures in the POW camp, which he is still reticent about, Chunchi had one last piece of bad luck to relate.

With the Russians advancing on the camp in 1945, the thorough Germans marched the entire camp to a waiting freight train and shipped them toward American lines. It was an unmarked train and subject to strafing, marauding Allied fighters.

In one of those bad-luck incidents of the war, the train was caught in daylight and hammered by P-47's. Over 50 percent of the POW officers died on the last days of the war. Chunchi lived.

I remember Chunchi when he came home. He seemed the same smiling, good-natured guy, but he was prone to staring out in space for long periods at a time. He had a wad of money, for he had a few years' back-pay coming. He had a great new car, and could be found at the Chatterbox Bar as soon as the sun went down. He drank but he didn't talk.

Eventually he went to F.S.U. where, he relates, he would look out the window, seeing nothing, hearing the chatter of intercom voices, the hard banging of fifty calibers, the roar of four huge engines, and the screeching, other-worldly voices saying their "May Day! May Day!" until silence took over and the only sound was the whistling of the cold clear air through the parachute cords.

Teachers of that postwar GI Bill period learned to recognize the thousand-yard stare, and acted as if they didn't notice. Somehow, after four years the noises seemed farther away, and there were more "Bombs Aways" than "May-Days," and Chunchi graduated.

It took twenty years before he related the story of his war to me. We both were in the air force during the Korean War, and he hosted me at his house at Randolph Field, and I spent many a wet evening at the Officer's Club hearing war stories. Early in the evening they were mostly funny or bizarre war stories, but as time drew on, the flak got heavier, the intercom started screaming in their heads—"ME 109's twelve o'clock high!"—and voices got strained, eyes moistened up, and the drinking got serious. That air war hung on in the deep recesses of their minds, and it was hard to let go.

Chunchi did his full time in the air force and retired. Taught school and retired. He is happy and can now talk with humor about his days in the skies over Europe.

For those who have the curiosity of a cat, let me answer your question. Yes, the navigator survived the war. Chunchi found him and they wrote after the war. According to his last note, he is retired in Nebraska.

And no, Goldberg never sent Chunchi a thank-you note.

The Big War ended in August 1945. By the end of six months our returning boys were in the 52-20 Club—twenty bucks a week for fifty-two weeks—and living it up in the bars of Franklin Street, on the Clearwater beaches, and at the Matinees. Ybor City families were bursting with pride to have their sons back.

They had seen the world. They would never again define their world by streets. It was not limited by Nebraska Avenue and 22nd Street. There were better ball parks than Cuscaden, they had seen Yankee Stadium. There were better football fields than Phillips Field, they had seen Chicago's Soldier's Field. The Tampa Terrace night club was nothing compared to the Copa in New York. What's 7th Avenue on a Saturday night when you've been in Times Square and walked Broadway? A fight in Benjamin Field seemed insignificant compared to Madison Square Garden fights.

Ybor City boys had seen the Himalayas, sailed the Pacific, struggled through the jungles of Guadalcanal, the deserts of Tunisia, the frozen wastes of the Aleutians, and the forest of the Ardennes. Fought through the villages of Sicily, the big city streets of Naples and Manila, the caves of Saipan, the volcanic ash of Iwo Jima, the tough house-to-house combat of Aachen. Ybor City boys had covered the world.

How were they ever to settle down in the peaceful, happy little town of Ybor City after that?

Some didn't and moved on. Some, like Chunchi, couldn't stay away from the military life and went back in. But most stayed home. They took advantage of the GI Bill and flooded the schools. A few followed in their fathers' footsteps and went back to the cigar factories, but they were few, for the cigar industry was collapsing, and Ybor City crenating into a wrinkled reminder of what was once a utopia. The Ybor City they knew was dying.

Our heroes, Captain Huerta and the beribboned Captain Joe Benito, met back in Ybor City, two guys waiting for their final discharge papers to come through. They had had a long, full, and honorable war. They had made it.

When they were high school heroes it was the thing to do to put on your letter sweater and stand in front of Walgreen's Drug, downtown by the railroad tracks on Franklin and Polk. The theory was that people (read "girls") coming out of the movie show at the Tampa or Franklin theaters would walk by, or stand on the corner to catch the streetcar. No one who ever saw the handsome Chelo Huerta, standing there in his red sweater with the big black H embossed on his left side, with three stripes and a star above them on his left arm, could possibly forget him. He was the epitome of a high school hero.

Well, the war had been over for a few months, and one Saturday night Chelo convinced Joe Benito to go stand in front of Walgreen's wearing their best Class A uniforms, with wings, campaign ribbons, and captain's bars shining under the street lights.

There probably has never been a more attractive uniform in the history of the military than the Air Force officer's winter uniform. The peaked officers hat was worn without a grommet, so it was soft and floppy, crushed by the air phones a pilot used in combat. It was called the fifty-mission crushed hat and it looked absolutely Hollywoodish. The sunglasses by Ray-Ban added the final rakish touch.

Hail the Conquering Heroes,
1943: "Let Me See Your
Orders." 1993. Ferdie
Pacheco.

The tunic was a dark green which was supposed to be olive drab but which looked more like forest green. It had four shiny buttons and a cloth belt. The four patch pockets were closed by brass buttons. On the lapels were military insignia, and the rank badges were placed on shoulder straps. The shirt was a dark green, with a tan tie.

The pants were straight-cut and of a pink cavalry twill. Yes, pink. Take my word for it, it was a killer combination. The shoes were highly polished half-boots with wraparound straps.

It was in this lavish, glamorous uniform that our two heroes stationed themselves to announce to the adoring girls of the town that they were back.

Before Chelo could get off a wave, two MPs stood in front of them, asking, in a not-too-courteous manner, who they were and what they were doing there. Anyone who knew Chelo could anticipate the resultant scene. Indignation fueled his already hair-trigger temper, and while Joe silently wished he could be up in his P-47 taking another shot at the bridge, Chelo dug them a deep hole with the Military Police.

They were discharged officers but had not received their papers as yet. They had no orders. They had no officer ID. Hadn't they read the board that orders the uniforms of the day? The MPs' voices had taken on a hard edge. The more Chelo yelled, the harder they got. The war ended unceremoniously for Chelo Huerta and Joe Benito as they were arrested for impersonating an officer.

After all, it's what's *supposed* to happen to guys from Ybor City.

The Captain's Vendetta: The Naval War Ashore

Among the young men of Ybor City there were a few boys who stood out for their legendary macho feats. I had to wait until Charles Bronson movies to find their equal.

Joe "Baby" Diaz, the bodyguard and driver of Charlie Wall, the crime overlord of Ybor City, was one. His escape from ambush by driving Wall's car in reverse down Nebraska was the talk of the town for years. But Baby was, and is, very modest and close-mouthed. Even today, still a trim, muscled man in his seventies, he refused to talk of his exploits. It was the Ybor City way. Big mouths talked about what they did, *real men* shut up.

Capt. Julian
Fernandez, mer-
chant marine,
1942. Courtesy of
Julian
Fernandez.

I grew up hearing about a man named Julian Fernandez who was
only a few years older than I, although in the period of the war a five-
year difference was considered a huge difference. He was quiet, refused
to allow insult, real or imagined, to himself, his family, his friends, or the
Spanish race in general. You can imagine he was active in the fighting
field. Luckily World War II came along and he was able to channel his
aggressive drive toward more socially acceptable enemies. He was not
tall, but he was shaped like a Basque stone-lifter. He had big shoulders
and enormous upper-body strength. He was a handsome boy in school
and carried himself with great dignity and the promise of sudden violence if his honor was questioned or compromised.

Once while at Hillsborough High School, he heard that the student body president, an Italian kid who was an excellent athlete and
a popular guy, was saying bad things about the Spanish boys from

Ybor City. Taking this personally, Julian Fernandez marched down the aisle to the stage during a student assembly. There, to the amazement of the assembled students, Julian punched out the student body president.

As the war heated up, it became apparent to anyone who knew Julian that he would be a great asset to the Allied cause. Julian joined the Merchant Marine and embarked on a remarkable fighting career. His progress was rapid, and he soon entered Officer Candidate School and graduated as a ship's officer. Then he went back to being torpedoed. His war years were punctuated with heroic episodes and epic struggles with the U-boat Wolf Packs of the Atlantic. Up and down the Florida coast the civilians could see tankers burning close to shore, and our beach shoreline was cluttered with debris and the bodies of merchant seamen in life preservers.

Julian, by this time called Captain Fernandez in Ybor City, stood out

Capt. Julian Fernandez patrolling the streets of Mobile, Alabama, 1944. Courtesy of Julian Fernandez.

*Las Novedades, 1930s. Courtesy of **La Gaceta**.*

in our minds as the embodiment of a Bronson-like hero. In those days servicemen on leave did not talk much about their exploits in the war, so Captain Fernandez set out upon a strange small war of his own in his hometown.

While most of the young men went off to war, some stayed at home by hook or crook. Our story concerns the crook. There was a young tough in Ybor City known simply as Rocky. He was a good-looking kid with a reputation for being a tough guy. He was alleged to be a hit man for hire, although the Tampa police, in their myopic way, never caught him in any violent mayhem. He was attractive to women who were attracted to dangerous men. He had a gang of young toughs who hung out with him and did some of his less important dirty work.

On one drizzly night in the middle of the war, Captain Fernandez and a shipmate were at the Seabreeze Restaurant chatting up two local beauties when Rocky came into the place. What he saw was two uniformed officers trying to pick up two local girls. He decided to teach them a lesson and summoned his little army to take the two officers outside and beat them severely. The odds were overwhelming and the two war heroes took a king-sized beating.

When Captain Fernandez recovered he went looking for the alleged hit man. He found him in Palmetto Beach, and on the spot, with a minimum of dialogue, lashed into him. The fight was short and brutal. When it was over and Rocky lay on the red brick street, Captain Fernandez relayed a cryptic message, a la Dirty Harry: "This beating was the good news. The bad news is that every time I see you on the streets of Ybor City you're going to get another beating."

Captain Fernandez shipped out once again to face the U-boat killers of the Atlantic. I'm sure Rocky prayed that he would take a Nazi torpedo down his throat and never come back to Ybor City. Such was not the case. The hardy Captain Fernandez survived many encounters and eventually returned to Ybor City to dry out.

On a quiet night Captain Fernandez had gone to Las Novedades Restaurant with his uncle, David Martinez, the mildest, most peaceful man in the Western Hemisphere. David, along with his wife Maria and brother-in-law Paco, had opened El Encanto Cleaners with the money they had saved up working in a cigar factory. He was a determined worker and the soul of gentility. Violence was an alien emotion in him.

On this night, as they sat eating their garbanzo soup, Rocky was sitting at the rear with a few friends. Captain Fernandez did not see him, but Rocky was told that his nemesis was there.

Pulling his .38 revolver, he walked to the front of the restaurant with his arms extended, pointing the pistol at Captain Fernandez. As he got to the table he had the gun against the captain's head before anyone could warn him.

"Now, let's stop this foolishness," said Rocky, cocking the gun. "Let's forget this stupid vendetta. I beat you up. You beat me up. We're even. Either forget it or I'll solve it right now."

The crowded restaurant had fallen silent, and people scrambled to get away from the scene of possible gunplay. Captain Fernandez stared defiantly at Rocky. The peace-loving David sat open-mouthed and white as a sheet.

From the rear of the restaurant came a waiter, a napkin over his hand.

He was hiding a butcher knife much as a torero hides the sword with his cape. Blithely he walked behind Rocky and, once out of his sight, whipped out the knife and placed it at Rocky's throat.

"You may shoot the captain, but you won't have a head after you pull the trigger."

It was a checkmate. Rocky had no choice but to put the .38 on the table, whereupon Captain Fernandez calmly unloaded the gun and put it on the floor.

"Now we're even again," the captain said, smiling thinly, "and we're going outside where you're going to get your *next* beating."

That one put him in the hospital.

In time, it got so bad that one night when Rocky was eating at the Barcelona Restaurant and saw Captain Fernandez come in, he resorted to calling the Tampa police to come get him out peacefully before the captain spotted him.

The war over, and several beatings later, Captain Fernandez moved to Miami to pursue the career of bar pilot. He had a long and brilliant career, rising to the top easily, and today, after retirement, continues as a consultant for the Port of Miami. He is much honored and respected. Few who knew him in his Miami days, and see him now as a white-haired, bewhiskered man, would suspect that under this courtly southern Iberian exterior there lies a time bomb waiting to explode. He is still fit and trim, and you get the feeling that if he ever ran across Rocky again he would be ready to administer another lesson.

The War at Sea

Bobby Mendez was one of the handsomest kids in our class, and certainly the most innocent. He was on the swimming team, and his main claim to fame was that he was the only kid at Jefferson High School to have an English thin-frame bicycle with hand brakes and skinny tires.

Bobby was itching to go to war. He had seen *A Yank in the RAF* with Tyrone Power and was swept away by the words of Winston Churchill: "Never in the field of human conflict was so much owed by so many to so few." He rode his English flyer down to the consulate, and reported.

The Equalizer.
1993. Ferdie Pacheco.

"I want to join the few," Bobby said.

"I'm sorry, there are far too many," said a weary Englishman, waving him off.

Undaunted, he went to the marines and found a line around the block. The navy office was flooded. In desperation Bobby tried the army. You see, Bobby had *not* seen *All Quiet on the Western Front*. Crushed, he returned to school only to find that if he enlisted in the merchant marine he would be given his high school diploma. This seemed like a great deal to Bobby, so he joined.

After a cursory training period Bobby found himself on a tanker leaving New York harbor for England. His new GI-issue clothes were warm and fit well. He had never been to sea before. He could not wait to experience the life of an able-bodied seaman.

The dim lights of New York Harbor were still in sight when a huge explosion tore the bottom out of the ship. It began to settle in the water. Fires had not yet started, and the experienced crew were jumping into the freezing sea as fast as they could and swimming hard to get away from the tanker before she blew up. The sea was covered with oil and the possibility of fire was big. Bobby and another oil-soaked seaman found a floating crate, climbed on, and paddled to shore.

They were picked up and taken to a military hospital. They were cleaned up and, there being no uniforms available, were given civilian clothes. Transport was called to take them back to the Brooklyn Navy Yard. A convoy was formed up and ready to head out, and they needed more able-bodied seamen.

As it turned out, the only form of transport available was the New York City subway. They were driven to the nearest station, given the fare, and told to report to the Brooklyn Navy Yard.

Bobby's entire life has been one of cataclysmic disaster resulting from simple events. This ride proved the first of many such occurrences.

As soon the two teen-agers got on board the subway, they sensed hostility in the crowd. Most of the passengers were middle-aged ship-yard workers. They looked at the two strapping kids with suspicious eyes, and the muttering began.

"Why ain't they in uniform?"

"I got a kid brother on Bataan."

"I lost a cousin in Pearl . . ."

Muttering soon turned to yelling, and yelling to pushing, and pushing to punches, and before Bobby could figure out what was happening he was on his way to the Navy Hospital, where he spent two weeks recovering from the beating.

This beating turned into a blessing, as Bobby's disasters always did, when it was reported that the convoy he would have sailed on had suffered 75 percent casualties on the way to Murmansk.

Bobby's luck continued hot and cold through the war. Once, when his ship was in harbor in Algiers he bet a shipmate that he could beat him swimming around the boat. Bobby was a great swimmer and the entire crew bet on him. Bobby was well in front as he swam around the bow, and he was encouraged by his shipmates, who lined the rails yelling and shouting. The effect on Bobby was electric, and he picked up his stroke. The faster he went, the louder the sound of the cheering. As he came to the Jacob's ladder at the finish line eager shipmates hauled him aboard. Worried faces greeted him. His opponent was nowhere in sight. He had vanished.

As Bobby was pushed on deck he was met by the stern-faced captain of the ship. By his side, looking relieved, was his opponent.

It was then that Bobby understood that the cheers had actually been frantic warnings. Bobby was being followed by a school of sharks as he swam around the boat. Once again, disaster followed close behind Bobby, and he had lucked out.

In Bari, Italy, Bobby's ship was held outside the harbor while the debris from a devastating Luftwaffe raid was cleared away. A British convoy had entered the harbor the previous day and had been caught flat-footed by Stuka dive bombers and badly mauled. What made it worse was that the convoy was made up of troop transports. It turned out to be a grisly massacre.

When the time came for Bobby's ship to enter the harbor, there were so many bodies floating in the water that Bobby was ordered with a crew of men to go ahead of his ship and push the bodies aside so that the ship would not run them over and mangle the bodies with the screw propellers. It was a grisly introduction to the realities of war.

Bobby was still a teen-ager, always looking for souvenirs in the form of weapons, uniform articles, or signs. He would bring home war souvenirs and in his generous way would give our friend Milo and me a few trinkets. Milo had a room decorated with traffic signs and a few street signs. Now, with the opportunity to rummage about in Bari, Bobby set out with a screwdriver to get a few signs.

In his innocence he did not realize that the British Army was very angry at the civilian population, blaming them for tipping off the Germans about the convoy's arrival, resulting in the bloody defeat. So he was surprised to find British MPs beating on the soles of his boots with truncheons. He had shinnied up a street lamppost and was unscrewing a sign that said BARI, 10 KM.

He was taken to the British Army police compound and interrogated. The British were a suspicious lot, and their method of interrogation proved to be rough. By the time the captain of the ship found him, Bobby was in the hospital again, and as always, the beating proved of therapeutic benefit. His ship had to sail without him and, of course, it was sunk in mid-Mediterranean. Once again, Bobby had stepped on a land mine and survived.

Bobby's war is the stuff of movies. He ended up the war in Red China looking for souvenirs behind the lines in a jeep. It was blown up by a land mine, and Bobby was airlifted to a hospital in Arabia, where he learned to enjoy Arabic food, including eating sheep's eyeballs. Bobby never saw a morsel of food he couldn't ingest.

Bobby has continued his flirtation with danger and disaster. He collected so many guns, bayonets, and swords that he had to move out of his apartment in order to find room to sleep. He recently retired after forty-five years with the Fire Department. During that time he completed law school and graduated. He worked for the U.S. Customs Service on his off-duty time and was assigned to drug stake-outs in the Everglades, where he dodged a few friendly bullets. He continues to be a peaceful, friendly, quiet, lovable man.

After a lifetime of adventure and gluttony Bobby is not as agile as he once was. He is still handsome, but is now rotund and rather immobile. There are only so many times one can fall off a fire truck, or fall through a flaming roof, before it affects one's mobility.

It is only fitting that we leave the dangerous life of Bobby Mendez

Fireman Bobby Mendez, 1950. Courtesy of Bobby Mendez.

with his latest escapade. On the steaming hot August day after Hurricane Andrew wrecked Miami, Bobby was walking down a tree-strewn street in Coconut Grove, trying to find an ice house. He was armed with a rapid-fire Italian automatic because the streets were fraught with marauders and crime was in the air. Bobby, a man intimately acquainted with street crime, was ready for any eventuality.

If there was trouble in the neighborhood, it would certainly find Bobby.

As he trudged through the debris he spotted two rough-looking characters approaching him. They had the look of desperate men. Bobby checked his automatic.

"We're looking for some money," one of the toughs said.

"So am I. If you find any, let me know where it is." Bobby tried to defuse the danger by using off-hand humor, a method that seldom works when faced with two determined professionals.

"We want your money," said the bigger man, balling up his fist, stepping closer to Bobby.

Bobby gripped the automatic and his thumb flicked the safety.

"Boy, have you got the wrong day," Bobby said, trying to recall the exact words of Dirty Harry. He pulled out the automatic and tried again.

"You can make my time," he said, coming closer, but still not right.

The two men, who knew the "Make my day" line perfectly, did not wait for Bobby to find the right words. Understanding his meaning very well, they turned on their heels, fled down the street, and broke Michael Jordan's records for airborne flight by vaulting a nine-foot concrete wall in one mighty leap. In the meantime Bobby increased their speed by spraying the street with flying bullets.

Later, Bobby reported with a satisfied smile, his doctor friend told him that two men had been admitted to the emergency room with bullet wounds in their feet. Bobby beamed when I gave him a videotape of *Dirty Harry*.

"My memory was bad, but my aim was good."

❦ Tampa Bananas served in all branches of the service and in every theater of war with honor and distinction. Few were the houses of Ybor City that did not boast of a family member in uniform. They all did well, and Ybor City demonstrated their pride in the men upon their return.

Some did not return. From my block, Manuel Arñiella's brother Tino and Danny Alvarez's brother John did not return. There were many such losses in Ybor City's blocks. They have not been forgotten.

Chapter 15

The University That Hid
in a Hotel

In the fall of 1944 I stepped into the halls of higher education. That is
what the brochure said.

World War II was at its peak. Manpower was scarce, so my father told
me that my presence was required at the family drug store, La Economica, in Ybor City.

I had been accepted into the University of Tennessee, where Dr.
Martorell, an alumnus, had arranged for a fraternity to rush me. If my
grades justified it, I would be accepted into medical school in the accelerated wartime program: two years of pre-med, three years of medical
school, and an internship in the service. In six years I would be a doctor.
I was sixteen years of age at the time. This meant that by the time I was
twenty-two years old I would be practicing medicine.

A lesser alternative was to attend the University of Tampa for one
year. If the war wound down, and men began returning, I'd be permitted to go to the University of Tennessee.

My first good look at the University of Tampa made my heart sink.
The facade was familiar to me. All Tampanians were used to seeing its
silver minarets, and the majority of postcards sent from Tampa had pictures of them. In fact, its design was so original that the architecture of
the downtown courthouse was a small replica of the university.

The freshman class of fifty boys and girls were crowded into an assembly hall which had formerly been the hotel ballroom. The walls were
dingy, the paint was peeling, and the place smelled like the inside of a
nursing home.

The class was largely female. The few men were either underage, too young for the draft, 4F, unfit for duty, or old. The popular song of that year was "They're Either Too Young or Too Old." The song was singularly appropriate to our class.

The university was housed in a relic of a bygone era. It had once been the Tampa Bay Hotel, the result of a dream of H.B. Plant, who had built the railroad to Tampa to bring people to his hotel on the shores of the Hillsborough River.

The structure was of Moroccan design. It was long rather than tall, so long that the occupants of the far wing had to be transported by coolie rickshaws to the main lobby. The halls were wide and spacious but the hotel rooms small and constricted. In those days most hotel rooms were spartan since they served only to accommodate the occupants' daily needs—sleep, a bath, and precious little else.

The hotel was completed during a decade of wealth and leisure in the 1880s. People came to sit on its broad verandas, to visit the zoo at the front of the hotel, sail on the bay, cruise on the Hillsborough River, ride horses in Hyde Park, and pass the time playing genteel parlor games. Dining was an attraction, followed by band concerts and dancing to an orchestra.

Built solidly, the hotel had thirteen minarets and cupolas, the number of months in the Arabic calendar. This information was conveyed to new students on the first day of indoctrination. I had the sinking feeling that while this had been a first-rate hotel, it was considerably less impressive as a teaching institution.

The classrooms were tiny. Not that large classrooms were needed, for the largest class rarely exceeded ten students. The rooms had once been the hotel bedrooms. By stretching the word they could be considered quaint. In the winter the hallways resembled a set from Dr. Zhivago, like the inside of a freezer, yet the classrooms were cozy. Each had its own wood-burning fireplace. The chairs, evenly placed at the beginning of the class, were lined against the far wall by the end of the class, as heat prompted the students to strip down to the bare minimum.

The biology and chemistry labs were at the end of the long building. The days of rickshaws and coolies had long since passed, and we premed students were left with the prospect of a long walk, carrying heavy books and equipment.

University of Tampa, 1944.
Burgert Bros. Studio. Courtesy
*of **La Gaceta.***

The professors were an odd lot. Our biology and chemistry professor was a refugee from his previous job, having taken off with a coed. He had sandy hair, rubbery lips, shaggy eyebrows, and wore high-heeled boots. His eyes rarely strayed far from the legs and the breasts of coeds who sat in the front row. He delighted in road trips to the shallow flats of the bay where he could watch as the girls hiked up their skirts and waded in the mud.

Our history professor was an odd duck; he was so dry he was brittle. He dressed in neat three-button suits with a vest, and wore bow ties and high-top shoes. He had a soft pasty face topped by a thin crew cut. He read from a prepared prospectus from which he had not deviated since the death of Queen Victoria. His one humanizing moment came when he showed us personal photographs of himself on his annual prewar European tour. One dreary postcard after another was exhibited. At this point you could strangle him if he showed as much as one more. Then he showed us his *pièce de résistance.*

There in a gondola in Venice sat Dr. Lamb, hands primly on his knees. He looked into the lens with the same humorless look we knew so well. But wait. Look behind him. There was a dowager old lady, looking every bit as grim as Dr. Lamb, but her legs were open, and she was not wearing her knickers. We tittered, then burst into a thunderclap of cheering. The next picture was the Leaning Tower of Pisa, followed by the Vatican. His album went on until June.

What the university lacked in scholastic talent, it could never make up in athletics. There were none. Not even intramural sports. There were no fraternities. No clubs. No dances. I began to suspect that I was being trained for a prisoner-of-war camp.

Each month's unremitting drudgery passed by, and each remarkably like the previous one. I began to despair. My high expectations for a scholastic life dwindled in the face of such intellectual doldrums.

Spring brought unexpected changes. For one thing, we had a new president. Our past president was a ghostly wraith who acted like a man who already had his bags packed and was waiting for his getaway car to show up.

Dr. Elwood Nance was a retired army chaplain, whose qualifications were many and who had attained the rank of full colonel. He was tall,

The distinguished new president, Elwood Nance, 1947. Courtesy of June Nance Bryant.

white-haired, and distinguished. He had a charming wife and two devilish teen-aged children. The boy was a heavy drinker at fourteen, his sister was a beautiful, witty girl named June.

One of my lifelong friends who went to the university was an architecture student named Johnny Rañon. His father, Domingo, was a builder who worked on the Columbia Restaurant and many houses in Ybor City. Before anyone could take a good look at June and make a determined run at her, Johnny was monopolizing her time. We formed a trio, and traveled around enjoying her company. How that worked I don't know, but it was a simpler time, and the psychodynamics of such an arrangement were not given much thought—the main preoccupation being "who can get the car tonight." The French examined this very well in their excellent film *Jules and Jim*. All I can remember is that June Nance was bright, beautiful, wonderfully witty, and a willing confederate in all our pranks and gags. I was always attracted to girls of this type, and all of my life sought them out. I recommend the type to all young folks. They are wonderful to marry, and laugh all the way through the divorce.

The low level of entertainment that spring was enlivened by a non-stop doubles Ping-Pong game on the veranda. It was a showcase for the natural comics and show-offs and an arena for the serious Ping-Pong players. Romances, such as they were, began here, and lifelong friendships were formed on the longest nonstop Ping-Pong tournament in college history.

It was a cool April afternoon, and we had taken June's father's Packard Clipper to the Colonnade. The day was clear. There wasn't a cloud in the sky. The bay was a crystalline green color and so calm it

Johnny Rañon, my running mate, 1946.

looked like a mirror. No B-17's flew that day to disturb the quiet of the sunny afternoon.

The Colonnade Drive-In was on Bayshore Boulevard. The rear parking area was spacious and interspersed with large, crooked oak trees, from which hung grey moss that dangled almost to the top of the car tops. The moss gave the parking area a ghostly look at night.

The loudspeakers, hung on the trees, suddenly crackled as a man said in a emotion-packed voice: "The president of the United States, Franklin D. Roosevelt, has just died. We ask a moment of silent prayer for our beloved president."

The impact was sudden and hard like a blow to the solar plexus. We stopped our horsing around, we stopped talking and became three statues. We didn't know what to do, what to say. June now clicked on the car radio. The details flowed from the dashboard, filling our heads.

Not since that December 7th Sunday had I been shocked into a profound silence. Roosevelt dead? Impossible.

FDR had been our president since 1933. I could not remember a day when he wasn't president. He was an absolute. The word *president* was synonymous with Roosevelt.

The Roosevelt family was our family. All of America believed we were part of a perfect, all-American, Hallmark card family. The president was warm, charming, sophisticated, and elegant. We never envisioned him as a handicapped person. In this era of TV coverage FDR would have been exposed immediately. But in that simpler era of news management, FDR's handicap was never mentioned. When he addressed Congress his braces were locked, and he was propped up against the podium. His "Fireside Chats" on radio were shown later in newsreels with FDR seated comfortably behind his familiar White House desk. Even his deterioration was never noticed, for we weren't shown the sickly, rapidly aging Roosevelt. When we saw him posing with Churchill and Stalin at Yalta, we were shocked to see him look grey and ill. We knew that soon we'd never hear his patrician voice on radio, making his good-natured cracks about Eleanor and her travels, his dog Fala, or one of his sons' latest escapades, or poking fun at Alf Landon, Wendell Willkie, or Tom Dewey. It did not seem fair. To think that on the threshold of the victory he had worked so hard for, he would be taken from us. It was too much to bear. Hitler, Churchill, Mussolini, and Stalin were all still alive. Only Roosevelt did not make it to the finish line.

Our good humor gone, we quietly drove back to the university, finding the students walking around with long faces. Even the longest nonstop Ping-Pong tournament had ground to a halt. June went to see her father, who knew FDR personally, and we all went home to our families.

There are days that stick with you for life, and you remember exactly what you were doing that day, and how you felt. Certainly Pearl Harbor Day was one, and Roosevelt's death the other. V-E Day came in May, but it was anticlimactic for us. We expected that; the feeling was more of relief than joy. We still had the Japanese to beat, and it affected all of us, for we were the wave to train for the assault on the main islands of Japan. Later, at the University of Tennessee, I was part of a memorable and riotous party celebrating V-J day. But after the atom bomb fell, it seemed anticlimactic. We knew it was coming, so the announcement did not stick in the mind. The last big jolt came much later with the assassination of John F. Kennedy. Again, the unexpected death of a beloved president made you remember exactly where you were when the news came on the radio.

❧ So the war was winding down. We were now seeing wounded servicemen enrolling. Some had "nervous" discharges, some were shot up, and all were shaky. The pace quickened. The flow of young pilots and gunners who came by looking for coeds dried up.

June's father was a perfect example of the absentminded professor. He simply couldn't remember facts or faces. No matter how many times he met me, he couldn't remember who I was or what I had last done to him.

It started in May, before V-E Day and a few weeks after FDR's death. Coming down the hall, I saw a small Latino carrying a large oil painting of FDR.

He seemed lost so I stopped to help. He was a Cuban political refugee. He was destitute, and wanted Dr. Nance to see his painting. Knowing Nance was a pal of FDR's and would be receptive, I took the refugee to his office. I told him to wait until I approached Nance.

Dr. Elwood Nance and
(seated, left to right)
daughter June, wife Helen,
and son John, 1947.
Robertson and Fresh Com-
mercial Photographers. Courtesy of June Nance Bryant.

Nance, still not recognizing me, blinked as he looked at the flattering painting of FDR. He loved it.

"He wants to donate it to the university. But he wants to do it in front of the assembly," I said, smiling.

Nance beamed, came out and shook hands with the Cuban. The secretary wrote out the date and time of presentation.

When we got outside the office I told the Cuban refugee that Dr. Nance had agreed to give him a $500 check and would present it to him in an assembly. Under no circumstances was he to hand over the painting without the check. I resolved to be absent from that assembly.

❦ Dr. Nance had high hopes of being appointed ambassador to a Latin American country. Before traveling to Peru he asked me to give him a catchy, slangy, but funny way to say "Pleased to meet you."

I responded with: "He tenido una diarrhea de placer en conocerla" (I've had a diarrhea of pleasure to meet you).

He came back confused at the reaction he got, but still not catching on that I was the last person to ask about Spanish phraseology. He consulted me again.

He had written a nice note to the president of Peru, but it had been translated by the Spanish professor, who was a costive, rigid man. The letter sounded as if it had been written by Cervantes. The eager-to-impress Dr. Nance had added a personal note on the bottom that he wanted me to check. He wanted to say: "Warmest regards to your wife." And he wrote: "Recuerdos a tu caliente mujer" (Regards to your hot wife).

"Send it, as it is," I said, feeling this was as good a way as any to end my freshman year in college.

❦ By the fall of 1945 I was ready to leave town, to seek my fortune, to find out what lay beyond Florida.

Larry Guerra had returned from his war in the Pacific, full of malaria and Japanese steel. He took his accumulated pay and bought a 1936 Dodge. Actually it was not the first thing he did on his release from the hospital.

Convinced that Grimaldi of the Draft Board had personally sent him to the Pacific, Larry withdrew all his money from the Columbia Bank as a form of protest. The withdrawal of $38.42 hurt the bank bad, and he decided to go off with me to Spring Hill College in Alabama to study dentistry so he could come back and drill Grimaldi properly.

Aside from a laughably loose steering wheel, the car looked like it would make it to Mobile, Alabama. What it needed was an interior. Seats, side panels, and rugs were badly needed. We added up our combined funds and found we had the $19.95 necessary for ready-made seat covers.

I have always felt that if you do things right, you take away more than you give to a university. Armed with a ruler and a big pair of upholstery scissors, Larry and I moved into the back of the University of Tampa Library, measured the necessary carpet, and cut the piece needed. The drapes were a matching red, and we cut the cloth we needed for the door panels.

The debonair author prepares to leave Ybor City and seek his fortune in the outer world. 1945

The car looked great, and we drove to Mobile in high spirits and low gear.

Things have a way of evening out. A few weeks after we started school we were out on a triple date in the Dodge when we were caught in a deluge. The inside of the car got hot and sweaty, but, engaged in our own discussions, we didn't notice. The following morning we were amazed to see our new suits smeared a bright red. Phone calls from the girls revealed that they too were victims of the Red Curse. That was embarrassing and solidly costly.

So, you see, as Don King says, "You does the crime, you does the time."

From that time on, I knew I had left Ybor City for good. Memories would fade, but most of it has remained forever imbedded in my mind, as I recall the carefree days of my youth, when the main thing I had on my mind was how to avoid boredom brought on by the sameness of things.

Ybor City
A New Face with an Old Look

I am certain you have enjoyed Ferdie Pacheco's reminiscences of old Ybor. His tales of growing up in a tri-cultural enclave of cigar makers provides an insight into one of the most unique communities in America. A way of life that is gone forever.

Today Ybor City is in transition. Its heart beats with a new spirit, but it still clings to its old traditions with a mix of enlightened eclecticism. At the Tropicana Café having their rich *café con leche,* the descendants of the old cigar makers can be heard discussing with optimism the future of Ybor City.

Ybor City has been designated as a National Historic Site. Thirty historical markers dot the area. These markers tell the story of three diverse cultures—Cuban, Spanish, and Italian—that formed a mosaic, instead of a melting pot.

One of the more enjoyable experiences for tourists is a walking tour of these markers.

A visit to Ybor City is not complete without visiting the historic Columbia Restaurant. Dining at the Columbia is an adventure into old Spain. The remembrances of this fascinating restaurant will remain ingrained in your mind—its cuisine, gentlemen waiters, fountains, patios, paintings, beautiful Sevillian ceramic decorations, and the fiery Andalusian dancers. You will walk away from the Columbia with delicious memories.

The old El Pasaje building with its twenty-four brick columns housed the Cherokee Club in the Gay Nineties. This once-plush men's club for tobacco tycoons now houses Café Creole, an outstanding New Orleans–style seafood restaurant. The metal tree-fountain in its tropical garden is a rare work of art. This is a must-see site.

The old cigar factory buildings stand as monuments to the Latin Quarter's unique past. Some of the buildings have been converted into offices and warehouses. The most historic is the Vicente Martinez Ybor Cigar Factory, now known as Ybor Square. This mammoth brick factory is a counterpart of San Francisco's Cannery. Therein are a variety of shops and restaurants, gift and antique boutiques, cafés, souvenir stores, and the Spaghetti Factory restaurant, where a full-size trolley car sits in the center—and the food is true Italian-style.

The Latin clubhouses, veritable palaces, were built by humble cigar makers. They are a marvel of architectural achievement. In addition to their social function, these clubs provided health insurance and thus are the forerunners of HMO's in America. The Centro Español, Centro Asturiano, Círculo Cubano, and Unione Italiana continue to keep Ybor City's Latin culture alive.

La Septima Avenida (7th Avenue) was not the usual American main drag. On Saturday nights the tabaqueros turned *la dolce via* into a carnival. The avenue was an actual stage of life, where courting, socializing, business, and politics held sway. The picturesque street was graced with wrought-iron balconies, quaint coffeehouses, and excellent stores. The bubbling mass of promenaders with admiring eyes and Latin smiles afforded a most delicious experience.

Today 7th Avenue is lined with sable palms, tropical shrubbery, and antique lampposts. Sadly, the cigar makers have vanished from the scene. The avenue may be compared with Denver's famous Larimer Square, with a series of tourist shops and bistros keeping the avenue alive with spark and pizzazz.

La Tropicana Café is the most celebrated gathering place. Here Roland Manteiga, the editor of *La Gaceta,* the trilingual newspaper, holds court at breakfast and lunch every day. La Tropicana is frequented by politicians, newsmen, businessmen, retirees, and former Latin residents of Ybor City who gather to reminisce about the good old days.

Tony Pizzo, 1980. Courtesy of Tony Pizzo.

Martí Park stands as a shrine of patriotism for Cuban exiles. The park is official Cuban soil commemorating the memory of Jose Martí and his revolution of 1895. To the Cubans in exile, Martí Park is their Mecca. The land called Ybor City will endure in history as the cradle of Cuban liberty. The idea for the revolution which freed Cuba from Spain began here.

Ybor City, which was once known as the largest cigar-manufacturing center in the world, will prevail as a living symbol of those heroic Latin pioneers who gave Tampa its famous cosmopolitan heritage.

Dr. Ferdie Pacheco is a favorite son of Ybor City. He is a special product of this dramatic community. He is a man of varied and rare talents: a picturesque raconteur, colorful writer, superb artist, and bon vivant. Dr. Pacheco has made significant contributions to the history and folklore of Ybor City. His marvelous book is a rare and vivid insight into Ybor City of the long ago, of another time, that is gone forever.

About the Author

Ferdie Pacheco, M.D., is the author of the novel *Renegade Lightning* and of two books of nonfiction, *Muhammad Ali: A View from the Corner* and *Fight Doctor,* an account of his life as a physician in the fight world. Dr. Pacheco practiced medicine from 1958 to 1980 and served as Muhammad Ali's personal physician from 1963 to 1977. In recent years, he has served as boxing color commentator for NBC-TV, Showtime, and Univision. In 1990, he received an Emmy for writing, producing, and narrating the NBC special "Ali Wins the Title." He is also a painter and has exhibited one-person shows in London, Paris, New York, Miami (where he now lives), and other cities throughout the United States.